THE ECUMENICAL CHRISTIAN DIALOGUES AND THE *CATECHISM OF THE CATHOLIC CHURCH*

Edited by
Jeffrey Gros, FSC, and
Daniel S. Mulhall

Paulist Press
New York/Mahwah, N.J.

Paulist Press has permission of the Pontifical Council for Promoting Christian Unity to cite excerpts from the agreed statements and reports of bilateral dialogues including those specifically identified that have not thus far been published in the *Growth and Agreement* series, namely, the International Methodist-Catholic Dialogue Commission's 2001 report *Speaking the Truth in Love;* and ARCIC's *The Gift of Authority* and *Mary: Grace and Hope in Christ.*

Cover and book design by Lynn Else

Library of Congress Cataloging-in-Publication Data

The ecumenical Christian dialogues and the Catechism of the Catholic Church / edited by Jeffrey Gros, and Daniel S. Mulhall.
    p. cm.
  ISBN 0-8091-4385-2 (alk. paper)
  1. Christian union—Catholic Church. 2. Catholic Church. Catechismus Ecclesiae Catholicae. I. Gros, Jeffrey, 1938- II. Mulhall, Daniel S.
  BX1784.E32 2006
  282—dc22

2006001227

Published by Paulist Press
997 Macarthur Boulevard
Mahwah, New Jersey 07430

www.paulistpress.com

Printed and bound in the
United States of America

CONTENTS

Contents

Dedication
To all Catholic catechists today who hand on the
faith in fidelity to the teaching of the
Second Vatican Council
and to the memory of
Brother John Joseph, FSC (+1942)
Brother Alphonsus Pluth, FSC (+1986)
and to their heirs at St. Mary's Press
in gratitude for their more than half century commitment to
handing on the teaching of the Catholic Church
to younger generations with fidelity and passion

ABBREVIATIONS

ACE	Assyrian Church of the East
ACE–RC	Assyrian Church–Catholic Common Declaration in GA II
ARCIC	Anglican Roman Catholic International Commission
ARCIC–M	Anglican–Roman Catholic Commission on the Theology of Marriage and Its Application to Mixed Marriage
ARCIC–Mary	Mary: Grace and Hope in Christ
ARCUSA	Anglican Roman Catholic Dialogue in the USA
BEM	Baptism, Eucharist, and Ministry (World Council of Churches)
Black Ch	Toward a Common Expression of Faith: A Black North American Perspective
BU	Building Unity
BWA	Baptist World Alliance
BWA/RC	Baptist–Catholic Dialogue, "Summons to Common Witness in Today's World"
CaC	ARCIC II, Church as Communion
CCC	Catechism of the Catholic Church (1992/1997)
CC/DC	Christian Church / Disciples of Christ
CC–C	Disciples–Catholic Dialogue (series noted I–III)
CDF	Congregation for the Doctrine of the Faith
COCU	The Consultation on Church Union
COF	Confessing the One Faith, World Council 1991
Coptic–RC	Common Declaration between Coptic and Catholic popes
CRC	Christian Reformed Church
CUIC	Churches Uniting in Christ

CW	Common Witness, A Study Document of the Joint Working Group of the Roman Catholic Church and the World Council of Churches
CWC	Church World Communions
Directory	Directory for the Application of Principles and Norms on Ecumenism (1993)
DH	*Dignitatis humanae*, Declaration on Religious Freedom, Vatican II
EF	*The Ecumenical Dimension in the Formation of Pastoral Workers*
ELCA	The Evangelical Lutheran Church in America
ERCDOM	Evangelical–Roman Catholic Dialogue on Mission in GA II
FU	Facing Unity in GA II
GA I	Growth in Agreement I
GA II	Growth in Agreement II
Gassmann	*Documentary History of Faith and Order*
GC	Growing Consensus
GC II	Growing Consensus II
GCD	*General Directory for Catechesis*
GofA	ARCIC II *Gift of Authority*
GS	*Gaudium et spes*, The Church in the Modern World, Vatican II
HC	*Heidelberg Catechism*
JDDJ	Lutheran–Catholic *Joint Declaration on the Doctrine of Justification* in GA II
JWG	Joint Working Group, World Council of Churches and Catholic Church
JW	Joint Worship at Ecumenical Gatherings, JWG 1965
LCUSA	Lutheran–Catholic Dialogue, USA (series noted I–X)
LinC	Life in Christ, Morals, Communion and the Church ARCIC II
L–RC	Lutheran–Catholic International Dialogues (series noted I–IX)
L/R/RC–M	The Theology of Marriage and the Problems of Mixed Marriages

LWF	Lutheran World Federation
NCCB	National Conference of Catholic Bishops [now US Conference of Catholic Bishops]
NCC	National Council of Churches of Christ in the USA
NDC	*National Directory for Catechesis*
OJC	Commission on Orthodox Participation in the WCC
OL	*Orientale lumen*, The Light of the East
Ox–C	Eastern Orthodox Roman Catholic Dialogue (international) (4 reports)
Ox–CUS	Eastern Orthodox Roman Catholic Dialogue in the US
PCPCU	Pontifical Council for Promoting Christian Unity
Peace I	The Apostolic Faith and the Church's Peace Witness
Peace II	The Fragmentation of the Church and Its Unity in Peacemaking
Pent–C	Pentecostal Catholic Dialogue (phases I–V)
Ref–C I	The Presence of Christ in the World, in GA I
Ref–C II	Toward a Common Understanding of the Church, in GA II
Ref–CUSA	Ethics and the Search for Unity in BU
S&C	Salvation and the Church, ARCIC II, in GA II
SBC	Southern Baptist Convention
SBC–CUSA	Southern Baptist Catholic Conversation in the USA (I–IV) in BU and GC II
ST	Scripture and Tradition, Lutheran Catholic US IX, in GC II
STt	Scripture, Tradition and the traditions, WCC, Montreal
TEV	Treasure in Earthen Vessels (Reflection on Hermeneutics) WCC
TSOF	Towards Sharing One Faith (study on the Nicene Creed), WCC
UR	*Unitatis redintegratio*, Decree on Ecumenism, Vatican II

USCC	United States Catholic Conference
USCCB	United States Conference of Catholic Bishops
UUS	*Ut unum sint*, That They May Be One
WARC	World Alliance of Reformed Churches
WCC	World Council of Churches
WEA	World Evangelical Fellowship [Alliance (since 2001)]
WMC	World Methodist Council
WMC–RC	World Methodist Council–Catholic dialogue (series noted I–VII)

Sources

Note: Asterisks after some sources refer to the following Web sites on which cited texts can be found:
    * http://www.prounione.urbe.it/dia-int/e_dialogues.html
    ** http://www.usccb.org/seia/dialogues.htm
    *** http://wcc-coe.org/wcc/what/faith/texts-e.html

Dialogue Volumes

BU Jeffrey Gros and Joseph Burgess, eds., *Building Unity* New York: Paulist Press, 1989. (US Dialogues with Roman Catholic Participation)

GA I Lukas Vischer and Harding Meyer, eds., *Growth in Agreement Reports and Agreed Statements of Ecumenical Conversations on a World Level*, New York: Paulist Press, 1984.

GA II William Rusch, Harding Meyer, Jeffrey Gros, eds., *Growth in Agreement II*, Geneva: World Council of Churches, 2000.*

GC I Joseph Burgess, Jeffrey Gros, eds., *Growing Consensus*, New York: Paulist Press, 1995. (US Dialogues)

GC II Jeffrey Gros, Lydia Veliko, eds., *Growing Consensus II*, Washington: US Conference of Catholic Bishops, 2004.**

Gassmann Gunther Gassmann, ed., *Documentary History of Faith and Order: 1963-1993*, Geneva: World Council of Churches, 1993.***

Dialogue Texts

WORLD COUNCIL TEXTS

Assemblies

All in Each Place, New Delhi 1961 in Gassmann

Conciliar Fellowship, Nairobi 1975 in Gassmann

The Church as Koinonia: Gift and Calling, Canberra 1991 in GA II***

Faith and Order

Scripture, Tradition and the traditions 1963 in Gassmann

Baptism, Eucharist and Ministry 1982 in GA I***

Confessing One Faith, Geneva: World Council of Churches, 1991

Toward Sharing the One Faith: A Study Guide for Discussion Groups, Geneva: World Council of Churches, 1996.***

Toward a Common Expression of Faith: A Black North American Perspective 1984 in GC II

The Apostolic Faith and the Church's Peace Witness 1991 in GC II

The Fragmentation of the Church and Its Unity in Peacemaking 1995 in GC II

Joint Working Group

Joint Worship at Ecumenical Gatherings 1965 (JW), see http://www.prounione.urbe.it/dia-int/jwg/doc/e_jwg_05.html

The Ecumenical Dialogue on Moral Issues: Potential Sources of Common Witness or of Divisions 1995 (JWG) in GA II, see http://www.prounione.urbe.it/dia-int/jwg/doc/e_jwg_n7db.html

Commission on Orthodox Participation in the WCC

A Framework for Common Prayer at WCC Gatherings 2002 (OJC), see http://www2.wcc-coe.org/ccdocuments.nsf/index/gen-5-en.html#Anchor—SECTIO-15275

ORTHODOX–CATHOLIC DIALOGUES

International

1) Mystery of the Church and the Eucharist in the Light of the Trinity 1982 in GA II*

2) Faith, Sacraments and the Unity of the Church 1987 in GA II*

3) The Sacrament of Order in the Sacramental Structure of the Church with Particular Reference to the Importance of Apostolic Succession for the Sanctification and Unity of the People of God 1988 in GA II*

4) Uniatism: Method of the Past: Dialogue as Today's Means of Seeking Unity 1993 in GA II*

United States

1) An Agreed Statement on Mixed Marriage 1971 in BU**

4) The Principle of Economy: A Joint Statement 1976 in BU**

5) An Agreed Statement on the Sanctity of Marriage 1978 in BU**

6) Joint Recommendations on the Spiritual Formation of Children of Marriages Between Orthodox and Roman Catholics 1980 in BU**

18) Baptism and "Sacramental Economy" 1999 in GC II**

20) The Filioque: A Church-Dividing Issue? 2003 in GC II**

ORIENTAL ORTHODOX–CATHOLIC TEXT

Common Declaration, 1973*

ASSYRIAN–CATHOLIC TEXT

Common Christological Declaration 1994 in GA II*

ANGLICAN–CATHOLIC DIALOGUES

Arcic

Anglican–Roman Catholic Commission on the Theology of Marriage and its Application to Mixed Marriage 1975 (ARCIC–M) in GA I*

1) *Final Report* 1982 in GA I*

2) Salvation and the Church 1986 in GA II*

3) The Church as Communion 1990 (CaC) in GA II*

4) Life in Christ, Morals, Communion and the Church (LinC) 1993 in GA II*

5) The Gift of Authority: Authority in the Church III (GofA) 1993*

6) Mary: Grace and Hope in Christ (ARCIC–Mary) 2004*

Arcusa

Five Affirmations on the Eucharist as Sacrifice 1994 in GC II

LUTHERAN–ROMAN CATHOLIC TEXTS

International Dialogue

3) The Eucharist 1978 in GA I*

6) The Ministry in the Church 1981 in GA I*

8) Facing Unity 1984 in GA II*

9) Church and Justification 1993 in GA II*

United States Dialogue

3) The Eucharist 1968 in BU

4) Eucharist and Ministry1970 in BU

5) Differing Attitudes Toward Papal Primacy 1973 in BU

6) Teaching Authority and Infallibility in the Church 1978 in BU

7) Justification by Faith 1983 in BU

8) The One Mediator, the Saints, and Mary 1990 in GC I

9) Scripture and Tradition 1995 in GC II

10) The Church as Koinonia: Structures and Ministries 2004 in GC II**

Agreement

Joint Declaration on the Doctrine of Justification 1999 in GA II*

METHODIST–ROMAN CATHOLIC TEXTS

International

1) *Denver Report*, 1971 in GA I*

2) *Dublin Report*, 1976 in GA I*

3) *Honolulu Report*, 1981 in GA I*

4) *Toward a Statement on the Church*, Nairobi, 1983 in GA II*

5) *The Apostolic Tradition*, Singapore, 1991 in GA II*

6) *The Word of Life*, Rio de Janeiro, 1996 in GA II*

7) *Speaking the Truth in Love*, Bristol, 2001*

REFORMED–CATHOLIC TEXTS

1) The Presence of Christ in Church and World 1977 in GA I*

2) Towards a Common Understanding of the Church 1989 in GA II*

3)"Report of the Interchurch Relations Committee Clarifying the Official Doctrine of the Roman Catholic Church Concerning the Mass, To the Synod of the Christian Reformed Church," Agenda for the Synod, 2002, pp. 274-294, see http://www.crcna.net/cr/crrs/crrs_art/crrs_synod_agenda02.pdf (Interchurch Relations Committee Appendix D) in GC II

4) Ethics and the Search for Unity 1980 in BU**

LUTHERAN–REFORMED–CATHOLIC TEXT

The Theology of Marriage and the Problems of Mixed Marriages 1976 in GA I*

DISCIPLES–CATHOLIC TEXTS

1) Apostolicity 1981 in GA I*

2) The Church as Communion in Christ 1992 in GA II*

3) Receiving and Handing on the Faith: The Mission and Responsibility of the Church 2002*

BAPTIST–CATHOLIC TEXTS

International

Summons to Witness to Christ in Today's World 1988 in GA II*

United States

II) Summary Statement 1984 in BU

IV) Report on Sacred Scripture 1999 in GC II**

EVANGELICAL–CATHOLIC TEXTS

The Evangelical–Roman Catholic Dialogue on Mission 1994 in GA II*

PENTECOSTAL–CATHOLIC TEXTS

1) Understanding of Both Traditions in Their Confessional Identities 1976 in GA I*

2) Understanding of Both Traditions in Their Confessional Identities 1982 in GA II*

3) Perspectives on Koinonia 1989 in GA II*

4) Evangelization, Proselytism and Common Witness 1997 in GA II*

Further Reading

TEXT BOOKS

Ann Riggs, Eamon McManus, Jeffrey Gros, *Introduction to Ecumenism*, New York: Paulist Press, 1998.

Fredrick Bliss, *Catholic and Ecumenical: History and Hope*, Ashland, OH: Sheed and Ward, 1999.

Jeffrey Gros, *That All May Be One: Ecumenism*, Chicago: Loyola University Press, 2000.

Gideon Goosen, *Bringing Churches Together: A Popular Introduction to Ecumenism*, Geneva: World Council of Churches, 2001.

Allan Laubenthal, *Catholic Teaching on Ecumenism*, Westlake, OH: Center for Learning, 2003.

REFERENCE BIBLIOGRAPHY

Michael Kinnamon, Brian Cope, eds., *The Ecumenical Movement: An Anthology of Basic Texts and Voices*, Grand Rapids: William B. Eerdmans, 1997. (Selected texts on the full range of ecumenical issues)

Ronald G. Roberson, *The Eastern Christian Churches*, Washington: US Catholic Conference, 1995. http://www.cnewa.org/generalpg-ver1.aspx?pageID=109

Michael Fahey, SJ, *Ecumenism: A Bibliographical Overview*, Westport, CT: Greenwood Press, 1992.

Nicholas Lossky, et al., eds., *Dictionary of the Ecumenical Movement*, Grand Rapids: William B. Eerdmans, 2002.

Vatican Texts
Directory for the Application of Principles and Norms on Ecumenism, Washington: US Catholic Conference, 1993. [Origins, 23:9] (Directory), see http://www.vatican.va/roman_curia/pontifical_councils/chrstuni/documents/rc_pc_chrstuni_doc_25031993_principles-and-norms-on-ecumenism_en.html

The Documents of Vatican II, ed. Walter M. Abbott, SJ. New York: America Press, 1966, see http://www.vatican.va/archive/hist_councils/ii_vatican_council/index.htm

The Ecumenical Dimension in the Formation of Pastoral Workers, Washington: US Catholic Conference, 1998. [*Origins* 27:39, March 19, 1998, 651–653] (EF)

Pope John Paul II, *Ut Unum Sint: On Commitment to Ecumenism*, Washington: US Catholic Conference, 1995 [*Origins*, 25:4, June 8, 1995, 49–72]. (UUS), see http://www.vatican.va/holy_father/john_paul_ii/encyclicals/documents/hf_jp-ii_enc_25051995_ut-unum-sint_en.html

FOREWORD

In his homily on the occasion of the solemn liturgy for the opening of the Second Vatican Council on October 11, 1962, Pope John XXIII again outlined the three main goals of the council as he envisioned them, namely, the renewal of the church, the reconciliation of the churches, and the transformation of the world by the gospel. Each of these goals is perennially rooted in the gospel of the kingdom proclaimed by Jesus of Nazareth during his earthly ministry. Each found new power and focus from the inspired teachings of the apostles and their disciples after the resurrection.

All the council documents are permeated by those same three purposes and hopes. With deepest respect for the ancient faith of the church and a zeal for expressing the perennial truths of faith in a language able to be embraced by Catholics poised to enter a new millennium, the council fathers labored to proclaim the truth of Christ in language both profoundly biblical and eminently contemporary in tone.

From the beginning, and with increasing interaction, official ecumenical observers and guests invited by the Holy See were present throughout the four sessions of the council's deliberations. These observers listened carefully to the speeches and presentations of the bishops; they were repeatedly encouraged to enter into informal discussions regarding all the ideas that were proposed. Friendships were forged across denominational lines. Expressions of a common Christian faith sometimes found more accurate formulation because of the respectful refinement made possible by that ecumenical exchange.

Renewal of the church was initiated by the council's effort to reclaim the fullness of the church's faith throughout the centuries. Reconciliation of the churches was begun anew by the rediscovery of profound commonalities in faith and deepened by the bond of charity that developed over the course of the four annual sessions of the council. The transformation of the world received new impetus as a result of the council's reaffirmation of the fundamental nature and mission of the church.

Sometimes the phrasing of the truth was reshaped or reworded because of informal suggestions from the ecumenical delegates, who were accorded a place of prominence near the section in the Basilica of St. Peter reserved for the cardinals. At times a more scriptural expression was found that might resonate among many or all of the church's ecumenical partners in the council's quest for greater understanding of the revealed mysteries of God's truth. Convergence and conversion often became the fruits of that journey together.

Immediately after the closing session of the council, the informal ecumenical discussions became official dialogues. Gradually, those formal conversations included the ancient Oriental Orthodox churches of the East and officially appointed representatives of the various national groupings of contemporary Orthodoxy as well as the churches and ecclesial communities of the Reformation in the West.

Elements of our common Christian heritage were explored, subject by subject and topic by topic, in order to understand the precise meaning of the formulae most cherished by each tradition. Repeatedly, those diverse phrases were discovered to hold virtually identical meanings across denominational boundaries. Some differences once presumed to be contradictory in the polemical debates of the past came to be understood as mutual enrichments.

Sometimes the different accents of faith revealed true differences that expanded our Catholic appreciation for the fullness of God's truth. Areas of diversity were probed in an effort to discover the common truth embodied in so many varied phrases and perspectives.

On still other occasions, ancient polemics had struggled over church-dividing issues that, as a result of years of patient scholarship and sustained prayer, became clarified and even at times resolved by the grace of God and the guidance of the Holy Spirit. The quest for unity in charity and truth has brought forth a great harvest over these past forty years.

Throughout the four decades of ecumenical dialogue, count-less reports had been written by the participants of each group. Summaries of convergence had found new expression, often begin-ning with the least controversial and then, by reason of mutual trust, moving toward more neuralgic topics. Each report and every statement of common agreement has its own history and its own fascinating tale. The role of the then Cardinal Ratzinger, for exam-ple, in reopening the final path toward the formal 1999 signing of the Lutheran–Catholic *Joint Declaration of the Doctrine of Justification* is well known. His recommitment of the entire church to this ecumenical task immediately after his election as Pope Benedict XVI is also recognized as a sign of the importance of this work for the future.

Clearly there still remain significant issues for mutual ecu-menical study and research. Some of them still seem church divid-ing at this time in history. Many such issues once presumed to fall within that category are now seen as elements of difference, not division. Thus the continued official study by ecumenically com-mitted theologians, the conversations of neighboring congrega-tions at the local level, and the prayers of all the churches remain an important task for all baptized Christians and an obligation for all Catholics.

During these same years, the Catholic Church heard a call for a new catechism that could present the teachings of the church in a manner that represented the ancient and fundamental truths of our faith and that reflected the work of the Second Vatican Council. Officially appointed bishops and scholars organized the presentation of those truths in a manner that revealed the interre-lationship of the mysteries of our faith but retained the biblical lan-guage that had become so cherished by everyone over the years. In 1992 Pope John Paul II promulgated the *Catechism of the Catholic Church*. In 1997 a slightly revised edition of that monumental work was published as a result of the further discussion inspired by the work itself. Theological and ecumenical dialogue had made yet another contribution toward the efficacy and clarity of the church's teaching ministry.

After these forty years of ecumenical collaboration, it has seemed obvious that some new compilation of these carefully crafted explorations into our common Christian faith might be useful for Catholic pastors, catechists, and teachers everywhere. It was agreed that by carefully selecting the most cogent expressions of faith from the ecumenical agreements, retaining the language of the original statements, and presenting them in a useable format, the text of the *Catechism* itself might be enhanced and made even more fruitful.

Thus the teachings of the whole church, East and West, Catholic and Reformed, can become an extraordinarily useful tool when carefully coordinated with the corresponding sections of the *Catechism of the Catholic Church*. A metaphor that has become increasingly common and familiar, perhaps especially because of its frequent use by the late Pope John Paul II, is the reference to the two lungs, Eastern and Western, by which the Church breathes the life-giving Holy Spirit and proclaims the truth of the gospel. A renewed experience of Pentecost can signal the Holy Spirit's impetus for reconciliation and unity among the Christian churches.

It is a great privilege and an honor to offer these few words of historical background and personal praise for the excellent work of Brother Jeffrey Gros, FSC, and Daniel Mulhall in the compilation of this work. *The Ecumenical Christian Dialogues and the "Catechism of the Catholic Church"* enables every reader to encounter the words of the *Catechism* together with the rich commentary provided, not merely by individual theological or catechetical writers alone, but by the very words from the various ecumenical dialogues themselves!

The Holy Spirit of Truth and Unity is clearly in our midst. May the Lord who began this good work bring it to perfection! May the three aims of the Second Vatican Council and the prayers of the entire church during its historic unfolding find success as God defines the term.

Bishop Richard J. Sklba, Chair
Bishops Committee for Ecumenical and Interreligious Affairs
United States Conference of Catholic Bishops

1

INTRODUCTION

Since its introduction in 1992, the *Catechism of the Catholic Church* frequently has been called a great gift to the Catholic Church. It certainly has become an important resource for Catholic educators and catechists in their task of evangelization. With the *Catechism* as a sure reference and guide, educators and catechists now have at their fingertips a brief presentation of the essentials of what the Catholic Church believes and teaches. With the *Catechism*, educators and catechists can feel confident that what they teach is what the church believes.

This compendium of teaching has also been a boon to those engaged in the effort to bring about visible unity within the church. The promotion of Christian unity is an essential aspect of the church's catechetical and evangelical mission. Although it may seem counterintuitive, strengthening the bonds of unity between churches also strengthens the church's ability to proclaim Jesus' message of salvation. In some cultures, especially those where religious illiteracy is a growing concern, the *Catechism* has stimulated Christian churches and ecclesial communities to collaborate in their efforts to pass on the gospel with integrity, clarity, and fidelity.

If the effort toward Christian unity is to be successful, however, teachers and catechists will need more than the knowledge of Catholic beliefs provided by the *Catechism*. They will also need to know about and understand the beliefs and practices of other Christian churches. This can be a daunting task. Learning what every other Christian church believes and teaches seems more the task of professional ecumenists then it does the average Catholic teacher or catechist. Unless they have a personal interest in ecumenism or a practical reason to know about a particular church (for example, an interchurch marriage in the family), few would be willing or able to make the effort needed to learn all that they need to know.

In addition to the sheer volume of materials one would need to learn, there is a larger hurdle to clear: How can one be sure that he or she understands the beliefs and practices of another church as the members of that church understand them? For our purposes here it is sufficient to say that people are shaped by the cultures in which they live. For example, people raised in the Catholic Church will understand Lutheran beliefs and practices from a Catholic perspective. They cannot understand them as a Lutheran does. Even though words used may be the same, the meaning and importance of those words may be entirely different, leading all too frequently to misunderstanding and conflict: a modern day Tower of Babel experience.

Because of the efforts at ecumenism over the last fifty years, such misunderstandings no longer need to happen. Through numerous official discussions between representatives of the Catholic Church and representatives from other Christian churches, points of belief have been clarified. During these discussions, Catholic theologians have explained to Lutheran theologians what they mean by a theological concept such as "justification by faith," and Lutheran theologians have been able to explain their beliefs right back. After many years of such discussions, the participants in these dialogues have produced written statements that explain clearly what each side believes and why it believes as it does. Where agreement is possible, it is so stated and written with one voice; where it is not, the differences in understanding are stated and each church explains for itself the differences in belief as they see it. Thus every church speaks for itself. These written statements are then taken back to the governing bodies of each of the churches for formal approval.

Over the years these ecumenical dialogues have produced a large number of statements covering many different topics. Because the dialogues have focused on the essential questions of the Christian faith, it should come as no surprise that many of the core beliefs presented in the *Catechism of the Catholic Church* (CCC) have also been treated in one or more discussions with other Christian churches. Thus, we no longer need to guess what another

Christian church believes about a core teaching—we can simply look it up!

This book was written to help you understand key aspects from the dialogues organized around the articles of faith as expressed in the *Catechism*. Chapters 4 through 10 are organized around foundational statements found in the *Catechism*. To these foundational statements we have added the corresponding statements from the ecumenical dialogues. What the Catholic Church believes and what other Christian churches believe on the same topic are gathered together for the reader's consideration.

This volume has been written with the following Catholic groups in mind: elementary and secondary level catechists and school teachers, school principals and parish DREs, high school and college campus ministers, those working with the Rite of Christian Initiation of Adults, those preparing educational and catechetical material, diocesan education and catechetical leaders, and anyone else who is interested in being a serious student of the faith. By using this book the reader will gain a deeper appreciation for the *Catechism*, encounter statements from the officially sponsored ecumenical dialogues, come to a deeper understanding of the faith that all Christians profess, and be empowered to build bridges toward Christian unity.

This book will also be useful for Christians catechized in other churches who are preparing to enter into full communion with the Catholic Church. It will help them to understand the common faith they have shared and the differences they are accepting by entering into the Catholic Church.

Finally, this text will be of great value for priests, deacons, and anyone else who works regularly with people from other Christian traditions. Although most of the materials presented here are taken directly from the dialogues themselves, reflection/discussion questions are provided, and suggestions are made for how to use these materials in pastoral settings.

While we have tried to make the materials in this book as easy to use as possible, we have not "dumbed them down." Most of what you will read here will be direct quotations from one or more dialogue reports. Because the dialogues are held among bishops, theologians, and other church leaders, the written reports are serious

theological works that many people who are not themselves theologians may find difficult to understand fully. Yet, as Pope John
Paul II made clear, what takes place in these dialogues and our
understanding of their reports is essential to the catechetical mission of the church.

> 80. While dialogue continues on new subjects or devel-
> ops at deeper levels, a new task lies before us: that of
> receiving the results already achieved. These cannot
> remain the statements of bilateral commissions but *must
> become a common heritage.* For this to come about and for
> the bonds of communion to be thus strengthened, a seri-
> ous examination needs to be made, which, by different
> ways and means and at various levels of responsibility,
> *must involve the whole People of God.* We are in fact deal-
> ing with issues which frequently are matters of faith, and
> these require universal consent, extending from the
> Bishops to the lay faithful, all of whom have received the
> anointing of the Holy Spirit. It is the same Spirit who
> assists the Magisterium and awakens the *sensus fidei.*
>
> Consequently, for the outcome of dialogue to be
> received, there is needed a broad and precise critical
> process which analyzes the results and rigorously tests
> their consistency with the Tradition of faith received
> from the Apostles and lived out in the community of
> believers gathered around the Bishop, their legitimate
> Pastor. (UUS 80, emphasis added)

If these technical texts are to become a common heritage and
if the whole people of God are to be engaged in understanding
them, then it is essential that those involved in the church's catechetical, preaching, and formation ministries know them well.
Educators and pastors with technical training know how to find
and use the complete dialogue statements in research volumes, on
the Web, or in periodical publications. For most educators, catechists, and pastoral workers, though, dialogue reports may seem
inaccessible or perhaps even unintelligible. The biggest obstacles of
all, however, will be the lack of awareness that any such materials

exist or that they might be of any interest whatsoever. The "why should I care" factor concerning the ecumenical dialogue reports is very high. The organization of this book addresses both of these obstacles head-on.

This volume attempts to provide a fairly basic selection of texts that have been produced by the Holy See or by the United States Conference of Catholic Bishops with their dialogue partners. The materials are offered in excerpted form, following the outline of the *Catechism of the Catholic Church*.

Some will use the volume as a reference, perhaps going to the section on baptism when teaching what the *Catechism* has to say on the subject of receiving adults into the Catholic Church who were previously baptized in another tradition. Others will use the volume as a companion to courses in doctrine, history, or ecumenism. For those interested in studying the ecumenical dialogues in depth, this text will serve as a useful primer for the ecumenical documents. To help these readers, the sources listed include the six reference volumes and three Web sites where most of the full texts can be found. Introductory vignettes and closing suggestions are included in each of the last seven chapters as a means to suggest practical pastoral uses of the information presented here.

Because each of the ecumenical dialogues is the fruit of years or even decades of research, dialogue, and exploration of the sources of the Christian faith, there is much that could not be included in this work. For example, the texts presented here include little of the rich historical, biblical, and theological background that makes the conclusions possible. Footnotes or background essays that are often published with the agreed statements of the dialogues have also been left out as a matter of expediency. These materials are available in the full dialogue text reports noted with each excerpt.

The reader is encouraged to dive deeply into this pool of writing, studying the original texts with interested and informed members of the dialogue churches. Such study can promote the Christian unity that is so greatly desired, and can be an opportunity for personal growth. Educators, in particular, will find it helpful to study with knowledgeable colleagues from these other churches. Through such dialogues they can explore how best to teach students, promote religious literacy in both communities, and gain a sense of the urgency for building the basis in faith that can lead to that unity for which Christ prayed.

This volume of selections begins with a chapter on Catholic ecumenical principles, and a chapter on the churches involved in the dialogue. Following these introductory chapters there will be seven chapters on agreements in faith, sacraments, the Christian life and spirituality, following the four parts of the *Catechism*. As you read these chapters, be prepared to use the *Catechism* itself as an accompanying support and guide.

Throughout the final seven chapters we have provided "Editor's Notes" to help the reader understand the context of the dialogues, the pertinent issues involved, and the significance of what has been addressed, all in clear, easy-to-understand language. This was done to help the reader understand the important points developed in each dialogue. These "Editor's Notes" will usually appear at the beginning of each section or in reference to a dialogue with a particular church or tradition. At times, however, they will appear within the dialogue texts, in brackets and in italics. In these situations, the "Editor's Notes" allow the reader to skip over large segments of dialogue text without losing the flow of the conversation.

The Holy Father's plea that these texts become a "common heritage" will occur only if educators, catechists, and pastoral leaders have the zeal for Christian unity, see this unity as integral to Catholic identity, and recognize that promoting this unity is an essential component of Catholic formation at every level: adults and children, cradle Catholics and catechumens, popular catechesis and ministry training.

This volume can only be an introduction, and in some cases a guide to the rich flowering of literature that has emerged over the last half century. It should whet the appetite for the reader to go beyond what is collected here to the original resources from which these brief selections are drawn.

In order to make the selected texts reader friendly, we have avoided footnotes but included references and abbreviations with each text, and noted where these are available on Web sites and in reference volumes. We have cited paragraph numbers rather than page numbers; where the paragraphs are not numbered in the original, the numbers presented here refer to the outline of the original text.

As Pope John Paul has reminded us, "[It] is absolutely clear that ecumenism, the movement promoting Christian Unity, is not just some sort of 'appendix' which is added to the Church's traditional activity. Rather, ecumenism is an organic part of her life and work, and consequently must pervade all that she is and does; it must be like the fruit borne by a healthy and flourishing tree which grows to its full stature" (UUS 20). In order for this to be the case, a clear knowledge of the results of ecumenical dialogue will need to become integral to every level of Catholic formation.

Unity among Christians can only be served by those who both know and are committed to their faith. Ecumenism is about the religious content of our Christian faith and the reconciliation of theological differences that have divided the Christian churches and ecclesial communities. Christians live together in interchurch families, collaborate together in Christian witness and service in their communities, and pray together regularly. However, there are also formal dialogues touching on all aspects of faith, where we share common beliefs, where there are differences that need to be resolved, and where we can deepen the relationships between, sadly, our still divided churches. These theological agreements serve to strengthen the faith summarized in the *Catechism* and are therefore an important resource for deepening Catholic identity.

Jeffrey Gros, FSC
Daniel S. Mulhall

2

CHURCH UNITY AND CATHOLIC EDUCATION

Whenever you speak with priests or parish catechists, one phrase will often be used to describe their work: "This is where the rubber hits the road." This apt metaphor makes the point that just as a tire on pavement is needed to make a car move, the priest or parish catechist is needed to make Catholic Church teaching come alive for most parishioners. Taking the analogy another step, just as the quality of a tire's tread will determine how well the car handles speed, pavement, and weather conditions, how well the priest or catechist understands the Catholic Church's teachings on ecumenical issues will determine how well those teachings are implemented or take root in the lives of the parish and its parishioners. And, finally, just as the car's contact with the road is through the wheels, the Catholic Church's most frequent contact with members of other faiths involves the priest or catechist: the priest as he deals with people seeking marriage to a spouse from another Christian faith, in counseling sessions, or at the time of death; the catechists when people seek to enter the Catholic Church through the Rite of Christian Initiation of Adults, or when they teach children whose parents belong to another Christian faith. What becomes clear here is that if the priest and catechists do not understand what is contained in the ecumenical dialogues, the dialogues will have little effect on the daily life of the Catholic Church or its members.

After years of working with both priests and catechists, it has become clear to us that while there are many people in each group who are interested in the church's dialogues with other Christians and who work diligently to build relationships between Christian churches, most priests and catechists will have their ministry enhanced by being better informed about the dialogues. This comment is not meant to be critical, but it is meant to be honest. Efforts within the Catholic Church to educate priests and catechists about the results of dialogues between churches are still in the process of development and have plenty of room to grow.

Part of the responsibility for this lack of progress must be placed on those of us involved in the ecumenical dialogues and those of us charged with handing on the church's teaching in this regard. While the written reports from the interchurch dialogues are readily available, many are written in a style only scholars find of interest. While this is necessary in order to be faithful to the words agreed to by the participating churches, the result is that few who work outside the ecumenical community ever manage to read the technical (some would say dry) language found in the reports.

Understanding the context of the ecumenical dialogues is often difficult, unless one is steeped in theology—both Catholic and that of the discussion partner—and aware of the history and tradition of each church. Reading in this field becomes a specialty, much like those who enjoy reading every act of Congress or who find keeping track of federal spending thrilling. Those of us charged with educating Catholics on these dialogues are just beginning to find ways to make the reports interesting or understandable to the average parishioner or usable by them. What passes as ecumenical education, then, often is little more than *ferverinos,* or pious exhortations: "Be inviting to our brothers and sisters in Christ. Make them feel welcome when they visit us." Such education leaves much to be desired.

This book grew out of a conversation between Christian Brother Jeffrey Gros, an active participant in the Catholic Church's ecumenical efforts for the past thirty years, and Daniel S. Mulhall, a catechist for twenty-five. The question that led to this book is "How do we take the teachings found in the ecumenical dialogue reports and make them accessible and of interest to priests and catechists?" This text is the result of that conversation.

The *Catechism of the Catholic Church* is used throughout to organize the work and to provide a context through which the dialogue teachings can be best understood. Because most Catholics are familiar with the language found in the Catechism, reading the dialogue responses in that context will make them easier to understand and more relevant than they otherwise might be. Second, by reading the dialogue statements in tandem with the *Catechism*, the reader will grow more aware of the depth of the church's teaching to which the *Catechism*, because of its limited scope, can only hint. Thus by reading this book, the reader is doubly served, gaining both a greater knowledge and appreciation for the beliefs and teachings of another Christian church and a fuller explanation for what the Catholic Church believes and teaches.

The texts presented in this volume provide new interpretations of the traditional Catholic faith, and therefore are aids in deepening our understanding of the formulations of faith as presented in the *Catechism*. The texts also provide a renewed way of looking at the present-day churches and ecclesial communities who have participated in the dialogues. Through these writings it is possible to overcome some of the misunderstandings that have developed from the early days of these churches when, in the crisis moments of history, the original divisions occurred.

Why the Ecumenical Dialogues Matter

The goal of the Catholic Church in the ecumenical movement is to be in full communion with all other Christians:

> The Catholic Church solemnly pledged itself to work for Christian unity at the Second Vatican Council. The Decree *Unitatis Redintegratio* explains how the unity that Christ wishes for his Church is brought about "through the faithful preaching of the Gospel by the Apostles and their successors—the Bishops with Peter's successor at their head—through their administering the sacraments, and through their governing in love," and defines this unity as consisting of the "confession of one faith,…the common celebration of divine worship,…the fraternal harmony of the family of God." This unity which of its very nature requires full visible communion of all Christians is the ultimate goal of the ecumenical move-

ment. The Council affirms that this unity by no means requires the sacrifice of the rich diversity of spirituality, discipline, liturgical rites and elaborations of revealed truth that has grown up among Christians in the measure that this diversity remains faithful to the apostolic Tradition. (Directory 20)

This unity is not achieved by compromise or negotiation, but by prayer, collaboration in all aspects of Christian life, internal renewal of the churches, and common theological dialogue. Relativism, indifferentism, and anti-intellectualism are all enemies of ecumenism and of the Catholic understanding of the faith, and thus are not part of these dialogues. These discussions between religious traditions have been frank, honest, and intense. Each church delegation enters into the conversations sure in its belief that God is present and active in its faith community. The purpose of these discussions is to find areas of agreement in theology and practice, and not to cast aspersions or challenge the legitimacy of any belief or tradition. The conversations take place because of the belief that when Jesus prayed, "Father, may they all be one" (John 17:21), he meant what he said. The churches all feel that by engaging in these discussions they are doing as Christ commanded.

Notes from the
General Directory for Catechesis

In 1997 the Vatican Congregation for the Clergy, which has responsibility for catechesis, published the *General Directory for Catechesis* (GDC). This *Directory* provides guidance to the universal church on how catechesis is to be done. In no. 197 of the GDC, the *Directory* calls for

[e]very Christian community…to recognize its ecumenical vocation in the circumstances in which it finds itself, by participating in ecumenical dialogue and initiatives to foster the unity of Christians. Catechesis, therefore, is

always called to assume an "ecumenical dimension" (98) everywhere. This is done, firstly, by an exposition of all of Revelation, of which the Catholic Church conserves the deposit, while respecting the hierarchy of truths. (99) In the second place, catechesis brings to the fore that unity of faith which exists between Christians and explains the divisions existing between them and the steps being taken to overcome them. (100) Catechesis also arouses and nourishes a true desire for unity, particularly with the love of Sacred Scripture. Finally, it prepares children, young people and adults to live in contact with brothers and sisters of other confessions, by having them cultivate both their own Catholic identity and respect for the faith of others.

In no. 198, the GDC adds,

The teaching of religion in schools attended by Christians of diverse confessions can also have an ecumenical value when Christian doctrine is genuinely presented. This affords the opportunity for dialogue through which prejudice and ignorance can be overcome and a greater openness to better reciprocal understanding achieved.

These ideas are also found in the new *National Directory for Catechesis* approved by the Holy See for use in the United States of America in December 2004.

The only way that the GDC's call for prejudice and ignorance can "be overcome and a greater openness to better reciprocal understanding achieved" is by making sure that catechists are confident in both their own understanding of the Catholic faith and in their familiarity with the teaching of other churches. This understanding and familiarity can be achieved by working with the reports from the various dialogues.

Conciliar Shifts

The Second Vatican Council (1962–1965) was called to help the Catholic Church better proclaim the gospel in a world that had experienced and continued to experience rapid changes. As a result of the council, the Catholic Church renewed the liturgy, empowered the lay faithful to full participation in the church's life, recommitted itself to evangelization, and made the quest for peace and justice integral to its daily life. On an equal footing with each of these mentioned changes, the church also committed itself to work for Christian unity. This "passion for unity" led to numerous conversations with many of the other churches in the world who say that they are Christian. As a result of these conversations, many positive changes have occurred. Consider for a moment these statements that express Catholic teaching:

- We recognize the real but imperfect communion that exists among our church and other churches and ecclesial communities, and we have begun to live into a deeper communion. (Decree on Ecumenism 1965)
- We no longer speak of "separated brethren" but of "fellow Christians." (UUS 1995)
- Common Baptism, those things we share in faith and our common scripture help Catholic identity to be formed within an understanding of our common Christianity. (Directory for the Application of Principles and Norms on Ecumenism 1993)
- We have moved from an ecumenism of "return" to a mutual respect, using dialogue as the means for disclosing our agreements, those things needing resolution on the common pilgrimage toward that unity for which Christ prayed. (Decree on Ecumenism)
- Our theological understanding has shifted from seeing the Roman Catholic Church as the one, true Church to an affirmation of the fact that the one, true Church "subsists in" the Catholic Church, but that elements of the true Church are alive and saving in other churches, and that we are all

wounded while the scandal of division remains. (Decree on Ecumenism)

As Pope John Paul reminded us: "The commitment to re-establishing full and visible communion among all the baptized does not apply merely to a few ecumenical experts; it concerns every Christian, from every diocese and parish, and from every one of the church's communities. All are called to take on this commitment, and no one can refuse to make his own the prayer of Jesus that all may be one; all are called to pray and work for the unity of Christ's disciples." (UUS)

All of these statements form the background for understanding the documents in this volume and the journey on which the Catholic Church has embarked.

Formation Principles

The 1998 text *The Ecumenical Dimension in the Formation of Pastoral Workers* outlines three dimensions from an ecumenical point of view that are essential in all Catholic education and formation: (1) an interpretive perspective, (2) an understanding of the hierarchy of truths, and (3) a knowledge of the results of the dialogues. This volume, which is a primer on the ecumenical dialogues, is designed to address this third priority. In order for the reader to understand the significance of these texts, however, a proper "interpretive horizon" first needs to be established.

This interpretive horizon entails, first of all, a conversion to the church's commitment to unity among the Christian churches. This presupposes that the reader is

- receptive to the idea that we share the same faith with the other Christian communities and churches with whom we share a common baptism, even if the communion between these churches and communities is not yet perfect.
- open to engaging in a dialogue of love and mutual respect that must precede the dialogue of truth and the theological interchange that has produced these texts.

- willing to look at the scripture through the eyes of the other, seeing what they see, understanding what they understand. This does not mean rejecting the Catholic understanding of scripture, but a willingness to learn from the other communities and churches.
- able to recognize the scripture's call to church unity and to reexamine its texts through the lenses of the various communities and churches that have interpreted it differently through the years.

This interpretive horizon also entails rereading church history with the intent of recognizing the Holy Father's call for a "healing of memories" (UUS 2). That is, Catholics will look at the history of separations—both East and West and the Reformation— and take full responsibility for the failings of their forebears, admitting that human failings on both sides contributed to the rupture in the Body of Christ.

Although ecumenical discussions have been occurring now for more than forty years, they are still in their early stages. No matter how committed each church is to the discussion, each moves at its own pace. Five hundred years of mistrust and animosity do not disappear overnight. New layers of trust have to be developed, ancient hurts must be healed through apologies offered and accepted. In those situations where theologies were developed in opposition to the teachings of the other churches, new expressions of beliefs must be found. In some cases, because of separated historical development, churches use the same words but understand them in different ways. These misunderstandings take time to sort out. The process is developmental, with each discussion laying the groundwork that will lead to the next conversation.

As new agreements have emerged, the churches have found new perspectives for seeing and interpreting the events of history and the historic formulations of faith that have emerged from them. For example, the 1999 *Joint Declaration on the Doctrine of Justification* (signed by representatives of the Catholic Church and the churches of the Lutheran World Federation) not only gives new interpretive principles for understanding the Council of Trent, but also offers a more positive way to tell the story of the Reformation and Luther's role in it.

We interpret justification, present-day Lutherans, and the history of the Reformation through a new lens now that the *Joint Declaration* has become an authoritative statement for Catholics. This gives us the opportunity of reinforcing the faith of the church as enunciated in the Catechism.

The second principle enunciated by the *Ecumenical Formation* text is the "hierarchy of truths." This statement recognizes that the faith revealed to us comes as a complex whole, centered on God's revelation in Jesus Christ, coming to clarification in the history of the church. While all of what the church teaches is to be believed, all of the truths of the faith are not related to one another in the same way. Some are foundational, providing the footing on which all other teachings rest, while others are structural: Like floor joists and studs in a building, they provide the framework that, built upon the solid foundation, holds the church together. Finally, some later explanations have been added that provide substance and texture. Thus, distinctions can be made between teachings that are dogmas of the church, teachings that support these dogmas, and teachings that are individual opinions or private devotions.

Therefore, in ecumenical dialogue it is important to order the truths of the faith accurately so that, where there are differences between communities, it's possible to determine whether the differences are related to the central message of the incarnation or to later interpretations that developed. This clarity will enable the parties in the dialogue to understand better what each believes about important Christian truths.

This text uses the structure of the *Catechism of the Catholic Church* to present a clear ordering of the truths. Each time that a section of agreed-to dialogue text is presented, an effort has been made to show where agreement exists between communities, where historical misunderstandings have been cleared up, where there is movement toward agreement on controversial issues, and where differences in theology still remain.

As noted before, the dialogue reports are written in precise theological language by scholars officially appointed to the discussions by the leaders of the various communities. The Holy See appoints the Catholic scholars to the international dialogues and the bishops of the U.S. Conference of Catholic Bishops appoint the U.S. representatives of the Catholic Church on the national dialogues. Thus, the texts produced for the church represent only the authority of the scholarship on which they are based. (Please note that some dialogue statements have been approved by the Holy See and thus carry the authority of church teaching. An example of this is the 1999 *Joint Declaration on the Doctrine of Justification*, or the Common Declaration with Eastern Patriarchs resolving the Christological differences of the Council of Chalcedon.) For that reason, it will be important for the reader to go back to the original, full text if the conclusions summarized here are not clear or do not seem to follow an intelligible line of reasoning. Where possible we have listed footnotes and background essays to the dialogues that further clarify how recommendations were reached.

The Dialogues

The methods used in the dialogue avoid compromise or negotiation. Rather, they seek the firm truth of the Tradition as embodied in scripture and the Christian heritage. Theologians, trying to get behind traditional interpretations and confessional uses of the text, carefully look at biblical passages seeking to find the intent of the original authors. The formulations of the councils of the church and of confessional positions of different churches are examined through the lenses of scripture and the Tradition to discern the original intent of the writers. Finally, new language is sometimes used to articulate the same faith but avoid old polemics.

Careful attention is given to how formulations of faith are used in the contemporary churches, how they can be interpreted today in the light of the best historical and biblical scholarship, and how they express the faith of the church today. New formulations may be developed in the dialogues, not to replace the historic positions of the churches but to clarify them or to deepen the understanding of both parties of the authentic faith of the church.

When the Catholic Church began to participate in the ecumenical movement, the Holy See produced a set of guidelines to be used in the dialogues. These same guidelines are still used today and provide an important summary of the procedures used in ecumenical interchange.

When these dialogues began forty years ago, few people would have predicted the great profusion of results that have emerged. Among the most significant for Catholics have been

- the Common Declarations with the patriarchs of the Eastern Churches,
- the *Joint Declaration* with the Lutherans,
- the Anglican/Catholic *Final Report* and its evaluation by the Holy See and the bishops of the Anglican Communion.

All of these documents represent milestones that have moved the Catholic Church from dialogue to decision. These decisions have changed the Catholic Church's relationships to these churches in fundamental ways.

Christians believe that they and their churches are in real, if imperfect, communion with one another. As noted above, Catholics hold that communion in faith, in sacramental life, and in bonds of communion (hierarchical communion in Catholic usage) are necessary if the full communion envisioned in the scripture is to be achieved. This communion reflects the communion (*koinonia*, communion) of the triune God: Father, Son, and Holy Spirit. One will note that the understanding of the church emerging from these dialogues is rooted in this same theology of communion central to Catholic self-understanding. Even where a dialogue deals with specific issues like the procession of the Holy Spirit, or the presence of Christ in the Eucharist, it is oriented toward perfecting that communion in Christ which is God's gift to the church.

There are many types of dialogues. The majority of texts in this volume will be the results of bilateral dialogues with a particular church, or cluster of Christians, like Pentecostal or Evangelical. Some of these dialogues, like those with the Orthodox, Lutherans, Disciples, Methodists, Reformed, and Anglicans, are oriented toward establishing full communion between the churches dialoguing. Obviously, these dialogues each move at their own pace, which are different one from another and take up different issues depending on the church's differences with the Catholic Church. Others, such as Catholic dialogues with Baptists, Pentecostals, and Evangelicals, are oriented toward mutual respect, understanding, and common witness between the churches. Because these churches, from their reading of the scripture, do not believe that visible unity is warranted, full communion is not on their dialogue agenda.

There are also texts from the Faith and Order commissions. The Faith and Order movement is a theological dialogue that began in the early twentieth century to help the Orthodox, Anglican, and Protestant churches to understand better one another's beliefs and theologies. For decades these Faith and Order commissions worked to improve relations between churches by holding discussions on the theology, sacramental life, and church structure of the various churches participating in the dialogue. In the 1950s these discussions moved from comparing differences between churches to studying the biblical and theological research coming from the various churches to see if agreement could be found there. Since 1969, following the Second Vatican Council and its 1965 Decree on Ecumenism, the Catholic Church has been a member of the Faith and Order commissions, both in the World Council of Churches and the United States National Council.

The bilateral dialogues sometimes produce results that claim full agreement or consensus. Sometimes they reach a mutual understanding of differences, clearly stated without stereotype or caricature. At other times the text produces a step toward agreement, called a convergence. Faith and Order Commissions, because of their diversity—often more than one hundred churches are represented in a discussion—are able to produce statements that only reach the level of convergence. But to be clear, even convergence-level statements are important because they clearly state what each church means and believes by its words, and thus lead to better understanding between churches and make the next round of conversations that much more hopeful.

The dialogues move along slowly and methodologically, sometimes offering proposals for interim stages toward full communion. Often advances in one area necessitate further study in another area. For example, agreement with the Lutherans on Eucharist has entailed the necessity of finding agreement on ordained ministry. Agreements with Anglicans on holy orders have necessitated work on authority, since differences about the ordination of women entail questions of authority.

In addition to Faith and Order and bilateral studies, there are also some texts here that are reports, such as those from a "Joint Working Group of the Catholic Church and the World Council," from the "Christian Reformed Church as a Result of Dialog with the Catholic Church," and from a "Commission of the Orthodox Churches and the World Council."

We will try to keep the status of the documents clear where that is appropriate. Those that express agreement affirmed by the churches are noted as *agreement.* Those which are *consensus* proposals, those that are *convergence* texts, and commonly articulated *differences* will be so noted. Some few are reports or recommendations. These differentiations will be signaled in later chapters when dialogue texts are quoted.

In referring to the full text, a more detailed explanation is usually given as to the origin, genesis, methodology, and standing of the dialogue text quoted. Notes here are kept to a minimum so that the excerpts themselves will be the major resource.

These texts, the decisions and understanding they enable, and the documents that stand behind them are an integral contribution to the new evangelization:

> The new evangelization is the order of the day....The task of evangelization involves moving toward each other and moving together as Christians, and it must begin from within; evangelization and unity, evangelization and ecumenism are indissolubly linked with each other....Because the question of the new evangelization is very close to my heart, as bishop of Rome, I consider overcoming the divisions of Christianity "one of the pastoral priorities." (Pope John Paul II, Germany, July 1996)

Resource List

The Catholic Church has developed important directives and resources that guide its ecumenical activity. The names of these resources are noted in the list of Vatican texts found in the Introduction. Those engaged in Christian formation should be familiar with these texts since they provide the foundation on which the church's ecumenical efforts rest. In addition to these formal church documents, the resource list also includes the names of several volumes, written as textbooks, that provide an overview of the history and ecumenism principles of the Catholic Church and help one to understand the developing relationships between the Catholic Church and her ecumenical partners. This volume can be used along with one or another of these texts, whether in a class on the church, doctrine, or ecumenism. For those engaged in catechist formation or adult faith development, the short volumes by Gros (2000) and Laubenthal (2003) can lead to a wealth of discussion.

3

WHO ARE OUR PARTNERS?

The Catholic faith is nurtured and enriched through dialoguing with fellow Christians. Such dialogues deepen the common faith believers share and clarify the differences that exist between them. Dialogue both promotes a common mission and fosters a spiritual sharing. As the *General Directory for Catechesis* says, the Christian community and its particular ecumenical make-up "becomes a point of concrete reference for the faith journey of individuals. This happens when the community is proposed as a source, *locus* and means of catechesis" (GDC 158). This means that as Catholics learn about particular churches, their history, their relationship to us, and their spiritual life, they are learning about what God has done and is doing in and through that community. They also learn how one's own spiritual and ecclesial life is enriched by the Holy Spirit's presence in these fellow Christians and how they live out this common calling to unity.

The Catholic Church has held formal dialogues with churches of both the East and West. Among the Eastern churches, dialogues have been held or are being held with these Orthodox churches: Assyrian, Eastern, and Oriental. Dialogues are also being held with the following Western churches: Polish National Catholic Church, Anglicans (Episcopalians), Lutherans, Methodists, Reformed, Presbyterian, United Church of Christ, Disciples of Christ, Mennonites, Baptists, Evangelicals, and Pentecostals. The Catholic Church also relates to a wide range of other churches through the Faith and Order Commissions of the World and National Councils of Churches.

The Eastern Churches

Any discussion of dialogues between the Roman Catholic Church and the Eastern churches must begin with a clarification. In addition to the Assyrian, Eastern, and Oriental Orthodox churches mentioned above, there are also several Eastern Catholic churches that are in full communion with Rome. These include the Byzantine (Melkite, Ukrainian, Ruthinian, Romanian, Bulgarian, Slovak, Hungarian), Coptic, Armenian, Ethiopian, Syriac, Syro-Malabar, Syro-Malankara, Maronite, and Chaldean churches. These Eastern Catholic churches were, until recently, commonly called "Eastern rite" churches. However, since the promulgation of the Code of Canons of the Eastern Churches in 1991, these communions have been recognized as "churches *sui juris* (with their own legal tradition)." Each of these churches has its own synodal governance and its own proper spirituality, law, liturgy, and theology.

Because the relationship between Rome and the Eastern Catholic churches is one of full communion, the relationship is not ecumenical. However, the Eastern Catholic churches often become the focus of the conversation in Orthodox/Catholic dialogues, especially those held with the Eastern (Byzantine) Orthodox. The Eastern Catholic churches often experience tension in their relationships with both Latin Catholics (with whom they share full communion) and with the Orthodox, whose traditions they share, but with whom relations have been strained for hundreds of years. That being said, note that the ecumenical dialogues are occurring with the Eastern Orthodox and not the Eastern Catholic churches.

The following information provides a snapshot to help you understand the various Eastern churches.

- The Assyrian Church of the East and the Chaldean Catholic Church are of the same tradition and developed in the Persian Empire beyond the borders of the Roman Empire. The Oriental Orthodox Churches were in Africa, Asia Minor, and Armenia on the borders of the Roman world.
- While the words *Oriental* and *Eastern* frequently are used as synonyms by Roman Catholics, the words have clear and

distinct meanings to the various churches that use them. The term *Oriental Orthodox* is used to distinguish those churches that have been separated from both Eastern Orthodoxy and Rome since the Council of Chalcedon (451).

- With the move of the center of the Roman Empire from Rome to Constantinople during the first centuries of Christianity, separated cultures began to take shape in each locale. As the Latin, Greek, and Slavic cultures diverged over the centuries, alienation developed between the churches in each locale. During the period between 1054 and 1204, the breakdown became complete. The churches of the East that resulted from this split are called Eastern or Byzantine Orthodox. The Eastern Orthodox believe that the Roman Catholic Church left the united communion of the first millennium. Roman Catholics feel that the divisions of 1054 and later were a schism that did not affect the apostolic faith, sacramental life, and episcopal structures of the churches, East and West. The Roman Catholic Church recognizes the sacramental character of these sister churches and insists that any study of the nature of the church take into full account the historical and theological developments of both East and West. Pope John Paul has written that the church must learn to breathe again "with both lungs." The unity shared during the first thousand years of Christianity serves as a common well to draw from during discussions of reform, renewal, and reunion.

- From the earliest days of the church, decisions were made for the church by bishops meeting together in councils. The decisions of the councils are recognized to be the highest authority in the church. During the second millennium of Christianity the Catholic Church in the West has come increasingly to rely on the ministry of unity provided by the pope, the bishop of Rome. The Roman Catholic Church, thus, is led by the central authority of the papacy. The churches of the East have remained much less centralized. They continue to make their decisions through councils known as "synods": the meeting of bishops around a patriarch to reach common decisions. A patriarch is the bishop of an ancient diocese and thus is held in high esteem. Patriarchal sees include Alexandria, Antioch, Rome, Jerusalem, and Constantinople. In addition to these foundational apostolic patriarchal sees, new patriarchates have also developed in both East and West, though none claim the primacy that has traditionally been attributed to Rome and Constantinople.

The dialogue with each of these three sister churches of the Eastern tradition is an important contribution to discerning the future God desires for us together.

ASSYRIAN CHURCH OF THE EAST

At the Council of Ephesus (431) the churches attempted to resolve the differences they had in speaking of Jesus' mother, Mary. Was she the mother of the humanity of Jesus Christ only, or was she the mother of Jesus, both human and divine? Those who were unwilling to speak of Mary as the "God bearer" *(theotokos)* seemed (to some) to question the full divinity of Christ, while to others the use of the title appeared to question his full humanity. The Persian Church with its patriarchate at Seleucia-Ctesiphon, called *Nestorian* by its critics, did not accept the council and fell out of communion with the five apostolic patriarchates.

The Assyrian Church of the East, as it is now called, flourished throughout Asia and the Middle East during the Middle Ages. Today, it primarily has members in Iran, Iraq, and the United States. The issue discussed at Ephesus on the nature of Mary as the mother of Jesus, human and divine, that divided the church has been resolved through dialogue. Pope John Paul and Patriarch Mar Dinkha (the See of his patriarchate is in Chicago) signed a common declaration in 1994 to this end.

ORIENTAL ORTHODOX CHURCHES

The Council of Chalcedon (451) dealt with christological issues that were raised by contentious debates between the theological schools of Antioch and Alexandria. At this council the bishops agreed that "[w]e teach . . . one and the same Christ, Son, Lord, Only-begotten, known in two natures, without confusion, without change, without division, without separation." Even after this definitive statement, this christological issue continued to be debated in various churches for centuries, and several councils were called by the Byzantine emperors, in collaboration with the patriarchs of Constantinople and Rome, attempting to heal the divisions in the church caused by the disagreement and to arrive at a formulation of the christological faith acceptable to all.

As a result of these debates, however, about half of the Patriarchate of Antioch (now the Syrian Orthodox Church) and most of the Church of Alexandria (now the Coptic Orthodox Church) separated from the patriarchs of Constantinople, Rome, and Jerusalem. The Armenian, Indian Syrian, and Ethiopian churches shared these christological views as well. These churches are now called Oriental Orthodox, but in the past were often stigmatized as *Monophysites*, which means that they believed that Christ had only one nature. These churches, in turn, characterized the Latin and Byzantine churches as *Dyophysite*, which means those who believe that Christ had two natures.

Recently, through the dialogues, christological agreements have emerged between these churches and the Byzantine patriarchs, Popes Paul VI and John Paul II, and some of the Reformation churches. Through the common declarations that have been issued it is now possible to say that Christians believe that Jesus Christ is truly human and truly divine, fully God and fully human. In 1981 Pope John Paul II and Syrian Orthodox Patriarch Ignatius of Antioch published a common declaration, setting to rest differences on christology and authorizing mutual eucharistic hospitality.

EASTERN (BYZANTINE) ORTHODOX CHURCHES

The Eastern Orthodox churches consider the West to have broken away from the common Tradition. This view has factual support in the events of 1054 and 1204. For example:

- In 1054 the representative of the pope in Constantinople excommunicated the patriarch, who returned the insult. There was, however, no pope alive at the time! These condemnations were "assigned to oblivion" by Pope Paul VI and Patriarch Athenagoras in 1964.
- In 1204, the Fourth Crusade from the Western Christians took over Constantinople, desecrated the cathedral, and set up a Latin bishop there. This sacrilege is still remembered in Orthodox churches. In 2000, Pope John Paul II publicly apologized to the archbishop of Athens for the misdeeds of his predecessors in the faith.

Over the years of separation, theology on both sides has continued to develop. Issues that still cause concern between the churches are things like the addition of the phrase "and the Son" *(filioque)* to the common creed, centralization of authority in the pope and papal infallibility, the Marian dogmas in Catholicism, and the ordination of women in Protestantism. The Orthodox see each of these developments as having been made unilaterally—not made in consultation with the faithful Church of the East—and hold that they have moved the church away from its apostolic heritage. Controversies also exist in sacramental theology and practice. The Orthodox have more difficulty recognizing as true the sacraments of the Catholic Church than Catholics have with recognizing as true the sacraments of the Orthodox churches.

The Orthodox Church has been unwilling to accept the claim of the Patriarchate of Rome to universal primacy. Because Constantinople became the "new" capital of the empire and thus has claims to being the new Rome, the Patriarchate of Constantinople claims an equal status with the Patriarchate of Rome. And while the Orthodox are willing to grant Rome's status as "first among equals"—more one of honor than authority—this issue has never been resolved and continues to cause tension. With the fall of Communism in the East, new tensions have developed because of the evangelization by Western Catholics of people who live in what is now Eastern Europe and the Balkans.

Most historians of both East and West now recognize that the Fourth Crusade of 1204 was the final blow to unity and trust. The

Byzantine Orthodox have never forgotten or forgiven the sacrilegious cruelty of the Western "Christian" invaders who sacked the cities and churches, replaced the canonical bishops with Latin prelates, and desecrated the holiest of sanctuaries.

Most of the patriarchates have members today in the United States: the Greeks and the Antiochean (Arabs), along with various Slavic groups; the Orthodox Church in America (Russian background, but now multiethnic), Serbian, Ukrainian, and so forth. The dialogues with the Orthodox in the United States have gone much easier than has the international dialogue, especially after the fall of Communism in 1989 when tensions in Eastern Europe reemerged.

Classical Protestant and Anglican Churches

Within the Latin Church of the West there were a series of divisions that developed during the Reformation of the sixteenth century. Some of the pre-Reformation divisions, such as those between rival popes in the fourteenth century, were healed, but not without a burden of distrust and cynicism concerning ecclesiastical institutions. Other problems, such as those with the Waldensians (excommunicated in 1183), with Wycliffe (1330–1384), and with the followers of the Bohemian reformer Jan Hus (c. 1372–1415), continued into the sixteenth century. They were eventually associated with Reformation churches in history, theology, and ecumenism. Waldensian and Moravian churches exist in the United States, but their numbers are small.

The context of the Reformation was complex and differed in the various parts of Europe. It is important to acknowledge that fault lies on both sides of the divisions. The Catholic Church now admits its complicity in the separation, and now approaches history with a sense of repentance and a commitment to the healing of memories (UUS 2).

LUTHERANS

Drawing on his pastoral experience, Martin Luther (1483–1546) began to pose academic questions in 1517 at the University of Wittenberg about the importance of good works to salvation. Luther was especially concerned with the sale of indulgences. His studies led Luther to a passionate conviction of the importance of preaching God's unmerited justification by grace through faith. This conviction, in turn, led him to question the emphasis placed on human effort and merit in achieving salvation by the church of his day. Luther originally had no intention of creating a schism in the church. He came to take more confrontational positions only after the questions he raised were rejected. Ironically, many of the reforms he advocated with regard to the preaching of indulgences were adopted by the Council of Trent half a century later, but not until after discussion with the Reformers had broken off.

In 1518, at the initiative of his Augustinian superior, Luther was released from his vows. Luther became an outlaw in the Holy Roman Empire after 1521 because he stood up for his convictions before Emperor Charles V at Worms. Luther placed emphasis on the authority of scripture in theology and in the church; he argued for the centrality of Christ, grace and faith over good works, and a gradual reform of ecclesial and sacramental practices. All of these issues brought him into the center of tensions that then existed between Germanic forces for reform and the established ecclesiastical and civil authorities of pope and emperor.

Luther's efforts at reform hardened into a formal separation following the publication of the Augsburg Confession (1530), which was drafted as an irenic statement of the evangelical princes within the Catholic empire. It became the theological platform for the protesting princes and their theologians against the leadership of the Catholic Church. From this point on, Reformation division had begun.

All dialogue ceased between Luther and Catholic officials in 1541 and reconciliation became impossible after the Council of Trent (1546–1563). Not until after the Peace of Augsburg in 1555 did the reality of separate church communities that eventually were to take on the name of "Evangelical" or "Lutheran" come into being. This reality was sealed by the Thirty Years War in the seventeenth century.

Lutheran churches emphasized the priesthood of all believers, the role of the civil leaders in church life, the centrality of scripture and its proclamation in worship, the real presence of Christ in the Eucharist—simplified and celebrated in the vernacular, the common language of the people—and above all else, the centrality of the gospel teaching on justification. Lutheran churches kept many Catholic practices: liturgical, spiritual, and artistic. This included, when possible, the episcopal structure of the church. The doctrinal tradition of the early church remains central to the Lutheran sense of fidelity to the apostolic church.

When Catholic history is taught in more detail, as much attention needs to be given to ecumenical history (1964 to the present) as might be given to a similar period in the sixteenth century (1517–1546). The Catholic dialogues have been conducted with the Lutheran World Federation, a communion of national Lutheran churches from around the world. In the United States, the Catholic Bishops Conference has been in dialogue with the Evangelical Lutheran Church and its predecessor bodies. The Lutheran Church–Missouri Synod was a member of the dialogue for the first nine rounds, and has been an observer at the tenth and most recent round. The Lutheran Church–Missouri Synod was not among the signers of the 1999 *Joint Declaration on the Doctrine of Justification.*

ANGLICANS

The Reformation in England took a very different course from the one in Germany. When the initial turmoil began in Europe, Henry VIII (reigned 1509–1547) was a staunch defender of the traditional faith and a persecutor of reformers. Henry's break with the church in Rome came later over efforts he made to obtain a divorce from his wife, Catherine of Aragon, who bore him no sons, so that he could marry someone else who could. For centuries afterward both continental Protestantism and continuing Catholic influences were in competition for the faith of the English people.

Thereafter, the English Reformation remained a confluence of Reformation and Catholic elements, with many Anglicans claiming continuity with, and even return to, the situation that prevailed in the medieval period.

Following Henry's death, England returned to papal obedience for a short time during the reign of his daughter Mary (1553–1558). Rome was again repudiated during the reign of her successor Elizabeth I (1558–1603). In 1559 the English monarch was named supreme governor of the English Church in an ecclesiastical settlement that featured a moderate *Book of Common Prayer* (Anglican "Missal")—which incorporated both Catholic and Reformation elements—and an episcopal ecclesiastical order that claimed continuity in the apostolic succession back to the apostles. Since the Second Vatican Council, the Catholic Church has acknowledged a special relationship with the Anglican tradition. As the council notes: "Among those [Reformation churches] in which Catholic traditions and institutions in part continue to exist, the Anglican Communion occupies a special place" (*Decree on Ecumenism* 13).

The dialogue between the Holy See and the worldwide Anglican Communion and the dialogue between the Catholic Church in the United States with the U.S. Episcopal Church have produced important agreements, pastoral proposals, and bases for mutual understanding. Because of these dialogues, many dioceses and parishes have developed covenants with their local counterparts in the other church.

REFORMED, METHODIST, AND DISCIPLES

While the dialogues between Episcopalians and Lutherans are best known among Catholics, important dialogues are also ongoing with other Protestant churches, including those with the Methodist and Baptist communities, the largest Protestant churches in the United States.

The Presbyterian Church and other Reformed churches, such as the Reformed Church in America and the Christian Reformed Church (both of Dutch background) and the United Church of Christ (UCC), owe their origins to the Swiss reform of John Calvin

(1509–1564), which spread to Scotland, Holland, and England. The word *reformed* is used to distinguish the Calvinist tradition from Lutheran and other Reformation churches. The Congregationalists (now UCC) and Presbyterians have had a strong influence on American forms of decision making as well as wider cultural issues. The United Church of Christ is to be distinguished from the Churches of Christ, which are a nineteenth-century American network of churches.

Calvin and Scottish Reformer John Knox (1514–1571) insisted on the full participation of the baptized in the governance of the church. Most Reformed churches have no bishops; there are both clergy and laity at every level of collegial decision making. Reformed churches are also sacramental, though their doctrine of the Eucharist has developed in a historically different and less catholic direction than the Anglican and Lutheran traditions. Catholics have had important international dialogues with the Reformed churches, including dialogues on important issues of ethics.

The Methodist churches (United Methodist and three African-American churches: African Methodist Episcopal, African Methodist Episcopal Zion, Christian Methodist Episcopal Churches) are the largest family in the U.S. ecumenical movement. They are, however, smaller internationally than Lutheran and Anglican communions. Their strong emphasis on spirituality and social involvement make them the natural ecumenical partner for U.S. Catholics.

Methodism began as a revival movement within Anglicanism. Its founder, John Wesley (1703–1791), felt that formal separation was necessary at the time of the American Revolution. He was devoted to sacramental as well as biblical and evangelistic renewal: He personally received communion several times a week. While Methodists recognize the office of bishop, they do not claim apostolic succession. Methodists are moving toward reconciliation with Anglican churches in the United States and in various other places around the world.

In 1969 the United Methodist Church revised its formula of faith to change those things that could be interpreted as being against the Catholic Church so they would no longer condemn

Catholicism. Catholic dialogues with the United Methodist Church in the U.S. and the World Methodist Council have been extensive, but less focused than with the Anglicans and Lutherans. However, a common sense of mission, the gift of these two churches for organization, similar ecumenical commitment, and a uniform distribution throughout the country make these churches important ecumenical partners.

Thomas Campbell (1763–1854) and Barton Stone (1772–1844) attempted to begin an ecumenical movement. They developed congregations with open membership, possessing no creed but Christ and practicing weekly Eucharist and adult baptism. From this movement emerged the Churches of Christ, the Christian Churches, and the Disciples of Christ. There has been an important Disciples/Catholic dialogue in this country and with the Holy See. Disciples, like Methodists, are among the most ecumenically active churches in any community.

The Reformation also produced the Mennonite Church, which clings to a strong peace commitment, as do the Quakers (Religious Society of Friends) and the Church of the Brethren that emerged in later centuries. These three traditions often work closely together as the historic Peace Churches. The dialogues with these churches, though modest, are important symbols, given the martyrdoms they have experienced at the hands of Catholics and other Christians.

The National Council of Churches (NCC) was created in 1950 by the Eastern and Oriental Orthodox and the ecumenically oriented Anglican and Protestant churches. Although the Catholic Church is not a member of the NCC, the Catholic Church does collaborate with the NCC on a variety of ecumenical issues and is a full member of the NCC Faith and Order Commission.

In addition to Protestant and Orthodox churches that are committed to the ecumenical movement, there are many other Christian groups more or less open to collaboration, common witness, and dialogue, but that do not relate formally to other churches in ecumenical work. We will briefly survey these churches and the Catholic relationships with them, where they exist.

Evangelical and Pentecostal Churches

All Christians consider themselves *evangelical* in the sense of being committed to the gospel of Jesus Christ. In Europe, the word *evangelical* is used as a name for the Lutheran churches to distinguish them from the Reformed or Calvinist churches. In the United States the word *evangelical* tends to designate conservative churches—Pentecostal, Baptist, Holiness, or independent churches—that do not belong to councils of churches, have a strong emphasis on the born-again conversion experience, have a history of polarization with the classical Protestant denominations, and have an aversion to Catholicism and Orthodoxy. However, there are many ecumenical spirits in the evangelical Protestant community. Fundamentalism is a specific movement within evangelicalism and by no means accounts for the majority of Evangelicals.

Evangelicals form a loose movement of churches, most of which do not belong to the traditional ecumenical movement. They have a vast web of connections among themselves, including a National Association of Evangelicals and a World Evangelical Alliance. They still have much mistrust of Catholicism and there is some prejudice among their members. However, their Christian seriousness, deep spiritual lives, and concern about pro-life, family issues, and interchurch marriages have created important bridges that encourage cooperation between Catholics and themselves. Full communion with the Catholic Church and other Christians is not their goal, however.

Baptists' insistence on the separation of church and state, on baptizing only believing adults, on understanding baptism and the Lord's Supper as ordinances rather than as sacraments, and on private interpretation of the scriptures sets them off from the earlier Reformation traditions. Baptists' emphasis on evangelism and congregational independence has contributed to their becoming the largest Protestant community in the United States today. The American Baptists are very ecumenically active. Other communities are not. The Holy See has had one round of dialogues with the Baptist World Alliance.

For over thirty years, the Catholic bishops of the United States have held a productive conversation with the Southern

Baptist Convention, the largest U.S. Protestant denomination. The conversation was ended in 2001 at Southern Baptist initiative. This dialogue is not well known. However, it is a very important resource for Catholics, especially in the South where this community is so large and active.

In the eighteenth and nineteenth centuries numerous divisions emerged among the Baptists and Methodists over issues of race, slavery, and a variety of doctrinal emphases. As a result of these problems in the United States, there developed three large African-American Baptist groups (National Baptist Convention of America, Progressive National Baptist Convention, and National Baptist Convention, USA) and three large African-American Methodist churches (African Methodist Episcopal, African Methodist Episcopal Zion, and Christian Methodist Episcopal). These churches are evangelical in their faith, while active ecumenically in the councils of churches and in the quest for social justice.

There are, additionally, a cluster of Wesleyan movements that have developed into the Holiness churches, such as the Church of the Nazarene, the Wesleyan Church, the Free Methodist, and Church of God (Anderson, Indiana).

The nineteenth-century urgency about the Second Coming of Christ at the end of time produced a variety of movements that have developed into churches, the most prominent of these being the Seventh-day Adventists. The millennial interest remains strong in certain sectors of the evangelical culture, as demonstrated by the popularity of the *Left Behind* novels.

After the turn of the twentieth century, a Pentecostal revival movement began, usually dated from a 1906 Azusa Street meeting in Los Angeles, California. This movement has developed into one of the fastest growing Christian communities in the early twenty-first century. Much of the theological impetus for this revival developed out of the Holiness movement and its Wesleyan emphasis on experience, the Holy Spirit, and a second work of grace. Speaking in tongues, faith healing, and baptism of the Holy Spirit are among the characteristics of this revival. It eventually gave rise to churches such as the Assemblies of God and Church of God in Christ. For thirty years there has been a Pentecostal-Catholic dialogue with many U.S. participants.

There is also an important Vatican dialogue with the World Evangelical Alliance and a United States dialogue with the National Association of Evangelicals.

Additional Resources

Arthur C. Piepkorn, *Profiles in Belief*, vols. 1–3. San Francisco: Harper & Row, Publishers, Inc., 1977–1979.

Ted Campbell, *Christian Confessions: A Historical Introduction*. Louisville: Westminster/John Knox, 1996.

4

THE PROFESSION OF FAITH: TRANSMISSION OF DIVINE REVELATION

Jim and Ted are walking home from high school, talking about their biology class. Ted argues that he can't believe evolution because his church teaches that when the Bible says God created the world in seven days, that's what it means, seven actual days. Jim says that his church reads the Bible differently. He's heard that there is no contradiction between what science reveals about the origin of living things and what the Bible teaches about God's care and creation of all things.

Ted makes the point that his church doesn't interpret the Bible and doesn't believe that there is a tradition that the church can rely on. Jim says that the Bible itself grew out of the life of the church, and its teaching is safeguarded by tradition and the teaching office of the church.

Can Jim and Ted find common ground between their churches before this discussion ruins their friendship? Can churches seeking full communion with one another but who disagree on the meaning of the Bible find a common understanding of God's revelation in Jesus Christ?

Editor's Notes: In dialogue with fellow Christians, Catholics deepen their understanding of divine revelation. Central to all of Christian life is our relationship to God in Jesus Christ and how we know the content of what he wills us to know through the power of the Holy Spirit. All Christians profess to know Christ through the holy scriptures and to find that scripture in the Christian Church. In the past, the relationship of the one revelation of God in Jesus Christ—mediated to us in the Great Tradition, communicated in scripture and the teaching of the church—has been a source of division among Christians. In our time, ecumenical dialogue has enabled us to come to a common appreciation of the roles of scripture, Tradition, and the church in passing on the apostolic heritage by the power of the Holy Spirit.

Apostolic Tradition (CCC #75–79)

Editor's Notes: Every Christian church believes each of these statements to be true about itself: (1) that the church is apostolic, (2) that it participates fully in that apostolic tradition, and (3) that it transmits the apostles' witness to divine revelation by passing on the faith, mission, and ministry that they have received.

Where churches differ historically is in their emphasis and understanding of the apostolic faith, apostolic mission, and apostolic ministry. These differences in understanding between churches have been sources of great conflict. Through interchurch dialogues, these differences in understanding have been discussed and many have been resolved.

The dialogues have dramatically deepened the common understanding of God's revelation in Jesus Christ, handed on in the church from the apostles. Even if all differences have not yet been resolved, the dialogues continue because the churches seek the unity for which Christ prayed.

Reflection Questions:

- How do Christians receive their revelation from Christ in history?
- What are the signs of continuity with the apostles that Catholics confess with other Christians?
- Where have historic differences over apostolicity begun to be healed?
- What can Christians do together to witness to the common tradition they have received from the apostles?

World Council of Churches Faith and Order

Editor's Notes: The wide variety of Christian churches discussing apostolic faith and ministry in Faith and Order research have developed a convergence in understanding that provides a context for the more precise agreements between Catholics and other particular churches (TSOF, see http://wcc-coe.org/wcc/what/faith/tsof.html).

Study Guide TSOF:
> 66. We proclaim that the Church is apostolic. Apostolicity of the Church expresses the identity of Christians throughout the ages as heirs of the tradition proclaimed and lived by those who were the first chosen witnesses. Apostolicity is the call to the churches to live on in continuity with the faith, life, witness and ministry of the apostolic community and all the faithful who follow them in the communion of saints.

Convergence, BEM in GA I:
> M34. In the Creed, the Church confesses itself to be apostolic....Apostolic tradition in the Church means continuity in the permanent characteristics of the Church of the apostles: witness to the apostolic faith, proclamation and fresh interpretation of the Gospel, celebration of baptism and the eucharist, the transmission of ministerial responsibilities, communion in prayer, love, joy and suffering, service to the sick and the needy, unity among the local churches and sharing the gifts which the Lord has given to each.
>
> B. Succession of the Apostolic Ministry
>
> M35. The primary manifestation of apostolic succession is to be found in the apostolic tradition of the Church as a whole. The succession is an expression of the permanence and, therefore, of the continuity of Christ's own mission in which the Church participates. Within the Church the ordained ministry has a particular task of preserving and actualizing the apostolic faith. The orderly transmission of the ordained ministry is therefore a powerful expression of the continuity of the

Church throughout history; it also underlines the calling of the ordained minister as guardian of the faith....

M36. Under the particular historical circumstances of the growing Church in the early centuries, the succession of bishops became one of the ways, together with the transmission of the Gospel and the life of the community, in which the apostolic tradition of the Church was expressed. This succession was understood as serving, symbolizing and guarding the continuity of the apostolic faith and communion.

⸺⸻⸺

Editor's Notes: Catholics have never questioned the apostolicity of Orthodox churches in their mission, faith, and ministry, but not all Orthodox churches have acknowledged the apostolicity of the Catholic Church. Therefore the dialogue, renewed after 1980, begins to turn a corner in the history of our relationship, and has helped us to grow toward mutual understanding in this area. Orthodox and Catholics agree that apostolic succession is broader than continuity in ordained ministry.

Eastern Orthodox

Consensus, Ox–C, Report 3 in GA II:

2. Our Churches affirm that ministry in the Church makes actual that of Christ himself....

3. This understanding prevents us seeing the economy Christ in isolation from the Spirit....

[All ministries are grounded in the Spirit sent by Christ as gifts, and no ministry has meaning apart from the church.] The ministry of the Twelve was unique and irreplaceable, *[but the apostles are the foundation of the church. The unity of the local church in universal communion is expressed through the episcopal college, into which a bishop is ordained as]* minister of a Church which he represents in the universal communion....Episcopal ordination...conferred by at least two or three bishops, expresses the communion of the

Churches,…as witnesses to the communion in the apostolic faith and sacramental life. (# 5, 20, 21, 26, 27)

Editor's Notes: For the Reformation churches, belief in the continuity of the apostolic tradition (manifested in faith and mission, and continually received by the whole people of God) is primary, though Anglicans also claim succession of ordinations by bishops from the earliest period of the church. Lutherans and some other Protestants claim succession ministry by ordinations by pastor/bishops through a theological position, common at the time of the Reformation, which recognized only a juridical and not a sacramental difference between priests/pastors and bishops. A bishop was a priest who was allowed to exercise powers given to him in the sacrament of ordination, like the ability to ordain and the responsibility to govern a diocese. Agreements on ordained ministry will be noted in the section on holy orders. (#1536–1589)

Anglican

Consensus, ARCIC II, GofA:

16. Apostolic Tradition is a gift of God which must be constantly received anew.…The handing on and reception of apostolic Tradition is an act of communion whereby the Spirit unites the local churches of our day with those that preceded them in the one apostolic faith. The process of tradition entails the constant and perpetual reception and communication of the revealed Word of God in many varied circumstances and continually changing times.…

17. Tradition expresses the apostolicity of the Church. What the apostles received and proclaimed is now found in the Tradition of the Church where the Word of God is preached and the sacraments of Christ celebrated in the power of the Holy Spirit.…

18. Tradition makes the witness of the apostolic community present in the Church today through its corporate memory. Through the proclamation of the Word and the celebration of the sacraments the Holy Spirit opens the hearts of believers and manifests the Risen Lord to them.…

31. Anglicans and Roman Catholics can agree in principle on all of the above, but need to make a deliberate effort to retrieve this shared understanding…they are called to recognize in each other elements of the apostolic Tradition which they may have rejected, forgotten or not yet fully understood.…

Lutheran

Consensus, L–RC VI in GA I:

15. The church stands once for all on the foundation of the apostles.…The post-apostolic church must forever maintain its relation to its apostolic beginning. The doctrine of the apostolic succession underscores the permanently normative character of the apostolic origin while at the same time intending to insist on the continuance of the missionary task.

Consensus, L–RC VIII, FU in GA II:

56. For the unity of our churches and especially for our task of preaching, common witness to the apostolic faith is of fundamental importance. If we apply the principle of the "'hierarchy' of truths," the Christological and Trinitarian center or "foundation of the Christian faith" is primarily at stake.…

57. This process is already under way:

—The starting point is the common affirmation of the faith of the Early Church.…"Together we confess the faith in the Triune God and the saving work of God through Jesus Christ in the Holy Spirit.…Through all the disputes and differences of the 16th century, Lutheran and Catholic Christians remained one in this central and most important truth of the Christian faith."

—The process of growth in common witness is advanced by a new consensus regarding the relationship between Holy Scripture and tradition, long the subject of controversy:

"This poses the old controversial question regarding the relationship of Scripture and tradition in a new way.

The Scripture can no longer be exclusively contrasted with tradition, because the New Testament itself is the product of primitive tradition. Yet as the witness to the fundamental tradition, Scripture has a normative role for the entire later tradition of the church."

⸙

Editor's Notes: Reformed, Methodist and Disciples' churches do not place the same emphasis on apostolic ministry.

Reformed

Convergence, Ref–C I I #94 in GA:

> *[However, we do confess with them the following, using the Reformed–Catholic statement as an example:]* The whole Church is apostolic. To be an apostle means to be sent, to have a particular mission. The notion of mission is essential for understanding the ministry of the Church.
>
> *[For Reformed and Catholics the role of the Holy Spirit is central for understanding the trinitarian character of the church's constitution.]*
>
> Guided by and instrumental to the work of God in this world, the Church has a charismatic character. *[See also WMC–RC V in GA II.]*

> 96. The extension of Christ's ministry, including his priestly office, belongs to all members of his body (cf. 1 Pet 2:5–9). Each member contributes to that total ministry in a different fashion; there is a distribution of diverse gifts (cf. 1 Cor 12:4–11), and every baptized believer exercises his or her share in the total priesthood differently. This calling to the priesthood of all those who share in the body of Christ by baptism does not mean that there are no particular functions which are proper to the special ministry within the body of Christ.

Editor's Notes: Thus Catholic and Reformed differences over apostolic ministry are understood within our common faith in the apostolic tradi-

tion and the missionary character of that apostolicity, the role of the Holy Spirit, and the ministry of the whole people of God.

<hr>

Disciples

Editor's Notes: The Disciples and the Methodist/Catholic dialogues reflect similar convictions, and the former further notes a dynamic development in this tradition.

Convergence, CC–C I in GA I #50:
> This Tradition reflects the *sensus fidelium* (the shared awareness of the faithful) of the primitive church as a whole. However, the *sensus fidelium* is not fixed in the past, but is ever dynamic and living through the dialectical interaction of Scripture and Tradition in the ongoing life of the Church from age to age.

<hr>

Tradition and Sacred Scripture (CCC #80–83)

Editor's Notes: Christians agree on the unique revelation of God in Jesus Christ. The unity of scripture and Tradition in God's single revelation in Jesus Christ (CCC #80), once divisive, has been moving toward resolution. If the unity for which Christ prayed is to be realized, a mutual understanding of our common source of revelation has to be one of the first issues resolved: We cannot deal with differences over sacraments and other elements of faith, and ways to speak together with authority to the world, without first agreeing on revelation.

Reflection Questions:

- How can Christians speak of "one source of revelation" and then affirm both scripture and Tradition?

- Scripture again plays a central role in Catholic life. What has this development meant for our relationships with other churches, especially Reformation churches?

Editor's Notes: In the first days of the Catholic discussions with Protestant and Orthodox scholars (1963), convergence agreement was reached on the sources of revelation. This agreement enabled Catholics and their fellow Christian partners to approach the Reformation debates in new and exciting ways. These agreements on the sources of revelation have made agreement on the sacraments and other elements of faith much easier. The reformulation of the Catholic faith in the Second Vatican Council, as reiterated in the Catechism, *has made this common position possible. This early convergence has made it easier for more detailed agreements to emerge in later dialogues.*

World Council of Churches Faith and Order

Convergence, STt:

> 45. Our starting point is that we are all living in a tradition which goes back to our Lord and has its roots in the Old Testament, and are all indebted to that tradition inasmuch as we have received the revealed truth, the Gospel, through its being transmitted from one generation to another. Thus we can say that we exist as Christians by the Tradition of the Gospel (the *paradosis* of the *kerygma*) testified in Scripture, transmitted in and by the Church through the power of the Holy Spirit. Tradition taken in this sense is worship, in Christian teaching and theology and in mission and witness to Christ by the lives of the members of the Church.

Editor's Notes: Lutheran and Reformed affirmations with Catholics show the dramatic development in a common understanding of God's revelation, its source in the Word of God, and the relationship of scripture and Tradition as witnesses to that one source. Lutherans and Reformed, while agreeing with Catholics, have different approaches to the development of doctrine.

Lutheran

Consensus, L–CUSA, ST in GC II:

64. Holy Scripture has preeminent status as the Word of God, committed to writing in an unalterable manner. Before the Old and New Testaments existed in written form, the Word of God was carried by tradition. Under the guidance of the Holy Spirit Scripture gives rise to the oral proclamation of law and gospel. The preeminent status of Scripture does not exclude the function of a teaching office or the legitimacy of doctrinal traditions that protect and promote the reliance of the faithful on the gospel message of Christ and grace alone. There are no historically verifiable apostolic traditions that are not attested in some way by Scripture. Not all true doctrine needs to be simply and literally present in the Bible, but may be deduced from it. The teaching of doctrine in the church is never above the Word of God, but must serve the Word and be in conformity with it.

Difference:

65. Lutherans and Catholics differ in their understandings of the development of doctrine. Lutherans recognize some developments, notably those declared by the early ecumenical councils, as expressing the true meaning of Scripture, but they do not accept developments that lack what Lutherans perceive as a clear basis in Scripture. For Catholics the supreme teaching authority of the church, with the assistance of the Holy Spirit, can proclaim doctrines expressing the faith of the whole church that go beyond the explicit statements of Scripture and beyond what can be strictly deduced from these statements.

Reformed

Consensus, Ref–C I in GA I:

25. Both on the Catholic and on the Reformed side today, the problem is no longer presented in terms of the battle

lines of post-Tridentine polemic.…Historical researches have shown not only how the New Testament writings are themselves already the outcome of and witness to traditions, but also how the canonization of the New Testament was part of the development of tradition.…

26. In the light of these facts, the customary distinction between Scripture and Tradition as two different sources which operate as norms either alternatively or in parallel has become impossible.

We are agreed that as *creatura Verbi* the Church together with its Tradition stands under the living Word of God and that the preacher and teacher of the Word is to be viewed as servant of the Word (cf. Lk 1:2) and must teach only what the Holy Spirit permits him to hear in the Scriptures.…

We are agreed that the development of doctrine and the production of confessions of faith is a dynamic process. In this process the Word of God proves its own creative, critical and judging power. Through the Word, therefore, the Holy Spirit guides the Church to reflection, conversion and reform.

Interpreting the Heritage of Faith (CCC #84–90)

Editor's Notes: As noted above, Christians all agree that Christ entrusted divine revelation to the church in scripture and the Tradition. We come to know Christ and his message by interpreting these witnesses to the common source. Yet, Christians still differ in how they relate the two, and on the role of the church in interpreting this heritage. Likewise, all churches have different means of teaching revelation (what Catholics call magisterium), but are only gradually moving toward resolving their differences on how this teaching is to be exercised in the structure of the Church, and by whom. Interpretation of the heritage of faith has been a major issue for common study. (TEV, see http://wcc-coe.org/wcc/what/faith/treasure.html)

Reflection Questions:

- When there is disagreement over interpretations of scripture and Tradition, how does the church decide which has precedence?
- How does the teaching office of the church help in discerning the truth of a particular interpretation of the gospel?
- What are the relationships between the individual, the whole people of God, and church leadership in interpreting the Word of God?

Editor's Notes: Of the theological agreements with Catholics on teaching and interpreting, none are more dramatic than those with Anglicans, though some issues remain unresolved.

Anglican

Consensus, ARCIC, Final Report, Elucidation on Authority I in GAI:

> 2. Tradition has been viewed in different ways. One approach is primarily concerned never to go beyond the bounds of Scripture....Another approach, while different, does not necessarily contradict the former. In the conviction that the Holy Spirit is seeking to guide the Church into the fullness of truth, it draws upon everything in human experience and thought which will give to the content of the revelation its fullest expression and widest application....Because these two attitudes contain differing emphases, conflict may arise, even though in both cases the Church is seeking the fullness of revelation. The seal upon the truthfulness of the conclusions that result from this search will be the reception by the whole Church, since neither approach is immune from the possibility of error.

Consensus, ARGIC I, Final Report in GA I:

> 18. In both our traditions the appeal to Scripture, to the creeds, to the Fathers and to the definitions of the councils of the early Church is regarded as basic and normative. But the bishops have a special responsibility for promoting truth and discerning error, and the interaction of bishop and people in its exercise is a safeguard of Christian life and fidelity...we believe that Christ will not desert his Church and that the Holy Spirit will lead it into all truth. That is why the Church, in spite of its failures, can be described as indefectible.

Consensus, ARGIC II, GofA:

> 23. The meaning of the revealed Gospel of God is fully understood only within the Church. God's revelation has been entrusted to a community. The Church cannot properly be described as an aggregate of individual believers, nor can its faith be considered the sum of the beliefs held by individuals....The faith of the community precedes the faith of the individual.... Individualistic interpretation of the Scriptures is not attuned to the reading of the text within the life of the Church and is incompatible with the nature of the authority of the revealed Word of God (cf. 2 Pet 1.20–21). Word of God and Church of God cannot be put asunder.

Editor's Notes: Catholics in dialogue with Lutherans have made considerable progress in understanding the infallibility of the church and relating this common understanding to the structures of ministry. However, full agreement on the role of bishops and the pope in teaching the truth of the Christian faith continues to be explored in dialogue.

Lutheran

Convergence, LCUSA—VI in BU:

> 41. The context within which the Catholic doctrine of papal infallibility is understood has changed. Lutherans

and Catholics now speak in increasingly similar ways about the gospel and its communication, about the authority of Christian truth, and about how to settle disputes concerning the understanding of the Christian message. One can truly speak of a convergence between our two traditions. The following instances of this convergence are significant. Our churches are agreed:

1) that Jesus Christ is the Lord of the Church, who discloses his gracious sovereignty through the proclamation of the apostolic gospel and the administration of the sacraments;

2) that the Word of God in the Scriptures is normative for all proclamation and teaching in the Church;

3) that the apostolic Tradition in which the Word of God is transmitted, while normative for all other tradition in the Church, is interpreted within the family of God with the assistance of tradition in the form of creeds, liturgies, dogma, confessions, doctrines, forms of church government and discipline, and patterns of devotion and service;

4) that in accordance with the promises given in the Scriptures and because of the continued assistance of the risen Christ through the Holy Spirit, the Church will remain to the end of time;

5) that this perpetuity of the Church includes its indefectibility, i.e., its perseverance in the truth of the gospel, in its mission, and in its life of faith;

6) that among the means by which Christ preserves the Church in the truth of the gospel, there is the Ministry, of the Word and sacrament, which will never perish from the Church;

7) that there are Ministries and structures charged with the teaching of Christian doctrine and with supervision and coordination of the ministry of the whole people of God, and that their task includes the mandate for bishops or other leaders to "judge doctrine and condemn doctrine that is contrary to the Gospel"....

Editor's Notes: Catholics agree with Reformed, Methodists, and Disciples on the fact that the scripture is interpreted in community, and not just by every individual. The Protestant churches place more emphasis, however, on the immediate role of scripture in the life of the Christian. Disciples, unlike Lutherans and Reformed, have resisted creeds as interpreters of the tradition.

Reformed

Difference, Ref–C I in GA I:

> 28. On the whole the Reformed sought a direct support for their doctrine in the apostolic witness of Scripture, whereas the Roman Catholic Church perceived the apostolic witness more strongly in the life of faith of the whole Church, in the measure that it constantly strove in the course of the centuries to apprehend the fullness of the divine truth.

Convergence, Ref–C II in GA II:

> 14. Historical scholarship today has not only produced fresh evidence concerning our respective roles in the Reformation and its aftermath. It also brings us together in broad agreement about sources, methods of inquiry and warrants for drawing conclusions....If we still inevitably interpret and select, at least we are aware that we do, and what that fact means as we strive for greater objectivity and more balanced judgment.

———

Editor's Notes: Disciples and Catholics are able to say, as are the other churches of the Reformation, that we recognize new situations that call for new interpretations of scripture and Tradition. Christians all recognize prophetic voices that seem to challenge traditional interpretations of the faith, and have ways of setting boundaries, though these differ.

Disciples

Convergence, CC-C, I in GA I:

> 53. Roman Catholics hold that the living transmission of the Gospel in and by the Church is necessary....While

the Scriptures are normative and the soul of all subsequent theological investigation, their adequate understanding is possible only within the life of the believing community.

54. Disciples believe that the New Testament is a sufficient expression of the essential faith, doctrine, and practice of the individual Christian…have not given a normative position to later expressions of the faith of the Church, and in particular have not used creeds and confessions as tests of eucharistic fellowship.…

55. Both Disciples and Roman Catholics are committed to the appropriation in their own lives of all that is good from the traditions of others, both in the past and today.

Convergence, CC–C III:

3.25. Disciples and Roman Catholics agree that the Church must always be sensitive to contemporary questions and to diversity of cultures when discerning authentic developments in its understanding of the Gospel.…

3.26. In many cases an immediate discernment is impossible because the community as such has to be involved in the complex dynamism of reception.…They recognize a process of development in the understanding of doctrine in the Church which can be traced through history. Reception plays a crucial part in this ongoing process. Disciples and Roman Catholics are not unanimous on the ways in which reception is achieved, but they agree on its necessity.

Difference, CC–C III:

4.6. Sometimes in the history of the Church individuals or groups, acting in obedience to the Word of God as they discerned it, have disagreed with the prevailing teaching or practice. Disciples and Roman Catholics respond to this situation differently. Disciples came into existence because their leaders were unwilling to accept the restrictions which Presbyterians placed on access to the Lord's Table....The nature of the history of the Roman Catholic Church means that it has no similar dominant memory; it also places a strong emphasis on the value of unity....Nevertheless Disciples and Roman Catholics agree that certain groups in the history of the Church have made an important and prophetic witness which has not immediately been recognized.

4.14. Among both Disciples and Roman Catholics teaching takes place within a set of limits or boundaries accepted by the community....Roman Catholics have emphasized that individuals cannot ignore the faith which the Church has received through the Holy Spirit when proposing a new understanding of some point....The Disciples' process encourages continued conversation as the Church seeks to identify those expressions of the faith that best show a clear relationship to the faith witnessed in the New Testament. When responding to people whose views or practice of the faith seem outside the common norms, the process is primarily pastoral.

4.15. In both communions, especially when crucial doctrinal and pastoral issues are at stake, it is the authority of the pastors, guided by the Holy Spirit, which is the instrument of God to keep the community in the right direction....Nevertheless bishops and pastors have not only to be aware of the needs of the community but also to weigh the various insights of the people and to "receive" those insights that are an authentic expression of the *sensus fidei* (sense of the faith) of the whole Church of God....

4.16. For both Roman Catholics and Disciples the authority of the Church's teaching derives from a combination of elements: the truths of revelation, the theological arguments based upon them to guide human thought and behavior, the position and experience of those responsible for teaching, and reception by the whole Church. However, the relative weight attached to the elements differs between Roman Catholics and Disciples. Thus the claims made for the authority of the Church in matters of conscience differ in our two communities. In the Roman Catholic Church those with episcopal or primatial oversight, who hold the apostolic teaching office conferred by ordination, can at times make decisions binding on the conscience of Roman Catholics. For Disciples ultimate oversight rests with a General Assembly or Conference (comprising both ministers and other church members), but their decisions do not bind the conscience of individual members....

Editor's Notes: Catholic and Methodist affirmations about the Holy Spirit's role in the Church's interpretation of tradition provide an example of the faith of many of the other Protestant churches. These agreements help Catholics understand the activity of the Holy Spirit, and the role of the whole people of God (along with their leaders), in interpreting the Christian faith.

Methodist

Convergence, WMC–RC VII:

117. Both Methodists and Catholics trust the unfailing presence and grace of the Holy Spirit to preserve them in faithfulness and to protect the truth of the Gospel they preach and teach. The Catholic Church recognizes this presence of the Spirit especially in the charism of unfailing truth and faith which is given to bishops in the Church....Methodists recognize the guidance of the Holy Spirit in Methodist Conferences though they do not ascribe to them a guaranteed freedom from error.

118. Both Catholics and Methodists recognize that it is the whole Church which abides in the truth because of the presence of the Holy Spirit in the community of believers....Most fundamentally, both Methodists and Catholics believe that it is the Spirit who preserves within the Church the truth of the Gospel proclaimed by Christ and the apostles, though there is not complete agreement on what constitute the essential components of that Gospel.

121. At the same time, while this report acknowledges obvious differences in ministerial structure for authoritative teaching and in theological interpretation of the reliability of these ministerial structures, there remains a common fundamental belief in the presence of the Holy Spirit and the use by the Holy Spirit of recognized bodies for teaching authoritatively to ensure the truth of the Gospel which is believed by both Methodists and Catholics....The experience of ordinary Methodists and Catholics...indicate that these perspectives may be much closer than the differing language might sometimes indicate.

⸻

Editor's Notes: While evangelical Christians are sometimes caricatured by Catholics as "fundamentalist," they share with Catholics a strong commitment to the historic faith and its embodiment in scripture. This agreement with some evangelical Christians shows common commitments to biblical authority and its careful interpretation in the community, while acknowledging some differences. Catholic understandings of interpretation are challenged and clarified by these divergent understandings. Both communities are cautious about interpreting the Word of God, but Catholics feel more certain of the Church's role in this discernment.

Evangelical

Convergence, ERCDOM in GA II:

1. 2. Roman Catholics affirm that Scripture must be seen as having been produced by and within the Church. It is mediated to us by the inspired witness of the first Christians....We cannot understand it in its truth unless we receive it in the living faith of the Church which, assisted by the Holy Spirit, keeps us in obedience to the Word of God.

Evangelicals acknowledge the wisdom of listening to the Church...but they insist that each believer must be free to exercise his or her personal responsibility before God, in hearing and obeying his Word. While the

Church's interpretations are often helpful, they are not finally necessary because Scripture, under the Spirit's illumination, is self-interpreting and perspicuous [clear]....Despite these differences we are agreed that since the biblical texts have been inspired by God, they remain the ultimate, permanent and normative reference of the revelation of God....Roman Catholics hold that "the task of giving an authentic interpretation of the Word of God whether in its written form or in the form of Tradition has been entrusted to the living, teaching office of the Church alone." This seems to Evangelicals to derogate from Scripture as "the ultimate, permanent and normative reference." Nevertheless, both sides strongly affirm the divine inspiration of Scripture.

1.3, a)...Christ also gives his Church teachers in the present (Eph 4:11), and it is the duty of Christian people to listen to them respectfully. The regular context for this is public worship in which the Word of God is read and expounded. In addition, we attend Church Synods and Councils, and national, regional and international conferences at which, after prayer and debate, our Christian understanding increases.

b) The regulation of Christian belief

We all agree that the fact of revelation brings with it the need for interpretation. We also agree that in the interpretative task both the believing community and the individual believer must have a share. Our emphasis on these varies, however, for the Evangelical fears lest God's Word be lost in church traditions, while the Roman Catholic fears it will be lost in a multiplicity of idiosyncratic interpretations.

This is why Roman Catholics emphasize the necessary role of the magisterium, although Evangelicals believe that in fact it has not delivered the Roman Catholic Church from a diversity of viewpoints, while admittedly helping to discern between them.

Evangelicals admit that in their case too some congregations, denominations and institutions have a kind of magisterium. For they elevate their particular creed or confession to this level, since they use it as their official interpretation of Scripture and for the exercise of discipline.…

We all believe that God will protect his Church, for he has promised to do so and has given us both his Scriptures and his Spirit; our disagreement is on the means and the degree of his protection.

Roman Catholics believe that it is the authoritative teaching of the Church which has the responsibility for oversight in the interpretation of Scripture, allowing a wide freedom of understanding, but excluding some interpretations as inadmissible because erroneous.

Evangelicals, on the other hand, believe that God uses the Christian community as a whole to guard its members from error and evil. Roman Catholics also believe in this *sensus fidelium*.

Sacred Scripture (CCC #101–119)

Editor's Notes: For the classical Protestant, Orthodox, and Catholic churches, scripture, interpreted in the church and studied with the tools of modern scholarship, is the norm for the Christian faith. Catholic understanding of scripture has been enriched by the ecumenical dialogue. Bible study among Christians that is based on common principles of interpretation can enrich our faith and spiritual life. But not all Christians agree on this format for reading the Bible. Pentecostal and evangelical churches, for example, depend on a more literal reading of the sacred text. While we are able to study the Bible with these Christians, the significant differences in our presuppositions make this study more difficult. In relating to other Christians we need to understand both where we agree and where we differ.

Reflection Questions:

- How do Christians together understand the Word of God in the sacred scripture?
- What role does scripture play for all Christians in the life of the church? In our relations with one another before the Word of God?
- What is the role of the church in interpreting scripture?

Editor's Notes: The agreement between Catholics and other classical Reformation churches on the authority of the scripture is articulated here in an example from the Anglican dialogue. As noted above, while the teaching offices and approaches to creeds and development of doctrine will differ in some degree between churches, Lutherans, Reformed, Methodists, and Disciples, like Catholics and Anglicans, all use the best critical scholarship to understand the scripture and its original meaning, and to help to keep it alive in the present life of the church. Each church recognizes the church's role in helping to discern and promulgate the Word of God.

Anglican

Consensus, ARCIC I, Final Report, Elucidation on Authority I in GA I:

2. The basis of our approach to Scripture is—the affirmation that Christ is God's final word to man—his eternal Word made flesh. He is the culmination of the diverse ways in which God has spoken since the beginning (Heb 1:1–3). In him God's saving and revealing purpose is fully and definitively realized....

The Church's essential task, therefore, in the exercise of its teaching office, is to unfold the full extent and implications of the mystery of Christ, under the guidance of the Spirit of the risen Lord.

No endeavor of the Church to express the truth can add to the revelation already given. Moreover, since the Scriptures are the uniquely inspired witness to divine revelation, the Church's expression of that revelation must be tested by its consonance with Scripture. This does not mean simply repeating the words of Scripture, but also both delving into their deeper significance and unraveling their implications for Christian belief and practice. It is impossible to do this without resorting to current language and thought. Consequently the teaching of the Church will often be expressed in words that are different from the original text of Scripture without being alien to its meaning....This combination of permanence in the revealed truth and continuous exploration of its meaning is what is meant by Christian tradition. Some of the results of this reflection, which bear upon essential matters of faith, have come to be recognized as the authentic expression of Christian doctrine and therefore part of the "deposit of faith."

⸺⸻⸺

Editor's Notes: Pentecostals, many Baptists, and most Evangelicals place special emphasis on the scriptures' role in the life of the church. Not all of these churches can accurately be called fundamentalists, however. Most of these churches are suspicious of diluting the meaning of God's revelation that is transmitted in the sacred texts. Some are suspicious of the church's role as interpreter of the Word of God. Yet, common Bible study among Catholics and Evangelicals is possible if these differences are kept in mind.

Evangelical

Convergence, ERCDOM in GA II:
    I. 2. c) Biblical criticism
      Since the Bible is God's Word through human words, therefore under the guidance of the Holy Spirit, who is the only one who leads us into the understanding of Scripture, we must use scientific critical tools for its elucidation, and we appreciate the positive gains of modern biblical scholarship. Human criticism and the Spirit of God are not mutually exclusive. By "criticism" we do not mean that we stand in judgment upon God's Word, but rather that we must investigate the historical, cultural and literary background of the biblical books.

We must also try to be aware of the presuppositions we bring to our study of the text….What we must seek to ensure is that our presuppositions are Christian rather than secular. Some of the presuppositions of secular philosophy which have vitiated the critical study of the Bible are (a) evolutionary (that religion developed from below instead of being revealed from above), (b) anti-supernatural (that miracles cannot happen and that therefore the biblical miracles are legendary), and (c) demythologizing (that the thought world in which the biblical message was given is entirely incompatible with the modern age and must be discarded). Sociological presuppositions are equally dangerous, as when we read into Scripture the particular economic system we favor whether capitalist or communist, or any other….

d) The "literal" sense

The first task of all critical study is to help us discover the original intention of the authors. What is the literary genre in which they wrote? What did they intend to say? What did they intend us to understand? For this is the "literal" sense of Scripture, and the search for it is one of the most ancient principles which the Church affirmed….

e) A contemporary message

To concentrate entirely on the ancient text, however, would lead us into an unpractical antiquarianism. We have to go beyond the original meaning to the contemporary message….

In this dialectic between the old and the new, we often become conscious of a clash of cultures, which calls for great spiritual sensitivity. On the one hand, we must be aware of the ancient cultural terms in which God spoke his word, so that we may discern between his eternal truth and its transient setting. On the other, we must be aware of the modern cultures and world views which condition us, some of whose values can make us blind and deaf to what God wants to say to us.

Southern Baptist

Differences, SBC–CUSA in GC II:

> [W]e share a great deal in our Christian faith concerning the authority and truth of the Bible, this report is…an account of the topics we have discussed, the processes we have followed and the clarification of terms at which we have arrived. While fully cognizant of our serious differences, our goal has been truth and clarity in charity. Our common and ongoing quest for the truth of Christ has deepened our appreciation for one another and strengthened our love for the Holy Scriptures….
>
> *Word of God:* The expression "Word of God" is used in at least three senses. First, Jesus, the Word made flesh, is the Word of God incarnate. Second, God's message of salvation, made known in the story of Israel and reaching its fullness in the life, death, and resurrection of Jesus, is the Word of God proclaimed. Finally, the Holy Scripture, both Old and New Testaments, is recognized as the Word of God inspired and written.
>
> *Inspiration:* The belief that the biblical books were fully inspired by the Holy Spirit, so that God may be said to be the primary and ultimate author (cf. 2 Tim 3:16–17).
>
> *Inerrancy:* The conviction that the Bible is "without error" in what it affirms. But there are different interpretations of what this actually means. For Southern Baptists, inerrancy means that the original biblical text was composed precisely as God inspired it and intended it to be because of God's superintendence: not just the thought comes from God, but every word with every inflection, every verse and line, and every tense of the verb, every number of the noun, and every little particle are regarded as coming from God….For Roman Catholics, inerrancy is understood as a consequence of biblical inspiration; it has to do more with the truth of the Bible as a whole than with any theory of verbal inerrancy….What is important is the qualification of "that truth" with "for the sake of our salvation."

Literalism: An interpretative approach which focuses only on the surface meaning of the text, without reference to authorial intent.

Fundamentalism: An early 20th century movement among Protestants in response to liberal Protestant theology, first marked by subscription to such doctrinal "fundamentals" as biblical inerrancy, the virgin birth, substitutionary atonement, bodily resurrection, and the second coming of Christ. In the mid 20th century, fundamentalism came to identify itself as strongly separationist. Outsiders came to identify fundamentalism with an anti-intellectual literalism and to extend the term to conservative non-Christian groups, such as "Islamic Fundamentalists." Because of the pejorative connotations, the Associated Press Stylebook appropriately suggests, "In general, do not use fundamentalist unless a group applies the word to itself."

Why It Matters

If Christians of all communities were to take seriously the points of agreement on what it means to be an apostolic Church, arguments such as those illustrated in the vignette at the beginning of this chapter would be fewer and less destructive. Although individual church structures continue to be different, the fact that each church, in its own way, continues to "live in continuity with the faith, life, witness, and ministry of the apostolic community" (TSOF, 66) is telling. Instead of looking at various church practices and seeing them as threats to our own beliefs, we can now examine them for the wisdom they contain.

The dialogues have helped Catholics to understand better the role that scripture plays in Catholic life and practice. That Catholics can say with other churches that "we exist as Christians by the Tradition of the Gospel…testified in Scripture, transmitted in and by the Church through the power of the Holy Spirit" (STt, no. 45) provides an impetus for a balance between the study of scripture and the study of the church's living teaching and tradition. For this to become a reality, more Catholics need to read the scriptures, study them for meaning, and learn more about them under the guidance of the Catholic Church. The more familiar Catholics become with scripture and how to understand it within a Catholic context, the more confident they will be when engaging in discussions with Christians from other churches. Then, perhaps, scripture discussions will become a way to seek truth, and not a weapon with which to bludgeon one's opponents.

Many Catholics participate in Bible study programs that are sponsored or produced by another Christian church. While participation in these studies can now be encouraged, Catholics do need to learn as much as they can about their church's understanding of scripture, otherwise they may be confused by some of what they see and hear. As the ARCIC II GofA statement no. 23 says so well, "The faith of the community precedes the faith of the individual....Individualistic interpretation of the Scriptures is...incompatible with the nature of the authority of the revealed Word of God."

Catholics engaged in Bible study or other discussions with Southern Baptists or other evangelical Christians would benefit from a familiarity with the definitions found in SBC–CUSA, GC II (see pages 61–62). Understanding what the Catholic and Baptist churches mean by such words and phrases as *Word of God, inspiration,* and *inerrancy* will lead to a greater understanding overall.

5
THE PROFESSION OF FAITH: THE CREED

Harry (a Lutheran) and Beatrice (a Catholic) have been happily married for twenty years. They attend their own church separately each Sunday, although from time to time they attend church together. They find that their churches, though separate, have nurtured their common commitment to Christ and common devotion to their churches.

When they are at the liturgy together in either of their churches, they profess the same Nicene Creed, affirm Christ presence in the Eucharist, and recognize a common liturgical tradition, even though they are not yet able to share communion. Their devotional life is somewhat different: Beatrice has a strong devotion to Jesus' mother, Mary, while Harry spends his time reading the Bible.

They are both involved as lay ministers in their congregations and work closely with their bishops and pastors, though they are often puzzled at the differences in their two churches. They are happy each time a new agreement between Lutherans and Catholics is announced, hoping that one day their bishops and pastors may lead them in a celebration of the full communion of their churches together.

More than a third of all married couples find themselves in Beatrice's and Harry's shoes, belonging to separate churches and unable to worship together regularly. This situation can divide families. What progress is being made to bring Christians to a common eucharistic table? Can Beatrice and Harry pray together in each of their favorite devotions and remain faithful to their church's teaching? Find out here in this chapter.

Editor's Notes: In addition to the scriptures, the Nicene Creed serves as the common basis of Christian faith for Catholics and Orthodox, and is also accepted as part of their heritage by the major Reformation churches: Anglican, Lutheran, and Reformed. While the creed expresses the faith commitment of many of the free churches, they may not use it in regular Sunday prayer as do the churches mentioned by name above. The Nicene Creed provides strong testimony to the common core of the faith shared by Christians. Major work has been done in numerous dialogues seeking mutual understanding of the statements found in the Nicene Creed.

The World Council's study document Confessing the One Faith *and its Study Guide* Towards Sharing One Faith *(http://wcc-coe.org/wcc/what/faith/tsof.html) can be useful companions to the* Catechism. *Texts selected here will relate to specific church-dividing issues that have moved or are moving toward resolution in the dialogues.*

The Father and the Son Revealed by the Spirit (CCC #246–249)

Editor's Notes: Before the separation of the Western (Latin Church) from the Eastern (Orthodox Church) or the earlier divisions between these traditions and the Assyrian and Oriental Orthodox churches, all Christian churches were united in the creed of AD 381. In its original form, this creed remains a witness to the unity in faith that still binds these Christians together in Christ.

During the centuries of gradual alienation because of cultural, linguistic, and, finally, theological differences, Western Christians unilaterally changed the common creed to include that the Holy Spirit "proceeds from the father and the Son." This change was made in response to real pastoral needs and theological concerns among Latin Christians. This change in the common faith formulation has never been accepted in the Orthodox East and is an ongoing source of tension between East and West.

The addition of the phrase "and the Son" (filioque) *to the common Nicene Creed by the Latin Church and the Latin Church's attempt to impose this statement of belief on the Eastern churches has been a divisive issue between the two churches for a millennium. A broad consensus exists on the place of the Holy Spirit in the Trinity.*

Reflection Questions:

- What does it mean to say that the Holy Spirit proceeds from the Father and the Son?
- What do you know about the beliefs and practices of the various Eastern churches? How are they similar to Roman Catholic beliefs and practices? How are they different?

World Council of Churches Faith and Order

Convergence, COF:

210. Despite the controversy created by the introduction of the term *filioque* by Western Christians to express this latter relation [between the Son and the Spirit], both Western and Eastern Christians have wished to be faithful to the affirmation of the Nicene-Constantinopolitan Creed that the Spirit proceeds from the Father, and both agree today that the intimate relationship between the Son and the Spirit is to be affirmed without giving the impression that the Spirit is subordinated to the Son. On that affirmation all Christians can agree and this enables an increasing number of Western churches to consider using the Creed in its original form.

———

Editor's Notes: Because of the theological agreement reached through the dialogue, it is now possible for Orthodox and Catholic scholars to recommend a solution to the problem.

Eastern Orthodox

Consensus, Ox–CUS, Filioque:

> We are convinced from our own study that the Eastern and Western theological traditions have been in substantial agreement, since the patristic period, on a number of fundamental affirmations about the Holy Trinity that bear on the Filioque debate:
>
> • both traditions clearly affirm that *the Holy Spirit* is a distinct hypostasis or person within the divine Mystery, equal in status to the Father and the Son, and is not simply a creature or a way of talking about God's action in creatures;
>
> • although the Creed of 381 does not state it explicitly, both traditions confess the Holy Spirit to be God, *of the same divine substance (homoousios)* as Father and Son;
>
> • both traditions also clearly affirm that *the Father is the primordial source* (arch') *and ultimate cause* (aitia) *of the divine being*, and thus of all God's operations…;
>
> • both traditions affirm that *the three hypostases or persons in God are constituted* in their hypostatic existence and distinguished from one another solely *by their relationships of origin*, and not by any other characteristics or activities;…
>
> Nevertheless, the Eastern and Western traditions of reflection on the Mystery of God have clearly developed categories and conceptions that differ in substantial ways from one another…

Editor's Notes: On the basis of this agreement Catholic and Orthodox scholars have made recommendations to their churches to return to the original common creed for worship and revisit historical judgments made of one another in the past. No final decision has been made on these recommendations by either of the churches.

True God and True Man (CCC #446–459)

Editor's Notes: The profession of the divinity and humanity of Christ is at the very core of who we are as Christians. Some of the most tragic divisions in the church emerged in the early centuries over how to formulate this faith in Christ, our savior. The issues that divided the church over the person and nature of Jesus Christ in the Council of Ephesus (431) with the Assyrian Church of the East, and the Council of Chalcedon (451) with the Oriental Orthodox churches, have been resolved now through the dialogue.

Reflection Questions:

- What is the significance of our common confession of the true divinity and true humanity of Christ?
- What do we mean when we say that Mary is the mother of God?
- Why is it important that we share with other Christians this common confession of faith in Christ as truly human and truly divine?

Assyrian Church of the East

Agreement, ACE–RC in GA II:

Christ therefore is not an "ordinary man" whom God adopted in order to reside in him and inspire him, as in the righteous ones and the prophets. But the same God the Word, begotten of his Father before all worlds without beginning according to his divinity, was born of a mother without a father in the last times according to his humanity. The humanity to which the Blessed Virgin Mary gave birth always was that of the Son of God himself. That is the reason why the Assyrian Church of the East is praying the Virgin Mary as "the Mother of Christ our God and Savior." In the light of this same faith the Catholic tradition addresses the Virgin Mary as "the Mother of God" and also as "the Mother of Christ." We both recognize the legitimacy and rightness of these expressions of the same faith and we both respect the preference of each Church in her liturgical life and piety.

This is the unique faith that we profess in the mystery of Christ. The controversies of the past led to anathemas, bearing on persons and on formulas. The Lord's Spirit permits us to understand better today that the divisions brought about in this way were due in large part to misunderstandings.

Whatever our christological divergences have been, we experience ourselves united today in the confession of the same faith in the Son of God who became man so that we might become children of God by his grace....

Living by this faith and these sacraments, it follows as a consequence that the particular Catholic churches and the particular Assyrian churches can recognize each other as sister Churches....

Editor's Notes: Common Declarations on the divinity and humanity of Christ between the Roman Catholic pope and the patriarchs and pope of the Oriental Orthodox churches (Coptic, Ethiopian, Eritrean, Armenian, Syrian [and Malankara Syrian]) have resolved the differences that have existed between the churches since Chalcedon. The Common Declaration between Catholic and Coptic popes illustrates this agreement. While there are other issues that still exist between Catholics and Oriental Orthodox churches, the dialogues continue bound fast in the common faith in the incarnation.

Oriental Orthodox Churches

Agreement, Coptic–RC:

In accordance with our apostolic traditions transmitted to our Churches and preserved therein, and in conformity with the early three ecumenical councils, we confess one faith in the One Triune God, the divinity of the Only Begotten Son of God, the Second Person of the Holy Trinity, the Word of God, the effulgence of His glory and the express image of His substance, who for us was incarnate, assuming for Himself a real body with a rational soul, and who shared with us our humanity but without sin. We confess that our Lord and God and Savior and King of us all, Jesus Christ, is perfect God with respect to His divinity, perfect man with respect to His humanity. In Him His divinity is united with His humanity in a real, perfect union without mingling, without commixtion, without confusion, without alteration, without division, without separation….We humbly recognize that our Churches are not able to give more perfect witness to this new life in Christ because of existing divisions which have behind them centuries of difficult history. In fact, since the year 451 A.D., theological differences, nourished and widened by non-theological factors, have sprung up. These differences cannot be ignored. In spite of them, however, we are rediscovering ourselves as Churches with a common inheritance and are reaching out with determination and confidence in the Lord to achieve the fullness and perfection of that unity which is His gift.

The Church Is One (CCC #813–832)

Editor's Notes: The church we confess is one, yet there are divisions among Christians. All ecumenical dialogue is oriented toward realizing the unity of the church. For this reason, understanding this article of the creed and how we agree and differ on it underlies all of our efforts to reconcile Christians.

The four marks of the church are shared by all Christians, but each church interprets the meaning of the marks in its own way. Through dialogue, the nature of the unity we seek has gradually been clarified. The churches have gradually been able to articulate together the elements needed for full communion, especially in the discussions with the World Council of Churches. Selections from three stages in these dialogues are noted here. The Nature and Purpose of the Church, *a current study of Faith and*

Order, provides an excellent resource to use along with the Catechism *on this point (http://wcc-coe.org/wcc/what/faith/nature1. html).*

Reflection Questions:

- How does the Catholic Church maintain the unity given to it in her tradition?
- What are the elements all churches, at least in World Council discussions, can agree upon as necessary for full visible unity?
- What are some of the elements of agreement on the nature of the unity of Christians that are most surprising? That most challenge Catholic understanding?

Editor's Notes: When the various churches began to engage in dialogue toward unity in the mid-twentieth century, they identified a minimal set of elements that would be necessary to help them move toward unity. The first statement by the 1961 Assembly was later expanded by the 1975 Assembly to envision the church as a conciliar communion (fellowship), and by the 1991 statement that enumerates the elements that must be resolved together as the pilgrimage toward full unity moves forward. Catholics have been involved in all of these dialogues, and they recognize that the three elements that the Catholic Church sees as necessary for unity—in faith, in sacraments, and in authority—have become ever more clearly shared by the other churches over this period of time.

World Council of Churches Assemblies

Convergence, New Delhi, 1961:

We believe that the unity which is both God's will and his gift to his Church is being made visible as all in each place who are baptized into Jesus Christ and confess him as Lord and Saviour are brought by the Holy Spirit into one fully committed fellowship, holding the one apostolic faith, preaching the one Gospel, breaking the one bread, joining in common prayer, and having a corporate life reaching out in witness and service to all and who at the same time are united with the whole Christian fellowship in all places and all ages in such wise that ministry and members are accepted by all, and that all can act and speak together as occasion requires for the tasks to which God calls his people.

Convergence, Nairobi, 1975:

The one Church is to be envisioned as a conciliar fellowship of local churches which are themselves truly united. In this conciliar fellowship, each local church possesses, in communion with the others, the fullness of catholicity, witnesses to the same apostolic faith, and therefore recognizes the others as belonging to the same Church of Christ and guided by the same Spirit. As the New Delhi Assembly pointed out, they are bound together because they have received the same baptism and share in the same Eucharist; they recognize each other's members and ministries. They are one in their common commitment to confess the gospel of Christ by proclamation and service to the world. To the end, each church aims at maintaining sustained and sustaining relationships with her sister churches, expressed in conciliar gatherings whenever required for the fulfillment of their common calling.

Convergence, Canberra, 1991:

2.1. The unity of the church to which we are called is a koinonia given and expressed in the common confession of the apostolic faith; a common sacramental life entered by the one baptism and celebrated together in one eucharistic fellowship; a common life in which members and ministries are mutually recognized and reconciled; and a common mission witnessing to the gospel of God's grace to all people and serving the whole of creation. The goal of the search for full communion is realized when all the churches are able to recognize in one another the one, holy, catholic and apostolic church in its fullness. This full communion will be expressed on the local level and the universal levels through conciliar forms of life and action. In such communion churches are bound in all aspects of life together at all levels in confessing the one faith and engaging in worship and witness, deliberation and action.

⸺ ⸙ ⸺

Editor's Notes: Catholics and Oriental and Eastern Orthodox churches claim to share in common major elements from the earliest centuries of Christianity, including a common faith in the Lord, common sacramental life, and common hierarchical structures of authority. Yet, centuries of separation have led to deep tensions and resentments between the churches, tensions and resentments that must be healed by dialogue and the power of the Holy Spirit before unity can happen. Giving careful attention to these wounds will enrich the Catholic faith and provide a missing balance to the Western tradition that was lost to the Western tradition as it developed in isolation for the last millennium.

Oriental (Coptic) Orthodox

Agreement, Coptic–RC:

> We have, to a large degree, the same understanding of the Church, founded upon the Apostles, and of the important role of ecumenical and local councils. Our spirituality is well and profoundly expressed in our rituals and in the Liturgy of the Mass which comprises the center of our public prayer and the culmination of our incorporation into Christ in His Church. We keep the fasts and feasts of our faith. We venerate the relics of the saints and ask the intercession of the angels and of the saints, the living and the departed. These compose a cloud of witnesses in the Church. They and we look in hope for the Second Coming of our Lord when His glory will be revealed to judge the living and the dead.

Eastern Orthodox

Consensus, Ox–C I in GA II:

> The body of Christ is unique. There exists then only one church of God. The identity of one eucharistic assembly with another comes from the fact that all with the same

73

faith celebrate the same memorial, that all by eating the same bread and sharing in the same cup become the same unique body of Christ into which they have been integrated by the same baptism....

[Orthodox and Catholic scholars go on to focus on] the local church which celebrates the eucharist gathered around its bishop.

[The communion of these local/diocesan churches demonstrates diversity or plurality as well as the sacramentality of the Church's unity.]

The universal church manifests itself in the synaxis of the local church, *[the text goes on to enumerate the conditions for unity]* catholicity in time, *[which means continuity with the apostolic church]* mutual recognition of catholicity as communion in the wholeness of the mystery...first of all at the regional level. *[Here we speak of patriarchal and diocesan unity among bishops and their local churches.* (III 1., 3, a, b)]

Consensus, Ox–C IV in GA II:

Editor's Notes: Among Catholics and Orthodox a problem has emerged with sections of Orthodox coming into communion with the Catholic Church and the bishop of Rome and leaving the Orthodox communion.

Unfortunately, none of these efforts succeeded in re-establishing full communion between the Church of the West and the Church of the East, and at times even made oppositions more acute....Because of the way in which Catholics and Orthodox once again consider each other in their relationship to the mystery of the Church and discover each other once again as Sister Churches, this form of "missionary apostolate" described above, and which has been called "uniatism," can no longer be accepted either as a method to be followed nor as a model of the unity our Churches are seeking.

[Of course, this does not mean that the Latin Church abandons its communion with these Eastern Catholic churches,

which it holds in greatest respect and with which it remains in full communion.]

The Oriental Catholic Churches who have desired to re-establish full communion with the See of Rome and have remained faithful to it, have the rights and obligations which are connected with this communion.... These Churches, then, should be inserted, on both local and universal levels, into the dialogue of love, in mutual respect and reciprocal trust found once again, and enter into the theological dialogue, with all its practical implications....*[However, as Pope John Paul II has said:]* We reject every form of proselytism, every attitude which would be or could be perceived to be a lack of respect. (#7, 8, 12, 13, 16, 18)

———

Editor's Notes: With the Reformation, different models of unity emerged in the various traditions. As the Second Vatican Council notes, we share a special relationship with the Anglican Communion (Episcopal Church, USA) because of the catholic elements it has retained: In addition to scripture and creeds, it also shares the ministry of priests, deacons, and bishops, and a sense of primacy. Agreement on the goal and shape of unity, then, has come more easily in the Anglican-Catholic dialogue.

Anglican

Consensus, ARCIC II, CaC in GA II:

45. In the light of all that we have said about communion it is now possible to describe what constitutes ecclesial communion....*[We share the common faith, scripture, creeds, baptism, a liturgy, and parish life centered on the Eucharist. We have shared commitment to mission, social concern, spirituality, and the ethical life, with an expectation of eternal life.]*

For the nurture and growth of this communion, Christ the Lord has provided a ministry of oversight, the fullness of which is entrusted to the episcopate, which has the responsibility of maintaining and expressing the unity of the churches. By shepherding, teaching and the celebration of the sacraments, especially the eucharist, this ministry holds believers together in the communion of the local church and in the wider communion of all the churches. This ministry of oversight has both collegial and primatial dimensions. It is grounded in the life of the community and is open to the community's participation in the discovery of God's will....Throughout history different means have been used to express...this communion between bishops: the participation of bishops of neighboring sees in episcopal ordinations; prayer for bishops of other dioceses in the liturgy; exchanges of episcopal letters. Local churches recognized the necessity of maintaining communion with the principal sees, particularly with the See of Rome. The practice of holding synods or councils, local, provincial, ecumenical, arose from the need to maintain unity in the one apostolic faith.

49. The convictions which this Commission believes that Anglicans and Roman Catholics share concerning the nature of communion challenge both our churches to move forward together towards visible unity and ecclesial communion....

58. Serious as these remaining obstacles may seem, we should not overlook the extent of the communion already existing between our two churches, which we have described in the last part of this Statement. Indeed, awareness of this fact will help us to bear the pain of our differences without complacency or despair. It should encourage Anglicans and Roman Catholics locally to search for further steps by which concrete expression can be given to this communion which we share. Paradoxically the closer we draw together the more acutely we feel those differences which remain. The forbearance and generosity with which we seek to resolve these remaining differences will testify to the character of the fuller communion for which we strive....

Editor's Notes: At the time of the Reformation, Lutheran and Reformed churches placed unity in faith at the core of the unity of the Church. Catholics and Lutherans have found agreement on doctrine to be as important as their agreements on sacraments and ministry. For Lutherans, the structures of the church are subordinate to and oriented toward the preaching of salvation. Therefore agreements on church and on grace go together. Historic polarizations about the invisible and visible dimensions of the church have begun to be overcome in the dialogues.

Lutheran

Consensus, L-RC IX in GA II:

> The far-reaching consensus in the understanding of justification noted during this and other Lutheran–Roman Catholic dialogues lead to testing the consensus on the critical significance of the doctrine of justification for all church doctrine, order and practice. Everything which is believed and taught regarding the nature of the church, the means of grace and the ordained ecclesial ministry must be grounded in the salvation-event itself and bear the mark of justification-faith as reception and appropriation of that event. Correspondingly, all that is believed and taught regarding the nature and effects of justification must be understood in the total context of assertions about the church, the means of grace and the church's ordained ministry….
>
> *[Lutherans and Catholics agree that the structures emerged through history, but:]* Our two churches give in part different and indeed controversial responses to the question of how far and to what degree these ecclesiastical realities which have arisen in history share in the enduring quality of the realities established when the church was founded. The reasons for the differences are certainly theological and ecclesiological, but very often they also reflect different experiences of the church. But it is not in dispute that (1) these realities arose in the history of the church and were not directly and explicitly established when it was founded, (2) they can certainly give expression to the continuity of the church and be of serv-

ice to it, and (3) they nevertheless remain capable of renewal and in need of renewal.

We may sum up by saying that in regard to all the problem(s)…we may not speak of a fundamental conflict or even opposition between justification and the church. This is quite compatible with the role of the doctrine of justification in seeing that all the church's institutions, in their self-understanding and exercise, contribute to the church's abiding in the truth of the gospel which alone in the Holy Spirit creates and sustains the church." (#168, 179, 242)

Reformed

Consensus, Ref–C I in GA I:

16. There was complete agreement in presenting ecclesiology from a clear Christological and pneumatological perspective in which the Church is the object of declared faith and cannot be completely embraced by a historical and sociological description.

Differences, Ref–C II in GA II:

102. Accordingly, our respective interpretations of the division in the sixteenth century are not the same. The Reformed consider that the Reformation was a rupture with the Catholic "establishment" of the period. This establishment had become greatly corrupted and incapable of responding to an appeal for reform in the sense of a return to the purity of the Gospel and the holiness of the early Church. Nevertheless, this does not mean that the resulting division was a substantial rupture in the continuity of the Church. For Catholics, however, this break struck at the continuity of the tradition derived from the apostles and lived through many centuries. Insofar as the Reformed had broken with the ministerial structure handed down by tradition, they had deeply wounded the apostolicity of their churches. The severity of this judgment is moderated today because ecumenical contacts

have made Catholics more aware of the features of authentic Christian identity preserved in those churches.

⊷⊷⊷

Editor's Notes: For Methodists, holiness and mission have been more important marks of the unity of the church than continuity in ministry and clarity of doctrine have been. Methodists and Catholics agree, however, that in a united church, holiness and mission are central to the unity of the church.

Methodist

Convergence, WMC–RC VII:

28. The ultimate aim of mission is to serve God's saving purpose for all of humankind. Just as the Church longs for the oneness of its members in love and prays for it in the liturgy, so it waits in hope for spiritual gifts that will lead it to a higher level of holiness, a more evident fullness of catholicity, and a greater fidelity in apostolicity. This striving after perfection in the God-given marks of the Church implies an ecumenical imperative. All Christian churches should pray and work toward an eventual restoration of organic unity. Visionary Methodists from John R. Mott onwards have been among the pioneers of the modern ecumenical movement, and Methodist Churches have wholeheartedly committed themselves to the recovery of the full visible unity of Christians. Likewise the Second Vatican Council committed the Catholic Church irrevocably to the same goal.…Catholics and Methodists have thus begun to enjoy a "union in affection" on their way to that "entire external union" for which Wesley in his time hardly dared to hope.

⊷⊷⊷

Editor's Notes: In the United States there are African-American Protestant churches—mostly Methodist, Baptist, and Pentecostal—whose faith is orthodox and commitment to the church is deep, but who emerged as separate denominations because of the racism in the predominate com-

79

munity. Therefore, their commitment to Christian unity is both visible and challenging to the other Christian churches.

Black Churches

Convergence, Black Ch:

I. We affirm that the unity of the Church not only expresses the unity of the Triune God, but is also a sign of the unity of humankind that holds together in one family the diversity of all races and cultures. In the economy of God each "tribe," each ethnic group and culture has its own vocation to bring its gift to the full household of faith. Notwithstanding the effort of some white Christians to disdain the contribution of Black folk to the faith and to its impact upon the institutions of the American church and society, we declare that the meaning of Blackness as cultural and religious experience edifies and enriches the universal message of the Christian faith. Blackness, in the religions of the African Diaspora, is a profound and complex symbol of a diversified yet united experience: servitude and oppression, faithfulness through suffering, identification with the exclusion, martyrdom and exaltation of Jesus as the Oppressed One of God who triumphs over enemies, a passion for justice and liberation, the exuberance of Black faith and life, rejoicing in the Risen Lord in Pentecostal fervor and in service to the "least" of Christ's brothers and sisters.

White Christians have too often treated unity as if it were only a spiritual reality. We believe that unity must not be spiritualized, but manifested in concrete behavior, by doing just and loving service to one another. The cost of unity in the Church is repentance and affirmative discipleship, (i.e., action). We have, therefore, a profound hermeneutical suspicion about any movement for unity that is dominated by North Atlantic attitudes and assumptions. We have observed that when our white brothers and sisters speak of unity they often mean being together on terms that carefully maintain their political, economic and cultural hegemony. Unity is frequently confused with

"Anglo-conformity"—strict adherence to premises and perspectives based upon the worldview and ethos of the North Atlantic community with its history of racial oppression. Christian unity is, however, based upon the worship of a common Creator who is no respecter of persons, obedience to a common Lawgiver and Judge whose commandment to break every yoke is not abrogated by the gracious justification of sinners, and upon participation in the earthly mission of a common Redeemer, the sharing of whose suffering and ordeal makes us truly one, though of many races and cultures….

Editor's Notes: Evangelical, Pentecostal, and Holiness churches seek a unity among Christians that is more spiritual than visible. This difference in the hope for church unity is, however, transcended by a profound spiritual bond in Christ. The text below from the Pentecostal dialogue is exemplary of Catholic agreements with other evangelical Christians. Personal conversion is often more important than church membership for these Christians.

Pentecostal

Differences, Pent–C in GA II:

5. Although the unity of the Church is a concern of Pentecostals and Roman Catholics alike, the dialogue has not had as its goal or its subject, either organic or structural union. These discussions were meant to develop a climate of mutual understanding in matters of faith and practice; to find points of genuine agreement as well as to indicate areas in which further dialogue is required….

76. The difficulties of some Pentecostals with their ecclesial institutions stem in part from frequent emphasis on their direct relation to the Spirit. They forget that the Spirit is given not only to individual Christians, but also to the whole community….Roman Catholics have rightly challenged Pentecostals to think of the whole

community, too, as a "temple of God" in which the Spirit dwells (1 Cor 3:16)....

83. Roman Catholics hold that some existing ecclesiastical structures (such as the office of a bishop) are "God given" and that they belong to the very essence of church order rather than serving only its well being.

84. While Pentecostals disagree among themselves concerning how the Church should best be ordered (the views range from congregational to episcopal), they accept the full ecclesial status of the churches ordered in various ways....

108. Roman Catholics believe that the contemporary Church is in continuity with the Church in the New Testament. Pentecostals, influenced by restorationist perspectives, have claimed continuity with the Church in the New Testament by arguing for discontinuity with much of the historical Church. By adopting these two positions, one of continuity, the other of discontinuity, each tradition has attempted to demonstrate its faithfulness to the apostolic faith "once for all delivered to the saints" (Jude 3).

The Hierarchical Constitution of the Church (CCC #871–913)

Editor's Notes: All Christian churches recognize God as the source of authority in the church; this authority is mediated through his Son, Jesus Christ. All recognize in the ministry of the church a "holy origin," and a "sacred order" (hierarchy), *though embodied in a variety of forms from the egalitarian Quakers to the intricate collegiality of the Presbyterians. In the churches' dialogues toward reconciliation, issues of authority and ministry are among the most difficult to resolve. Christians have differed on the questions of who, how, and what sources are to be used in this authority in service to the unity. All of these questions have been subjects of dialogue toward building common bonds of communion.*

Reflection Questions:

- What is the common ground in church order, authority, and ministry that the churches can share together?
- What are some of the developments of agreement about bishops, councils, decision making, and church leadership that expand our Catholic understanding of the hierarchical nature of the church?
- How are papal and other primacies seen to serve the unity of the Church?

Editor's Notes: Although the language of hierarchical communion is not used in the very inclusive discussions of the many churches represented in Faith and Order, there is a general convergence about the need for this ordered authority and its relationship to ordained ministry. This overarching convergence provides a context for the more particular consensus between Catholics and other partners in their bilateral dialogues. It outlines three dimensions of hierarchical authority that recur in Catholic dialogues with other churches: collegial, communal, and personal.

World Council of Churches Faith and Order

Convergence, BEM in GA I:

M13. The chief responsibility of the ordained ministry is to assemble and build up the body of Christ by proclaiming and teaching the Word of God, by celebrating the sacraments, and by guiding the life of the community in its worship, its mission and its caring ministry.

M15. The authority of the ordained minister is rooted in Jesus Christ, who has received it from the Father (Matt. 28:18), and who confers it by the Holy Spirit through the act of ordination….Since ordination is essentially a setting apart with prayer for the gift of the Holy Spirit, the authority of the ordained ministry is not to be understood as the possession of the ordained person but as a gift for the continuing edification of the body in and for which the minister has been ordained. Authority has the character of responsibility before God and is exercised with the cooperation of the whole community.

M16. Therefore, ordained ministers must not be autocrats or impersonal functionaries….Only when they seek the response and acknowledgment of the community can their authority be protected from the distortions of isolation and domination….

M26. Three considerations are important in this respect. The ordained ministry should be exercised in a personal, collegial and communal way. It should be personal because the presence of Christ among his people can most effectively be pointed to by the person ordained to proclaim the Gospel and to call the community to serve the Lord in unity of life and witness. It should also be collegial, for there is need for a college of ordained ministers sharing in the common task of representing the concerns of the community. Finally, the intimate relationship between the ordained ministry and the community should find expression in a communal dimension where the exercise of the ordained ministry is rooted in the life of the community and requires the community's effective participation in the discovery of God's will and the guidance of the Spirit.

M27. The ordained ministry needs to be constitutionally or canonically ordered and exercised in the Church in such a way that each of these three dimensions can find adequate expression. At the level of the local eucharistic community there is need for an ordained minister acting within a collegial body. Strong emphasis should be placed on the active participation of all members in the life and the decision-making of the community. At the regional level there is again need for an ordained minister exercising a service of unity. The collegial and communal dimensions will find expression in regular representative synodal gatherings.

EPISCOPAL COLLEGE AND POPE
(CCC #880–887)

Editor's Notes: Anglicans and Lutherans in their dialogues with Catholics have been able to formulate important agreements on authority, collegiality, episcopacy, and even primacy, though all of the differences over the exercise of papal primacy and the infallibility of the church remain unresolved.

Anglicans

Convergence, Final Report, Elucidation on Authority #5 in GA I:

Editor's Notes: The Anglican–Catholic dialogue elucidates why the word hierarchy is not used, while affirming what Catholics mean by it:

> We have been asked to clarify the meaning of what some of our critics call "hierarchical authority,"—an expression we did not use. Here we are dealing with a form of authority which is inherent in the visible structure of the Church. By this we mean the authority attached to those ordained to exercise *episcope* in the Church….Both our communions have always recognized this need for disciplinary action on exceptional occasions as part of the authority given by Christ to his ministers.

Convergence, Final Report, Authority II, #17:

Editor's Notes: For Anglicans and Catholics the exercise of the authority of the church by the bishop is an explicit common conviction. It is in this context that agreement on the papacy develops:

> This authority of the bishop, usually called jurisdiction, involves the responsibility for making and implementing the decisions that are required by his office for the sake of the koinonia. It is not the arbitrary power of one man over the freedom of others, but a necessity if the bishop is to serve his flock as its shepherd. So too, within the universal koinonia and the collegiality of the bishops, the

universal primate exercises the jurisdiction necessary for the fulfillment of his functions, the chief of which is to serve the faith and unity of the whole Church.

⋙

Editor's Notes: Lutheran and Catholic scholars were able to say, after extensive review of the history and agreement on recounting the different ways in which the papacy has operated within the hierarchical communion of the church, how a renewed understanding of the Petrine ministry and the office of the bishop of Rome might serve in a united church of the future.

Lutherans

Convergence, LCUSA–V in BU:

(20) The bishop of Rome is head of the college of bishops, who share his responsibility for the universal church. His authority is pastoral in its purpose even when juridical in form. It should always be understood in its collegial context.

(21) We thus see from the above that the contemporary understanding of the New Testament and our knowledge of the processes at work in the history of the church make possible a fresh approach to the structure and operations of the papacy. There is increasing agreement that the centralization of the Petrine function in a single person or office results from a long process of development. Reflecting the many pressures of the centuries and the complexities of a world-wide church, the papal office can be seen both as a response to the guidance of the Spirit in the Christian community, and also as an institution which, in its human dimensions, is tarnished by frailty and even unfaithfulness. The Catholic members of this consultation see the institution of the papacy as developing from New Testament roots under the guidance of the Spirit. Without denying that God could have ordered the church differently, they believe that the papal form of the unifying Ministry is, in fact,

God's gracious gift to his people. Lutheran theologians, although in the past chiefly critical of the structure and functioning of the papacy, can now recognize many of its positive contributions to the life of the church. Both groups can acknowledge that as the forms of the papacy have been adapted to changing historical settings in the past, it is possible that they will be modified to meet the needs of the church in the future more effectively.

(35) This brings us to a thorny problem between Lutherans and Roman Catholics which the group has had to discuss. Whatever primacy the Lutheran reformers accorded to the bishop of Rome was seen as a matter of historical development, and therefore of human right *(de iure humano)*, rather than something rooted in the teaching of the scriptures. Over against this position the Roman Catholic view of the papal primacy claimed divine sanction *(de iure divino)* for certain papal prerogatives....Rather than using the traditional terminology of divine and human right, therefore, both Lutherans and Roman Catholics have been compelled by their historical studies to raise a different set of questions: In what way or ways has our Lord in fact led his church to use particular forms for the exercise of the Petrine function? What structural elements in the church does the gospel require for the ministry which serves the unity of the empirical church?

(36) Structures invested with powerful symbolic meaning cannot be created at will. Therefore we do not anticipate that a concrete Ministry of unity to serve the church of the future will be something completely new. It will have to emerge from the renewal and the restructuring of those historical forms which best nurture and express this unity. We recognize that among the existing signs or structures for the Ministry of unity in the whole church, the papacy has a long history marked by impressive achievements in spite of all the things we have regarded as faulty in it.

[Even before Pope John Paul offered to renew the papacy (1995), with advice from our ecumenical partners, to serve better the unity of Christians, Lutheran and Catholic scholars were able to say:]

(41) We ask our churches earnestly to consider if the time has not come to affirm a new attitude toward the papacy "for the sake of peace and concord in the church" and even more for the sake of a united witness to Christ in the world. Our Lutheran teaching about the church and the Ministry constrains us to believe that recognition of papal primacy is possible to the degree that a renewed papacy would in fact foster faithfulness to the gospel and truly exercise a Petrine function within the church. If this is indeed what Lutherans hold, ought they not to be willing to say so clearly and publicly?

[On the basis of these agreements on the papacy and church structure the dialogue raised some questions that have been answered positively in subsequent actions by the Lutheran and Catholic churches, such as the 1999 Joint Declaration on the Doctrine of Justification. Other questions enable Christians to look more deeply at the role of authority in the church and its exercise:]

Has not the time come for our churches to take seriously the possibility of what we have come to call "magisterial mutuality"? Should we not recognize the Spirit of Christ in each other's church and acknowledge each other's Ministers as partners in proclaiming the gospel in the unity of truth and love? Should we not listen to each other in formulating teaching, share each other's concerns, and ultimately develop a more unified voice for Christian witness in this world?…Should not creative efforts be made to discover a form of institutional relationship between the Catholic and the Lutheran churches which would express magisterial mutuality and would correspond to the converging state of their traditions? (# LCUSA–VI in BU, 55)

Editor's Notes: Anglicans have preserved the episcopacy and early in relationships with the Catholic Church have been willing to speak about a new relationship with the bishop of Rome. The Anglican–Catholic dialogue has one of the most developed treatments of authority, which is found in three documents. The agreements (1) recognize the centrality of God's authority in Christ mediated by the Holy Spirit, an authority to which the church responds, but which is also exercised by those in the church entrusted with leadership; (2) speak of the authority of holiness, the limitations of all human expressions of authority, and the role of the whole people of God—recognizing specific gifts and responsibilities within the community.

Anglican

Consensus, ARCIC I, Final Report, Authority I in GA I:

8. The authoritative action and proclamation of the people of God to the world therefore are not simply the responsibilities of each church acting separately, but of all the local churches together. The spiritual gifts of one may be an inspiration to the others. Since each bishop must ensure that the local community is distinctively Christian he has to make it aware of the universal communion of which it is part. The bishop expresses this unity of his church with the others: this is symbolized by the participation of several bishops in his ordination.

[Episcopal authority is situated within the universal and conciliar constitution of the church as it has developed from the earliest ages:]

10. This form of *episkope* is a service to the Church carried out in co-responsibility with all the bishops of the region; for every bishop receives at ordination both responsibility for his local church and the obligation to maintain it in living awareness and practical service of the other churches.

[Within this conciliar exercise of the office of bishop, the dialogue outlines the emergence of the role of the bishop of Rome as servant of this unity:]

12. The teaching of these councils shows that communion with the bishop of Rome does not imply sub-

mission to an authority which would stifle the distinctive features of the local churches. The purpose of this episcopal function of the bishop of Rome is to promote Christian fellowship in faithfulness to the teaching of the apostles.

[The form and exercise of this role has varied greatly over history and can further develop in the future church in which Anglicans and Catholics would live in full communion.]

Yet the primacy, rightly understood, implies that the bishop of Rome exercises his oversight in order to guard and promote the faithfulness of all the churches to Christ and one another. Communion with him is intended as a safeguard of the catholicity of each local church, and as a sign of the communion of all the churches.

[The church's teaching of the truth of faith takes a variety of forms in history: preaching, worship, reflection on the Word, and especially local, regional, and worldwide/ecumenical councils. The role of councils and bishops was particularly important in defining the limits of the faith.]

19. In discharging this responsibility bishops share in a special gift of Christ to his Church. Whatever further clarification or interpretation may be propounded by the Church, the truth expressed will always be confessed. This binding authority does not belong to every conciliar decree, but only to those which formulate the central truths of salvation. This authority is ascribed in both our traditions to decisions of the ecumenical councils of the first centuries.

[The role of primate bishops becomes important in times of crisis.]

20. The primacy accorded to a bishop implies that, after consulting his fellow bishops, he may speak in their name and express their mind. The recognition of his position by the faithful creates an expectation that on occasion he will take an initiative in speaking for the Church.

[In the context of this argument for the episcopal and conciliar constitution of the church, and the evolution of prima-

cies, especially the primacy of the bishop of Rome, the dialogue is able to suggest:]

> 23. The only see which makes any claim to universal primacy and which has exercised and still exercises such *episkope* is the see of Rome, the city where Peter and Paul died. It seems appropriate that in any future union a universal primacy such as has been described should be held by that see.

Editor's Notes: Furthermore, this primacy is intimately related to the unity of local churches and the roles of local dioceses and their bishops: Convergence, ARCIC I, Final Report, Authority II in GA I:

> 21. The purpose of the universal primate's jurisdiction is to enable him to further catholicity as well as unity and to foster and draw together the riches of the diverse traditions of the churches. Collegial and primatial responsibility for preserving the distinctive life of the local churches involves a proper respect for their customs and traditions, provided these do not contradict the faith or disrupt communion. The search for unity and concern for catholicity must not be divorced.

Editor's Notes: Later ARCIC dialogues are able to go even further with agreements on the authority of bishops and the infallibility of the church, exercised in certain situations by the pope.

Consensus, ARCIC II, GofA:

> 44. The duty of maintaining the Church in the truth is one of the essential functions of the episcopal college. It has the power to exercise this ministry because it is bound in succession to the apostles, who were the body authorized and sent by Christ to preach the Gospel to all the nations. The authenticity of the teaching of individual bishops is evident when this teaching is in solidarity with that of the whole episcopal college. The exercise of this teaching authority requires that what it teaches be faithful to Holy Scripture and consistent with apostolic Tradition....

47. [T]he Bishop of Rome offers a specific ministry concerning the discernment of truth, as an expression of universal primacy....Every solemn definition pronounced from the chair of Peter in the church of Peter and Paul may, however, express only the faith of the Church....It is this faith which the Bishop of Rome in certain circumstances has a duty to discern and make explicit. This form of authoritative teaching has no stronger guarantee from the Spirit than have the solemn definitions of ecumenical councils. The reception of the primacy of the Bishop of Rome entails the recognition of this specific ministry of the universal primate. We believe that this is a gift to be received by all the churches.

[As with the Lutherans, Catholics and Anglicans make specific suggestions as to how their churches can give more structure to the "hierarchical communion" on which they agree:]

58. Anglican and Roman Catholic bishops should find ways of cooperating and developing relationships of mutual accountability in their exercise of oversight. At this new stage we have not only to do together whatever we can, but also to be together all that our existing koinonia allows...bishops meeting regularly together at regional and local levels and the participation of bishops from one communion in the international meetings of bishops of the other. Serious consideration could also be given to the association of Anglican bishops with Roman Catholic bishops in their ad limina visits to Rome. Wherever possible, bishops should take the opportunity of teaching and acting together in matters of faith and morals. They should also witness together in the public sphere on issues affecting the common good. (#59)

60. Both Roman Catholics and Anglicans look to this *[papal]* ministry being exercised in collegiality and synodality—a ministry of *servus servorum Dei*. We envisage a primacy that will even now help to uphold the legitimate diversity of traditions, strengthening and safeguarding them in fidelity to the Gospel.

[In suggesting that the primacy of the pope can be developed in both Anglican and Catholic churches even before full communion is reestablished, they base this re-reception in both churches on the principles that:]

62. Anglicans be open to and desire a recovery and re-reception under certain clear conditions of the exercise of universal primacy by the Bishop of Rome; that Roman Catholics be open to and desire a re-reception of the exercise of primacy by the Bishop of Rome and the offering of such a ministry to the whole Church of God.

Editor's Notes: Some Methodist churches have bishops; all have structures of decision making and communion. The dialogues with Catholics have shown a willingness to consider common structures of authority and even a re-reception of the papacy.

Methodists

Convergence, WMC–RC IV in GA II:

[The dialogue traces a common record of the rise of the episcopacy, councils, and authority in the church, but is] not agreed on how far this development of the ministry is now unchangeable.…Practically, however, the majority of Methodists already accept the office of bishop, and some Methodist Churches that do not, have expressed their willingness to accept this for the sake of unity.…It is the belief of the Roman Catholic Church and these Methodist Churches that for the exercise of their ministry the bishops receive special gifts from the Holy Spirit through prayer and the laying-on of hands. (#29, 34)

[While Methodists have no experience of primacy within their own life, with Catholics they are able to give a common account of the rise of councils and the papacy and come to the conclusion:]

48. Methodists accept that whatever is properly required for the unity of the whole of Christ's Church must by that very fact be God's will for his Church. A universal primacy might well serve as focus of and min-

istry for the unity of the whole Church. *[and]* A clearer recognition of this today would make it easier for Methodists to reconsider whether the bishop of Rome might yet exercise this ministry for other Christians as well as for those who already accept it. (#50) It would not be inconceivable that at some future date in a restored unity, Roman Catholic and Methodist bishops might be linked in one episcopal college and that the whole body would recognize some kind of effective leadership and primacy in the bishop of Rome. In that case Methodists might justify such an acceptance on different grounds from those that now prevail in the Roman Catholic Church. (#62)

[Methodists and Catholics are not yet agreed about infallibility, especially as exercised by the papacy, but they are able to say:]

75. In any case Catholics and Methodists are agreed on the need for an authoritative way of being sure, beyond doubt, concerning God's action insofar as it is crucial for our salvation.

Editor's Notes: Methodists and Catholics agree about the theology of the Church as teacher, but continue to differ on the exercise of this teaching office.

Convergence, WMC–RC VII:

118. Most fundamentally, both Methodists and Catholics believe that it is the Spirit who preserves within the Church the truth of the Gospel proclaimed by Christ and the apostles, though there is not complete agreement on what constitute the essential components of that Gospel….

119. Both recognize the role of the laity in the development of the faith through living it, preaching and teaching it, and meditating upon it. In Methodism lay people participate as members of Conference in the authoritative determination of the precise content of the Church's faith. The Catholic Church, on the other hand,

maintains that the authoritative determination of the precise content of the Church's faith is properly the ministry of bishops.

———⊷⊶———

Editor's Notes: Most Reformed churches do not have bishops, but they affirm with Catholics the unique role of the minister of Word and Sacrament, and the transmission of orders by the church through the laying on of hands and prayer to the Holy Spirit. These ministers have a teaching office.

Reformed

Convergence, Ref–C in GA I:

97. Within apostolicity in general there is a special ministry to which the administration of Word and Sacrament is entrusted. That special ministry is one of the charismata for the exercise of particular services within the whole body. Ordination, or setting apart for the exercise of these special services, takes place within the context of the believing community. Hence consultation with that community, profession of faith before that community, and liturgical participation by that community belong to the process of ordination. This is important to underline because we need to go beyond an understanding of ordination which suggests that those consecrated to the special ministry are given a *potestas* and derive a dignity from Christ without reference to the believing community.

102. We agree that the basic structure of the Church and its ministry is collegial. When one is consecrated to the special ministry, one accepts the discipline of being introduced into a collegial function which includes being subject to others in the Lord and drawing on the comfort and admonition of fellow ministers.

This "collegiality" is expressed on the Reformed side by the synodical polity, and, on the Roman Catholic side, by the episcopal college, the understanding of which is in process of further development. In the Reformed polity, the synod functions as a corporate episcopacy, exercising oversight of pastors and congregations.

—————

THE LAY FAITHFUL (CCC #897–913)

Editor's Notes: All Christian churches profess the centrality of baptism, the priesthood of all believers, and the universal ministry of the whole people of God. The churches differ in how they understand the relationship of the ministry of the whole people of God to the ordained ministry and to the authority structures of the church. We agree in a theology that gives an important place to the ministry of all baptized but we are divided in our practice of how we incorporate the baptized faithful into the leadership of our churches. It is particularly important for Catholics to explore the teaching of the church in this matter. Unlike Orthodox and Reformation churches, Catholics do not have a place for the lay faithful in the governance structures of the church.

Reflection Questions:

- How does the Holy Spirit empower the whole people of God for ministry?
- What are the important differences among the variety of gifts given to the baptized?
- What are the agreements among Christians in their faith in the common ministry of all Christians?

World Council of Churches Faith and Order

Editor's Notes: As an overarching convergence among the churches, the World Council statement on ministry begins with an extensive review of the biblical basis for the calling of all baptized Christians to ministry, concluding:

Convergence, BEM in GA I:
    M5. The Holy Spirit bestows on the community diverse and complementary gifts. These are for the common good of the whole people and are manifested in acts of

service within the community and to the world. They may be gifts of communicating the Gospel in word and deed, gifts of healing, gifts of praying, gifts of teaching and learning, gifts of serving, gifts of guiding and following, gifts of inspiration and vision. All members are called to discover, with the help of the community, the gifts they have received and to use them for the building up of the Church and for the service of the world to which the Church is sent.

M6. Though the churches are agreed in their general understanding of the calling of the people of God, they differ in their understanding of how the life of the Church is to be ordered. In particular, there are differences concerning the place and forms of the ordained ministry. As they engage in the effort to overcome these differences, the churches need to work from the perspective of the calling of the whole people of God. A common answer needs to be found to the following question: How, according to the will of God and under the guidance of the Holy Spirit, is the life of the Church to be understood and ordered, so that the Gospel may be spread and the community built up in love?

⊷

Editor's Notes: Because Catholics and Orthodox share a common sacramental and ministerial understanding of the church, they differ very little in their understanding of the ministry of the baptized. In order to come to a full understanding of the nature of the church, however, it is necessary to see the ordained ministry in the context of the calling of the baptized.

Orthodox

Consensus, Ox–C 3, #17, 18 in GA II:
Invisibly present in the Church through the Holy Spirit, whom he has sent, Christ then is its unique High Priest. In him, priest and victim, all together, pastors and faithful, form a "chosen race, a royal priesthood, a holy

nation, a people he claims as his own" (1 Pt 2:9; cf. Rv 5:10). All members of the Churches, as members of the Body of Christ, participate in this priesthood, called to become "a living sacrifice holy and acceptable to God" (Rom 12:1; cf. 1 Pt 2:5). Head of the Church, Christ has established, to make himself present, apostles chosen among the people, whom he endowed with authority and power by strengthening them through the grace of the Holy Spirit.

Editor's Notes: In the dialogues, Anglicans and the other Reformation churches cannot address questions of authority, episcopacy, and primacy without first making a strong affirmation of the role of all of all the baptized in the church.

Anglicans

Consensus, ARCIC I, Final Report, Elucidation on Ministry #2 in GA I:

> The ordained ministry can only be rightly understood within this broader context of various ministries, all of which are the work of one and the same Spirit....The Priesthood of the whole people of God (1 Peter 2:5) is the consequence of incorporation by baptism into Christ. This priesthood of all the faithful is not a matter of disagreement between us....The word priesthood is used by way of analogy when it is applied to the people of God and to the ordained ministry. These are two distinct realities which relate, each in its own way, to the high priesthood of Christ, the unique priesthood of the new covenant, which is their source and model.

Editor's Notes: In discussions of authority, Catholics and Anglicans articulate a common faith in the role of the Christian faithful.

Consensus, ARCIC II, G of A:

> 28. The people of God as a whole is the bearer of the living Tradition. In changing situations producing fresh challenges to the Gospel, the discernment, actualization and communication of the Word of God is the responsibility of the whole people of God. The Holy Spirit works through all members of the community, using the gifts he gives to each for the good of all. Theologians in particular serve the communion of the whole Church by exploring whether and how new insights should be integrated into the ongoing stream of Tradition. In each community there is an exchange, a mutual give-and-take, in which bishops, clergy and lay people receive from as well as give to others within the whole body.

> 29. In every Christian who is seeking to be faithful to Christ and is fully incorporated into the life of the Church, there is a *sensus fidei*. This *sensus fidei* may be described as an active capacity for spiritual discernment, an intuition that is formed by worshipping and living in communion as a faithful member of the Church.

> *[Anglican and Catholic dialogue partners have placed questions to one another, including:]*

> 57. The Second Vatican Council has reminded Roman Catholics of how the gifts of God are present in all the people of God....However, is there at all levels effective participation of clergy as well as lay people in emerging synodal bodies?

Editor's Notes: A major emphasis in the Reformation was the priesthood of all believers over against what Reformers thought was an overemphasis in the church on the sacramental priesthood. Agreements with Lutherans and other Reformation churches enable Catholics to deepen their appreciation of the common teaching of the church. This text, from a document on ordained ministry, is illustrative of agreements with Methodist, Disciples, and Reformed churches on this theme.

Lutheran

Consensus, L–RC VI in BU:

> 13, 14. The Reformation was against emphasizing a special clerical class within the people of God and stressed the universal priesthood of the baptized. In both our churches, consciousness of this calling of the whole people of God diminished greatly in recent centuries. In contemporary Protestant teaching regarding the church, the universal priesthood of all the baptized is once again stressed. The Second Vatican Council expressly emphasized the common priesthood of the faithful. Within this priestly people of God, Christ—acting through the Holy Spirit—confers manifold ministries: apostles, prophets, evangelists, pastors and teachers "to equip the saints for the work of ministry, for building up the body of Christ" (Eph 4:11f.).

Mary—Mother of Christ (CCC #864–871)

Editor's Notes: While all Christian churches recognize Mary as the mother of God, they differ on the place she holds in the doctrine of the church. Devotional practices vary widely between churches, and even within the Catholic Church. While devotional preferences are not church dividing, doctrinal differences on the role of Mary will need to be resolved as the pilgrimage toward reconciliation moves forward.

Reflection Questions:

- How does our belief in Mary and her role in our salvation relate to Christ?
- How are our Catholic and Orthodox devotions to Mary related to our faith in Christ and in Mary's role in redemption?

- How do Protestant concerns about Catholic and Orthodox devotion to Mary help to purify our faith and deepen our understanding of the church's devotional life?

World Council of Churches Faith and Order

Editor's Notes: In the context of the Nicene Creed's affirmation of Christ's birth, a broad convergence is enunciated among Christians.

Convergence, COF, #122, 123:

All Christians share in the confession affirmed by the Council of Ephesus (431) that Mary is "Theotokos," the mother of him who is also God, through the creative work of the Spirit of God. In referring to the motherhood of Mary, the Creed shows the Son of God to be a human being like us, one who shares our experience in being born and loved by a mother, and nurtured by parental care. But Mary is also the disciple who hears the word of God, responds to it and keeps it. In her obedience to God and her utter dependence on the Holy Spirit, Mary is the example par excellence of our discipleship….In her complete reliance on God, her active response of faith and her expectation of the kingdom, Mary has been seen as a figure *(typos)* of and an example of the Church. Like Mary, the Church cannot exist on its own; it can only rely on God; it is the vigilant servant waiting for the return of the Master.

―――

Anglicans

Editor's Notes: Anglicans have retained most Marian feasts, and devotion to Our Lady is a regular part of Anglican life. However, the Marian dogmas of the last two centuries and some Catholic practices are alien to Anglican life. For this reason, the agreements reached have taken account of authority questions as well as the piety of the churches.

Convergence, ARCIC–Mary:

> 76. We together reaffirm…:
> • any interpretation of the role of Mary must not obscure the unique mediation of Christ;…
> • Mary was prepared by grace to be the mother of our Redeemer, by whom she herself was redeemed and received into glory;…
> 77…
> • This study has led us to the conclusion that it is impossible to be faithful to Scripture without giving due attention to the person of Mary.
> • In recalling together the ancient common traditions, we have discerned afresh the central importance of the *Theotokos* in the Christological controversies….
> • We have reviewed the growth of devotion to Mary in the medieval centuries, and the theological controversies associated with them. We have seen how some excesses in late medieval devotion, and reactions against them by the Reformers, contributed to the breach of communion between us, following which attitudes toward Mary took divergent paths….
> • This growing convergence has also allowed us to approach in a fresh way the questions about Mary which our two Communions have set before us. In doing so, we have framed our work within the pattern of grace and hope which we discover in Scripture—"predestined…called…justified…glorified."(Rm 8:30)
> 78. As a result of our study, the Commission offers the following agreements…:
> • The teaching that God has taken the Blessed Virgin Mary in the fullness of her person into his glory as consonant with Scripture, and only to be understood in the light of Scripture;
> • That in view of her vocation to be the mother of the Holy One, Christ's redeeming work reaches "back" in Mary to the depths of her being and to her earliest beginnings;

• That the teaching about Mary in the two definitions of the Assumption and the Immaculate Conception, understood within the biblical pattern of the economy of hope and grace, can be said to be consonant with the teaching of Scripture and the ancient common traditions;

• That this agreement, when accepted by our two Communions, would place the questions about authority which arise from the two definitions of 1854 and 1950 in a new ecumenical context;

• That Mary has a continuing ministry which serves the ministry of Christ, our unique mediator, that Mary and the Saints pray for the whole Church and that the practice of asking Mary and the saints to pray for us is not communion-dividing.

79. We agree that doctrines and devotions which are contrary to Scripture cannot be said to be revealed by God nor to be the teaching of the Church. We agree that doctrine and devotion which focuses on Mary, including claims to "private revelations," must be moderated by carefully expressed norms which ensure the unique and central place of Jesus Christ in the life of the Church, and that Christ alone, together with the Father and the Holy Spirit, is to be worshipped in the Church.

Editor's Notes: Luther had a personal devotion to Mary and believed in the Immaculate Conception and the Assumption even though, in his time, these were not dogmas of the Catholic Church. The churches of the Reformation, however, were very cautious about any devotion that seemed to detract from the centrality of Christ. This included devotion to Our Lady. The Lutheran–Catholic dialogue in the United States has done a thorough common treatment of the history of Marian doctrine and devotion through the ages, concluding with some common observations.

Lutherans

Convergence, L–CUSA VIII in GC I:

(99) With regard to the mediatory role of Mary, our dialogue has not revealed any tendency on the part of Catholics to look upon Mary as a propitiator or to consider that her mercy is anything but an expression and reflection of the mercy of Christ himself. Catholics today do not commonly speak of Mary's heavenly "mediation," if they use the term at all, except to express her intercessory role with her son.

(101) From the Lutheran side, one may recall the honor and devotion paid to the Mother of God by Luther himself, including his own attitude to the Immaculate Conception and the Assumption, which he accepted in some form. The Lutheran Confessions offer high praise for Mary as foremost of all the saints. When confronted with contemporary abuses, however, the Confessions warn of "idolatry" with regard to the saints and express the fear that Mary "in popular estimation...has completely replaced Christ." Lutheran reactions, where voiced to the dogmas about Mary's Immaculate Conception (1854) and Assumption (1950), were negative. The statements of the Second Vatican Council, however, demonstrate that the sole mediatorship of Christ can be asserted and the role of Mary further interpreted by Roman Catholics in ways that old Lutheran fears can be diminished. The Lutherans of this dialogue are of the opinion that, as long as the sole mediatorship of Christ is clearly safeguarded, these two Marian dogmas need not divide our churches provided that in a closer future fellowship Lutherans as members would be free not to accept these dogmas.

(102) In the greater fellowship we envisage between our churches, continuing efforts would have to be made together to apply hermeneutical principles to the Marian dogmas. Lutherans and Catholics would have to try to see together how far decisions since the separation have

been stamped with a certain particularization in thought and language, and how they could be reread in the context of the whole tradition and with a deeper understanding of Scripture. In this way it might be possible to transcend differences regarding the definitions of 1854 and 1950 without doing violence to the essential content. Unless and until such agreed reinterpretations can be achieved, the two Marian dogmas must be acknowledged as an obstacle to full fellowship between our churches, though they need not prevent a significant advance in the relationship that already exists.

<hr />

Editor's Notes: Evangelical, Pentecostal, and Holiness churches have even more difficulty with the place of honor Mary holds in the Catholic Church and Catholic piety toward Mary than the classical Reformation churches have had. However, careful theological dialogue has clarified these differences and dispelled some of the mutual misunderstanding.

Pentecostals

Convergence, difference, Pent–C II, #58–76 in GA II:
Both classical Pentecostals and Roman Catholics were surprised that they had entertained unreal perceptions of the others' views on Mary....Both Roman Catholics and Pentecostals agree that Mary is the Mother of Jesus Christ who is the Son of God and as such she occupies a unique place.

[Both affirm the Council of Ephesus definition of Mary as mother of God.]

Roman Catholics and classical Pentecostals concur in the special respect due to Mary as the mother of Jesus....For Pentecostals, certain Roman Catholic practices of Marian veneration appear to be superstitious and idolatrous. For Roman Catholics there is an apparent failure among Pentecostals to take account of the place of Mary in God's design as indicated in Holy Scripture....Both Pentecostals and Roman Catholics teach that Mary in no way substitutes for, or replaces, the one Savior and Mediator Jesus Christ....Catholics believe that intercessory prayers directed to Mary do not end in Mary but in God Himself. Pentecostals would not invoke the intercession of Mary or other saints in heaven because they do not consider it a valid biblical practice.

[The dialogue situates the Immaculate Conception and Assumption within the hierarchy of truths and demonstrates, to Pentecostals, how they relate to the unique and central role of Christ.]

Both Pentecostals and Roman Catholics agree that Mary was a virgin in the conception of Jesus and see in the texts which state it an important affirmation of the divine Sonship of Christ....Pentecostals acknowledge Catholic assurances that the special grace claimed for Mary is a redeeming grace that comes from Jesus. She stands among the redeemed and is a member of the church. However, Pentecostals cannot find any basis for the doctrine of Mary's Immaculate Conception in Scripture. Furthermore, Pentecostals do not see any value for salvation in this doctrine. Roman Catholics see in the Pentecostal attitude a failure to appreciate fully the implications of the incarnation and the power of Christ's saving and sanctifying grace.

[A similar discussion clarifies differences over the Catholic doctrine of the Assumption.]

The Pentecostal difficulty rests in the absence of biblical evidence. There is a generally accepted view that Mary, as one of the faithful, awaits the day of resurrection when she, along with all Christians, will be united bodily with her Son in glory. Pentecostals see a parallel between Mary's "assumption" and the Pentecostal understanding of the "bodily resurrection" or the "rapture of the church" (1 Thess 4:13–18, cf. esp. v. 17), but differ as to when this will take place for Mary.

Editor's Notes: The Evangelical/Roman Catholic Dialogue on Mission also took up this theme, in the context of salvation. Catholics explained their Marian faith and devotion in great detail to clarify the christocentric and biblically grounded base of these beliefs and practices. However, Evangelicals still voiced their concerns over some excesses in Marian piety, as did Catholics.

Evangelicals

Convergence, difference, ERCDOM, #3, Appendix (b) in GA II:
Yet a certain Evangelical uneasiness remained. First, the traditional Catholic emphasis on Mary's role in salvation (e.g. as the "New Eve," the life-giving mother) still seemed to them incompatible with the much more modest place accorded to her in the New Testament. Secondly, the vocabulary used in relation to Mary seemed to them certainly ambiguous and probably misleading. Is it not vitally important, they asked, especially in the central doctrine of salvation through Christ alone, to avoid expressions which require elaborate explanation (however much hallowed by long tradition) and to confine ourselves to language which is plainly and unequivocally Christ-centered? At the same time Roman Catholics are troubled by what seems to them a notable neglect by Evangelicals of the place given by God to Mary in salvation history and in the life of the Church.

Why It Matters

An alien visiting Earth would certainly have a hard time understanding how Christian churches that all express the Nicene Creed could interpret it in such a vast array of diverse lifestyles and attitudes. But that's the nature of reality when family feuds develop and ripen over time.

But the fact that there is agreement on the creedal statements between most Christian churches is a sign of hope for those who are in interchurch marriages. While there are still issues that must be resolved before regular sacramental communion is possible between churches, sharing these common beliefs can strengthen a marriage instead of being a source of division.

When couples of different Christian traditions are being prepared for marriage, a discussion of the common beliefs and differences in interpretation between churches would seem appropriate. Couples have a right to know how they can and cannot share in each church's worship and devotional life. They have a right to know how both churches interpret the creedal statements. They can take comfort in knowing that their marriage to a spouse from another Christian tradition does not separate them in any way from Christ or from their own church. And they should not be misled to believe that shared sacramental worship or communion is near at hand.

Understanding how the various Christian churches interpret the creed is of significant importance for those responsible for assisting baptized seekers into the Catholic Church. It is not enough that a person professes the creed; the person should also have a Catholic understanding of its beliefs and a commitment to them.

6

CELEBRATING THE MYSTERIES: SACRAMENTS OF INITIATION

Grandmother Graham is visiting for the weekend. She is a Baptist. Her daughter Lillian became Catholic when she married Stephen. Their five children have all been raised Catholic. Grandma is especially fond of the youngest, Jane, who is seven months old.

Grandma is particularly bothered by the knowledge that Jane and her other grandchildren have been baptized. Infant baptism isn't accepted in her church. She thinks the children should have a chance when they are older to accept Jesus as their personal Lord and Savior, and then be baptized when they have had personal experiences of faith.

To make matters more confusing, Stephen's sister-in-law is Ukrainian Catholic and is constantly asking why baby Jane and the other young children don't receive communion with the family. Lillian and Stephen feel caught between these various religious traditions and are unsure of what to do.

The different approaches to the sacraments of initiation among Christians are a source of tension for many families. Some of these differences are divisive, while others are simply appropriate actions of diverse customs. Which is which? Read on to find out.

The Seven Sacraments of the Church (CCC #1113–1130)

Editor's Notes: Christians share a common baptism, a common faith in Christ, and a common goal of unity among Christians. This unity in the Spirit is at the very heart of Catholic identity as a sacramental people. Therefore, we also recognize that on the sacramental level not all divisive differences have been resolved. The fact that significant progress is being made is integral to a Catholic understanding of our sacramental life together because it both illumines our Catholic faith and brings us closer to that goal of sacramental unity for which we pray.

We hunger for communion together at the Lord's Table, but this unity can only occur when we share the same belief and the same understanding of Christ's presence in our midst that draws us together. It is important to note that agreement on sacramental issues is more advanced with some churches than with others.

The World Council's Baptism, Eucharist, and Ministry text is a good companion to this section of the Catechism *(http://wcc-coe.org/wcc/what/faith/bem1.html).*

The church did not definitively set the number of sacraments at seven until the Council of Trent. Before that time a variety of rites were included, or the number was reserved to baptism and the Eucharist. In the early Middle Ages Scholastic theologians began to introduce the list of seven. Catholics and Orthodox recognize the same seven sacraments, although they will, at times, use different names for the sacraments.

Both churches say that baptism and Eucharist are central to the life of the church and that the other sacraments can be understood only in relationship to these two. While the Reformation churches focus on these two central sacraments, which are clearly attested to in the scriptures, their acceptance of other sacraments differs for each church. Some churches include rites other than the traditional Catholic seven in their sacramental practice, such as foot washing.

Reflection Questions:

- How does the relationship that Orthodox and Catholics share in the sacramental life build communion between churches?

- How does agreement with other churches strengthen the Catholic understanding of sacrament?
- What is the role of grace and of faith in the sacraments of initiation?
- How do the reservations of Baptists and Pentecostals about the baptismal understanding of Catholics, Orthodox, and other Protestants help us deepen our understanding of the relationship of grace, conversion, faith, and the role of the church?

Eastern Orthodox

Consensus, Ox–C 2:

3. Given this fundamental character of faith, it is necessary to affirm that faith must be taken as a preliminary condition, already complete in itself, which precedes sacramental communion; and also that it is increased by sacramental communion, which is the expression of the very life of the Church and the means of the spiritual growth of each of its members. This question has to be raised in order to avoid a deficient approach to the problem of faith as a condition for unity. It should not, however, serve to obscure the fact that faith is such a condition, and that there cannot be sacramental communion without communion in faith both in the broader sense and in the sense of dogmatic formulation.

[The churches together have clarified how God's initiative and human response are both active in Christian faith, which is at the base of sacramental life. While Latin and Byzantine liturgical traditions differ, both churches see faith coming to full expression in worship and accept the legitimate differences in liturgical rites.]

15. The sacraments are both gift and grace of the Holy Spirit, in Jesus Christ in the Church. This is expressed very concisely in an Orthodox hymn of Pentecost: "The Holy Spirit is the author of every gift. He makes prophecies spring forth. He renders priests perfect. He teaches wisdom to the ignorant. He makes

fishermen into theologians and consolidates the institution of the Church."

16. Every sacrament of the Church confers the grace of the Holy Spirit because it is inseparably a sign recalling what God has accomplished in the past, a sign manifesting what he is effecting in the believer and in the Church, and a sign announcing and anticipating the eschatological fulfillment....

25. Identity of faith, then, is an essential element of ecclesial communion in the celebration of the sacraments. However, a certain diversity in its formulation does not compromise the koinônia between the local churches when each church can recognize, in the variety of formulations, the one authentic faith received from the Apostles....

36. Communion in faith and communion in the sacraments are not two distinct realities. They are two aspects of a single reality which the Holy Spirit fosters, increases and safeguards among the faithful.

Protestants

Editor's Notes: Among the churches of the Reformation, the Lutherans in dialogue with Catholics have proposed a solution to the differences over the number of sacraments and their relative importance.

Consensus, L-RC VIII in GA II:
84. Nevertheless, even here we must not strive after a questionable homogeneity. Just as in the case of the understanding of faith, the common sacramental life needed for unity must not be mistaken for uniformity. Room must be left for legitimate diversities. This is true not only in relation to the understanding and shaping of the individual sacraments or sacramental ecclesial acts, but also in relation to the concept of sacrament as such. The open questions remaining, especially regarding the number of sacraments, are ultimately rooted in an open

concept of sacrament. Not only between our two churches, but also within our churches the concept of sacrament is not fixed in every last detail. A certain fluctuation historically in determining the number of sacraments as well as the differentiation between or "ranking" of the sacraments (and a conjunctive "analogue-use" of the sacramental concept)—all point in this direction.

~~~

Pentecostals and Evangelicals

Editor's Notes: Pentecostal and Evangelical Christians are generally suspicious of the Protestant, Catholic, Anglican, and Orthodox understanding of sacrament. This suspicion is clearly articulated in this joint statement.

Convergence, Pent–C III:

> 86. Some Pentecostals observe what appears to be a "mechanical" or "magical" understanding of the sacraments, especially among Roman Catholic laity, and do not accept the grace-conveying role of the sacraments distinct from their function as a visible Word of God. Roman Catholic theology, however, maintains that the sacraments are not "mechanical" or "magical" since they require openness and faith on the part of the recipient. In Catholic understanding, the grace of the sacraments is not bestowed automatically or unconditionally, irrespective of the dispositions of the recipient. What Paul says in 1 Cor 11:27 ("profaning the body and blood of the Lord") is common teaching in the Roman Catholic Church....Furthermore, the efficacy of the sacraments is not dependent upon the personal piety of those who minister them, but rather, is ultimately dependent upon the grace of God.

~~~

The Sacrament of Baptism (CCC #1213–1274)

Editor's Notes: In baptism, all Christians are related in Christ and to the church. Nevertheless, some Protestant Christians do not accept the baptism of infants. Divisions over baptism between churches have focused on some churches' understanding of it as a sacrament administered to both infants and adults or only to professing adults. To a lesser degree, differences over the form of baptism—by immersion only, or either by immersion or pouring—has also been a cause for disagreement. Churches who baptize both infants and adults may have different theological emphases, but these have not caused them to question one another's baptism.

Reflection Questions:

- Why is the question of baptism by immersion or by pouring a divisive issue among Christians?
- What makes baptism valid among most Christian churches?

World Council of Churches Faith and Order

Editor's Notes: This Faith and Order text is a comprehensive convergence on baptism among the churches. Believers' Baptist, Orthodox, Catholic, and Protestant scholars articulate a common understanding of the institution, meaning, and biblical basis of baptism. The text makes clear the relationship of baptism to conversion, repentance, cleansing, and the reception of the Holy Spirit. Furthermore, it outlines how baptism is a participation in the death and resurrection of Christ, an incorporation into the church, and a sign of the kingdom. In speaking of faith, it attempts to focus on the traditional differences in emphasis, as both a gift of grace and an eliciting of a human response.

Convergence, BEM in GA I:

> B9. Baptism is related not only to momentary experience, but to life-long growth into Christ....The life of the Christian is necessarily one of continuing struggle yet also of continuing experience of grace. In this new

relationship, the baptized live for the sake of Christ, of his Church and of the world which he loves, while they wait in hope for the manifestation of God's new creation and for the time when God will be all in all (Rom. 8:18–24; 1 Cor. 15:22–28, 49–57).

[Churches can agree on a common understanding of faith, development in the Christian life, and the human response to grace. This agreement enables further common reflection on differences in practices among the churches.]

B11. While the possibility that infant baptism was also practiced in the apostolic age cannot be excluded, baptism upon personal profession of faith is the most clearly attested pattern in the New Testament documents.

In the course of history, the practice of baptism has developed in a variety of forms. Some churches baptize infants brought by parents or guardians who are ready, in and with the Church, to bring up the children in the Christian faith. Other churches practice exclusively the baptism of believers who are able to make a personal confession of faith. Some of these churches encourage infants or children to be presented and blessed in a service which usually involves thanksgiving for the gift of the child and also the commitment of the mother and father to Christian parenthood.

All churches baptize believers coming from other religions or from unbelief who accept the Christian faith and participate in catechetical instruction.

B12. Both the baptism of believers and the baptism of infants take place in the Church as the community of faith. When one who can answer for himself or herself is baptized, a personal confession of faith will be an integral part of the baptismal service. When an infant is baptized, the personal response will be offered at a later moment in life. In both cases, the baptized person will have to grow in the understanding of faith.

For those baptized upon their own confession of faith, there is always the constant requirement of a continuing growth of personal response in faith. In the case of infants, personal confession is expected later, and Christian nurture is directed to the eliciting of this confession. All baptism is rooted in and declares Christ's faithfulness unto death. It has its setting within the life and faith of the Church and, through the witness of the whole Church, points to the faithfulness of God, the ground of all life in faith. At every baptism the whole congregation reaffirms its faith in God and pledges itself to provide an environment of witness and service. Baptism should, therefore, always be celebrated and developed in the setting of the Christian community.

[Because the churches have developed areas of common agreement concerning baptism and its importance to church life, the churches have been able to agree on other steps that should be taken to illustrate the sacrament's importance.]

B15. Churches are increasingly recognizing one another's baptism as the one baptism into Christ when Jesus Christ has been confessed as Lord by the candidate or, in the case of infant baptism, when confession has been made by the church (parents, guardians, godparents and congregation) and affirmed later by personal faith and commitment. Mutual recognition of baptism is acknowledged as an important sign and means of expressing the baptismal unity given in Christ. Wherever possible, mutual recognition should be expressed explicitly by the churches.

B16. In order to overcome their differences, believer baptists and those who practice infant baptism should reconsider certain aspects of their practices. The first may seek to express more visibly the fact that children are placed under the protection of God's grace. The latter must guard themselves against the practice of apparently indiscriminate baptism and take more seriously their responsibility for the nurture of baptized children to mature commitment to Christ.

Editor's Notes: From a Catholic view of the church, there has never been a question of the validity of Orthodox baptism, though in historical practice Catholics have occasionally rebaptized Orthodox—either out of ignorance or ideological conflict; Orthodox have not always recognized Catholic baptism either. In order to build unity between these two traditions, the churches have had to reconsider the sacramental nature of the church and baptismal recognition.

Eastern Orthodox

Consensus, Ox–C 2 in GA II:

4. [W]e have also considered in our meetings the relation of what are called sacraments of initiation—i.e. baptism, confirmation or chrismation and eucharist—to each other and to the unity of the Church. At this point it is necessary to examine if our two Churches are confronted simply with a difference in liturgical practice or also in doctrine, since liturgical practice and doctrine are linked to one another. Should we consider these three sacraments as belonging to one sacramental reality or as three autonomous sacramental acts? It should also be asked if for the sacraments of initiation a difference in liturgical practice between the two traditions raises a problem of doctrinal divergence, which could be considered as a serious obstacle to unity….

38. The history of the baptismal rites in East and West, as well as the way in which our common Fathers interpreted the doctrinal significance of the rites, shows clearly that the three sacraments of initiation form a unity. That unity is strongly affirmed by the Orthodox Church. For its part, the Catholic Church also preserves it….

48. In the East, the temporal unity of the liturgical celebration of the three sacraments was retained, thus emphasizing the unity of the work of the Holy Spirit and the fullness of the incorporation of the child into the sacramental life of the Church.

In the West, it was often preferred to delay confirmation so as to retain contact of the baptized person with the bishop. Thus, priests were not ordinarily authorized to confirm.

Editor's Notes: Scholars in the U.S. dialogue have been particularly strong about the mutual recognition of baptism.

Consensus, Ox–CUS, Baptism II, B, 4, C in GC II:
The Non-Repeatability of Baptism: It is our common teaching that baptism in water in the name of the Holy Trinity, as the Christian's new birth, is given once and once only....As the definitive entry of an individual believer into the Church, it cannot be repeated....The Orthodox and Catholic members of our Consultation acknowledge, in both of our traditions, a common teaching and a common faith in one baptism, despite some variations in practice which, we believe, do not affect the substance of the mystery. We are therefore moved to declare that we also recognize each other's baptism as one and the same. This recognition has obvious ecclesiological consequences. The Church is itself both the milieu and the effect of baptism, and is not of our making. This recognition requires each side of our dialogue to acknowledge an ecclesial reality in the other, however much we may regard their way of living the Church's reality as flawed or incomplete. In our common reality of baptism, we discover the foundation of our dialogue, as well as the force and urgency of the Lord Jesus' prayer "that all may be one."

Editor's Notes: The importance of the mutual recognition of baptism among the Anglican, Protestant, and Catholic churches is a foundation for other ecumenical developments. This agreement is so central that some dialogues, like the Lutheran/Catholic one, began with this theme and others, like the Anglican/Catholic one, felt no need to repeat their mutual recognition of baptism in formal statements. The Methodist dialogue text seen here can be taken as an example of the texts in these dialogues.

Reformation Churches

Consensus, WMC–RC IV in GA II:

> 15. The sacraments are effective signs by which God gives grace through faith. Their efficacy should not be conceived in any merely mechanical way. God works through his Spirit in a mysterious way beyond human comprehension, but he invites a full and free human response.
>
> 16. Salvation is ultimately a matter of our reconciliation and communion with God—a sharing in God's life which is effected through real union with Christ. Those actions of the Church which we call sacraments are effective signs of grace because they are not merely human acts. By the power of the Holy Spirit they bring into our lives the life-giving action and even the self-giving of Christ himself. It is Christ's action that is embodied and made manifest in the Church's actions which, responded to in faith, amount to a real encounter with the risen Jesus. And so, when the Church baptizes it is Christ who baptizes....

Editor's Notes: From the time of the Reformation there were some churches that baptized only believing adults, considering that both a personal conversion and a profession of faith were needed prior to baptism. While the Anabaptists of the sixteenth century initiated this position, it has been appropriated by subsequent Baptist, Pentecostal, and some other free churches.

Baptists

Difference, BWA/RC in GA II:

> 18. As Baptists and Catholics we both strive to "be converted and believe in the good news" (Mk 1:14). Yet, conversion and discipleship are expressed differently in our ecclesial communions. Baptists stress the importance of an initial experience of personal conversion wherein the believer accepts the gift of God's saving and assuring

grace. Baptism and entry into the church are testimony to this gift, which is expressed in a life of faithful discipleship. For Catholics baptism is the sacrament by which a person is incorporated into Christ and is reborn so as to share in the divine life. It is always consequent upon faith; in the case of an infant, this faith is considered to be supplied by the community. Catholics speak of the need for a life of continual conversion expressed in the sacrament of reconciliation (penance), which in the early church was sometimes called a "second baptism." In both of our communions changes in church practice challenge us to consider more deeply our theology of conversion and baptism. In the recently instituted Rite for the Christian Initiation of Adults, Roman Catholics affirm that the baptism of adults is the paradigm for a full understanding of baptism. In some areas of the world Baptists receive baptism at a very early age....

49. The conversations revealed growing common concern among Baptists and Roman Catholics about authenticity of faith, baptism, and Christian witness. There are, however, obvious divergences. Baptists, viewing faith primarily as the response of the individual to God's free gift of grace, insist that the faith response precede baptism. Baptist congregations, however, vary in the way they receive persons baptized as infants in other congregations. Practices range from rebaptism of all persons who have not received baptism at the hands of a Baptist minister to acceptance of all persons baptized by any mode, whether as infants or as adults. Roman Catholics regard the sacraments, such as baptism, in a context of faith, as an exercise of the power of the risen Christ, comparable to that exercised by Jesus when he cured the sick and freed the possessed. Emphasizing the corporate as well as the individual nature of faith, they baptize infants and catechize them through a process culminating in full participation in the church.

Editor's Notes: Most Pentecostals practice adult baptism, though in some parts of the world, like Chile, there are formal agreements for the mutual recognition of baptism in which Pentecostals and Catholics participate. The discussion with Pentecostals is further complicated by the practice of "baptism in the Holy Spirit," and an interest in the role of the Holy Spirit in the process of Christian initiation. Catholics and Pentecostals continue to discuss what was the practice and intent of the early church in formulating the role of the Holy Spirit in initiation.

Pentecostals

Convergence, Pent–C I, #22–25 in GA I:

> In discussing infant baptism, certain convergences were noted:
>
> (a) Sacraments are in no sense magical and are effective only in relationship to faith.
>
> (b) God's gift precedes and makes possible human receiving. Even though there was disagreement on the application of this principle, there was accord on the assertion that God's grace operates in advance of our conscious awareness.
>
> (c) Where paedobaptism is not practiced and the children of believing parents are presented and dedicated to God, the children are thus brought into the care of the Christian community and enjoy the special protection of the Lord.
>
> (d) Where paedobaptism is practiced it is fully meaningful only in the context of the faith of the parents and the community. The parents must undertake to nurture the child in the Christian life, in the expectation that, when he or she grows up, the child will personally live and affirm faith in Christ.

The Sacrament of Confirmation (CCC #1285–1314)

Editor's Notes: For Catholic and Orthodox churches, confirmation/chrismation has been seen as integral to the initiation process, although its practice has differed significantly in East and West. Confirmation has not been part of the sacramental thinking of most Protestants.

Reflection Questions:

- How do the dialogues about confirmation help to clarify the sacramental theology between churches?
- How do the dialogues concerning confirmation help us to a fuller understanding of the sacrament?

World Council of Churches Faith and Order

Difference, BEM:

> B14. In God's work of salvation, the paschal mystery of Christ's death and resurrection is inseparably linked with the pentecostal gift of the Holy Spirit. Similarly, participation in Christ's death and resurrection is inseparably linked with the receiving of the Spirit. Baptism in its full meaning signifies and effects both.
>
> Christians differ in their understanding as to where the sign of the gift of the Spirit is to be found. Different actions have become associated with the giving of the Spirit. For some it is the water rite itself. For others, it is the anointing with chrism and/or the imposition of hands, which many churches call confirmation. For still others it is all three, as they see the Spirit operative throughout the rite. All agree that Christian baptism is in water and the Holy Spirit.

Editor's Notes: As noted in the dialogue on baptism, Orthodox and Catholic practice of chrismation/confirmation has diverged over the cen-

turies, but both churches are able to give a common account and recognize a common pattern.

Eastern Orthodox

Consensus, Ox–C 2 in GA II:

40. The early pattern included the following elements:

41.1: for adults, a period of spiritual probation and instruction during which the catechumens were formed for their definitive incorporation into the Church;

42.2: baptism by the bishop assisted by his priests and deacons, or administered by priests assisted by deacons, preceded by a profession of faith and various intercessions and liturgical services;

43.3: confirmation or chrismation in the West by the bishop, or in the East by the priest when the bishop was absent, by means of the imposition of hands or by anointing with holy chrism, or by both;

44.4: the celebration of the holy eucharist during which the newly baptized and confirmed were admitted to the full participation in the Body of Christ.

45. These three sacraments were administered in the course of a single, complex liturgical celebration. There followed a period of further catechetical and spiritual maturation through instruction and frequent participation in the eucharist.

46. This pattern remains the ideal for both churches since it corresponds the most exactly possible to the appropriation of the scriptural and apostolic tradition accomplished by the early Christian churches which lived in full communion with each other....

51.[I]n certain Latin Churches...the practice has become more and more common of admitting to first communion baptized persons who have not yet received confirmation, even though the disciplinary directives which called for the traditional order of the sacraments of Christian initiation have never been abrogated. This inversion, which provokes objections or understandable reservations both by Orthodox and Roman Catholics, calls for deep theological and pastoral reflection because pastoral practice should never lose sight of the meaning of the early tradition and its doctrinal importance. It is also necessary to recall here that baptism conferred after the age of reason in the Latin Church is now always followed by confirmation and participation in the eucharist.

52. At the same time, both churches are preoccupied with the necessity of assuring the spiritual formation of the neophyte in the faith. For that, they wish to emphasize on the one hand that there is a necessary connection between the sovereign action of the Spirit, who realizes through the three sacraments the full incorporation of the person into the life of the Church, the latter's response and that of his community of faith and, on the other hand, that the full illumination of the faith is only possible when the neophyte, of whatever age, has received the sacraments of Christian initiation.

Editor's Notes: The Catholic/Lutheran description of differences with confirmation is representative of the approaches of most Protestant churches.

Lutheran

Difference, L–RC VIII in GA II:
81. In the Lutheran Reformation confirmation disappeared completely. Later it was reintroduced as a rite of admission to the Lord's Supper and/or the celebration of coming of age. As such it was closely linked with previous catechetical instruction. In the Catholic Church confirmation is understood to be an integral part of sacramental initiation into the church, although here, too, it is not devoid of catechetical aspects. In both churches the promise of the gifts of the Holy Spirit is central. Even in the Lutheran understanding confirmation is an act of blessing performed through the prayer of the congregation, and in which grace is promised and granted to the confirmand. Catholics and Lutherans

both participate in the ecumenical discussion of the questions about a proper relationship of confirmation to baptism and Christian witness.

⚬⚬⚬

The Sacrament of the Eucharist (CCC #1322–1405)

Editor's Notes: For Catholics, the Eucharist is the source and summit of our personal and ecclesial life. Therefore, zeal for full unity around the Lord's Table is a characteristic of Catholic piety and affects its relations with fellow Christians. It is important to understand differences in our faith and practice; however, understanding the common faith we share as we move toward full communion in the Body of Christ is even more important.

Reflection Questions:

- How does our faith in Christ's presence among us in the Mass lead us to a hunger for unity of all Christians around the eucharistic table, the source and summit of our Christian life?
- What have we learned about the richness of Christ's sacrifice by our dialogue with fellow Christians?
- If we share so much in faith with fellow Christians, how do we identify the things we share and the things that keep us apart?

World Council Faith and Order

Editor's Notes: After fifty years of dialogue, liturgical reform, and a return to common sources from the earliest centuries of the church, Protestants, Orthodox, Catholics, and Anglicans have reached an amazing convergence in their common understanding of the Eucharist. Through bilateral dialogue, biblical exploration, individual research, and common worship renewal a very diverse group of churches have begun to solve differences

125

concerning such matters as the real presence of Christ in the Eucharist and how the one sacrifice of Christ is related to the sacrifice of the altar.

Convergence and *difference*, BEM in GA I:

E8. The eucharist is the sacrament of the unique sacrifice of Christ, who ever lives to make intercession for us. It is the memorial of all that God has done for the salvation of the world. What it was God's will to accomplish in the incarnation, life, death, resurrection and ascension of Christ, God does not repeat. These events are unique and can neither be repeated nor prolonged. In the memorial of the eucharist, however, the Church offers its intercession in communion with Christ, our great High Priest....

E13. The words and acts of Christ at the institution of the eucharist stand at the heart of the celebration; the eucharistic meal is the sacrament of the body and blood of Christ, the sacrament of his real presence. Christ fulfills in a variety of ways his promise to be always with his own even to the end of the world. But Christ's mode of presence in the eucharist is unique. Jesus said over the bread and wine of the eucharist: "This is my body...this is my blood...." What Christ declared is true, and this truth is fulfilled every time the eucharist is celebrated. The Church confesses Christ's real, living and active presence in the eucharist. While Christ's real presence in the eucharist does not depend on the faith of the individual, all agree that to discern the body and blood of Christ, faith is required....

[In this convergence, however, the churches are honest about issues still in need of resolution.]

Many churches believe that by the words of Jesus and by the power of the Holy Spirit, the bread and wine of the eucharist become, in a real though mysterious manner, the body and blood of the risen Christ, i.e., of the living Christ present in all his fullness. Under the signs of bread and wine the deepest reality is the total being of Christ who comes to us in order to feed us and transform our entire being. Some other churches, while affirming a real presence of Christ at the eucharist, do not link that presence so definitely with the signs of bread and wine. The decision remains for the churches whether this difference can be accommodated within the convergence formulated in the text itself.

E14. The Spirit makes the crucified and risen Christ really present to us in the eucharistic meal, fulfilling the promise contained in the words of institution. The presence of Christ is clearly the centre of the eucharist, and the promise contained in the words of institution is therefore fundamental to the celebration....Being assured by Jesus' promise in the words of institution that it will be answered, the Church prays to the Father for the gift of the Holy Spirit in order that the eucharistic event may be a reality: the real presence of the crucified and risen Christ giving his life for all humanity.

E15. It is in virtue of the living word of Christ and by the power of the Holy Spirit that the bread and wine become the sacramental signs of Christ's body and blood. They remain so for the purpose of communion....

E19. The eucharistic communion with Christ who nourishes the life of the Church is at the same time communion within the body of Christ which is the Church....It is in the eucharist that the community of God's people is fully manifested. Eucharistic celebrations always have to do with the whole Church, and the whole Church is involved in each local eucharistic celebration. In so far as a church claims to be a manifestation of the whole Church, it will take care to order its own life in ways which take seriously the interests and concerns of other churches....

E28. The best way towards unity in eucharistic celebration and communion is the renewal of the eucharist itself in the different churches in regard to teaching and liturgy. The churches should test their liturgies in the light of the eucharistic agreement now in the process of attainment.

The liturgical reform movement has brought the churches closer together in the manner of celebrating the Lord's Supper. However, a certain liturgical diversity compatible with our common eucharistic faith is recognized as a healthy and enriching fact. The affirmation of a common eucharistic faith does not imply uniformity in either liturgy or practice....

E32. Some churches stress that Christ's presence in the consecrated elements continues after the celebration. Others place the main emphasis on the act of celebration itself and on the consumption of the elements in the act of communion. The way in which the elements are treated requires special attention. Regarding the practice of reserving the elements, each church should respect the practices and piety of the others.

Editor's Notes: While Orthodox and Catholic traditions have had very different liturgical practices and eucharistic devotion, faith in the Eucharist has never been a divisive issue between us. However, both base their understanding of the nature of the church on the Eucharist as the center of the communion within and among the local (diocesan) churches, although each emphasizes this teaching in its own unique way.

Eastern Orthodox

Consensus, Ox–C 1 in GA II:

I. 6. Taken as a whole, the eucharistic celebration makes present the Trinitarian mystery of the church. In it one passes from hearing the word, culminating in the proclamation of the Gospel the apostolic announcing of the word made flesh to the thanksgiving offered to the Father and to the memorial of the sacrifice and to communion in it thanks to the prayer of *epiclesis* uttered in faith. For the *epiclesis* is not merely an invocation for the sacramental transforming of the bread and cup. It is also a prayer for the full effect of the communion of all in the mystery revealed by the Son.

[Orthodox have emphasized the role of the Holy Spirit, and the liturgical prayer to him (epiclesis) in effecting Christ's presence, while the Western churches have emphasized the words of institution, "This is my body...this is my blood."]

In this way the presence of the Spirit itself is extended by the sharing in the sacrament of the word made flesh to all the body of the church...we can already say together that this Spirit, which proceeds from the Father (Jn 15:26) as the sole source in the Trinity and which has become the Spirit of our sonship (Rom 8:15) since he is also the Spirit of the Son (Gal 4:6), is communicated to us particularly in the eucharist by this Son upon whom he reposes in time and in eternity (Jn 1:32).

That is why the eucharistic mystery is accomplished in the prayer which joins together the words by which the word made flesh instituted the sacrament and the *epiclesis* in which the church, moved by faith, entreats the Father, through the Son, to send the Spirit so that in the unique offering of the incarnate Son, everything may be consummated in unity....

II. 2. The unfolding of the eucharistic celebration of the local church shows how the koinonia takes shape in the church celebrating the eucharist. In the eucharist celebrated by the local church gathered about the bishop, or the priest in communion with him, the following aspects stand out, interconnected among themselves even if this or that moment of the celebration emphasizes one or another.

[The text goes on to outline the eschatological, pneumatological, kerygmatic, and ministerial character of the Eucharist in the context of the local church, presided over by a bishop and in communion with other bishops.]

3. The function of the bishop is closely bound to the eucharistic assembly over which he presides. The eucharistic unity of the local church implies communion

between him who presides and the people to whom he delivers the word of salvation and the eucharistic gifts.

III. 1. [T]he local church which celebrates the eucharist gathered around its bishop is not a section of the body of Christ. The multiplicity of local synaxes does not divide the church, but rather shows sacramentally its unity. Like the community of the apostles gathered around Christ, each eucharistic assembly is truly the holy church of God, the body of Christ, in communion with the first community of the disciples and with all who throughout the world celebrate and have celebrated the memorial of the Lord.

—⁂—

Editor's Notes: Anglicans and Catholics were able to formulate a consensus on Christ's real presence in the Eucharist and the sacrificial character of its celebration as early as 1982. After certain clarifications were made, the Holy See and the bishops representing the worldwide Communion of Anglicans were able to recognize in this agreement an adequate formulation of the faith of the church. Here are a few brief excerpts from that extensive agreement and its elucidations and clarifications.

Anglican

Agreement, ARCIC I, 10, 11 in GA I:
>The Lord who thus comes to his people in the power of the Holy Spirit is the Lord of glory. In the eucharistic celebration we anticipate the joys of the age to come. By the transforming action of the Spirit of God, earthly bread and wine become the heavenly manna and the new wine, the eschatological banquet for the new man: elements of the first creation become pledges and first fruits of the new heaven and the new earth.

Consensus, ARCUSA 5, Affirmations in GC II:
>According to the traditional order of the liturgy the consecratory prayer *(anaphora)* leads to the communion of the faithful. Through this prayer of thanksgiving, a word

of faith addressed to the Father, the bread and wine become the body and blood of Christ by the action of the Holy Spirit, so that in communion we eat the flesh of Christ and drink his blood.

We Affirm that in the eucharist the Church, doing what Christ commanded his apostles to do at the Last Supper, makes present the sacrifice of Calvary. We understand this to mean that when the Church is gathered in worship, it is empowered by the Holy Spirit to make Christ present and to receive all the benefits of his sacrifice.

We Affirm that God has given the eucharist to the Church as a means through which all the atoning work of Christ on the Cross is proclaimed and made present with all its effects in the life of the Church. His work includes "that perfect redemption, propitiation, and satisfaction, for all the sins of the whole world" (Cf. Art. 31 Episcopal *Book of Common Prayer*, p. 874). Thus the propitiatory effect of Christ's one sacrifice applies in the eucharistic celebration to both the living and the dead, including a particular dead person.

We Affirm that Christ in the eucharist makes himself present sacramentally and truly when under the species of bread and wine these earthly realities are changed into the reality of his body and blood. In English the terms *substance, substantial* and *substantially* have such physical and material overtones that we, adhering to *The Final Report*, have substituted the word *truly* for the word *substantially* in the clarification requested by the Vatican *Response*. However, we affirm the reality of the change by consecration as being independent of the subjective disposition of the worshipers.

Both our Churches Affirm that after the eucharistic celebration the body and blood of Christ may be reserved for the communion of the sick, "or of others who for weighty cause could not be present at the celebration" (BCP [USA], pp. 408–409). Although the American *Book of Common Prayer* directs that any consecrated bread and wine not reserved for this purpose should be consumed at the end of the service, American Episcopalians recognize that many of their own Church members practice the adoration of Christ in the reserved sacrament. We acknowledge this practice as an extension of the worship of Jesus Christ present at the eucharistic celebration.

We Affirm that only a validly ordained priest can be the minister who, in the person of Christ, brings into being the sacrament of the eucharist and offers sacramentally the redemptive sacrifice of Christ which God offers us.

Editor's Notes: At the time of the Reformation Lutherans affirmed that, in the Eucharist, the bread and wine were changed to become the body and blood of Christ, though they did not agree with the theories Catholic theologians then gave to explain this change. Biblical and historical scholarship that lies behind the texts excerpted here has enabled the differences over the sacrifice of the Mass and explanations of Christ's presence to be overcome.

Lutheran

Convergence, L-RC-II in GA I:

48. Catholic and Lutheran Christians together confess the real and true presence of the Lord in the Eucharist. There are differences, however, in theological statements on the mode and therefore duration of the real presence.

49. In order to confess the reality of the eucharistic presence without reserve the Catholic Church teaches that "Christ whole and entire" becomes present through the transformation of the whole substance of the bread and the wine into the substance of the body and blood of Christ while the empirically accessible appearances of bread and wine *(accidentia)* continue to exist unchanged. This "wonderful and singular change" is "most aptly" called transubstantiation by the Catholic Church. This terminology has widely been considered by Lutherans as

an attempt rationalistically to explain the mystery of Christ's presence in the sacrament; further, many suppose also that in this approach the present Lord is not seen as a person and naturalistic misunderstandings become easy.

50. The Lutherans have given expression to the reality of the Eucharistic presence by speaking of presence of Christ's body and blood in, with and under bread and wine—but not of transubstantiation. Here they see real analogy to the Lord's incarnation: as God and man become one in Jesus Christ, Christ's body and blood, on the one hand, and the bread and wine, on the other, give rise to a sacramental unity. Catholics, in turn, find that this does not do sufficient justice to this very unity and to the force of Christ's word "This is my body."

51. The ecumenical discussion has shown that these two positions must no longer be regarded as opposed in a way that leads to separation. The Lutheran tradition agrees with the Catholic tradition that the consecrated elements do not simply remain bread and wine but by the power of the creative Word are bestowed as the body and blood of Christ. In this sense it also could occasionally speak, as does the Greek tradition, of a "change." The concept of transubstantiation for its part is intended as a confession and preservation of the mystery character of the Eucharistic presence; it is not intended as an explanation of how this change occurs.

***

Editor's Notes: At the time of the Reformation the Calvinist Reformed tradition developed in debate with the Catholic Church and the Lutheran Reformers, over Christ's real presence in the Eucharist. While the Reformed always affirmed a real presence of Christ in the Lord's Supper, they did not affirm the change of the bread and wine. In the modern ecumenical dialogues, some Lutherans and Reformed have reconciled these differences. Catholics and Reformed have been able to deepen their understanding of one another and their common faith in Christ's presence, though all areas of disagreement have yet to be overcome.

Reformed

Editor's Notes: Among the Reformed creeds is the Heidelberg Catechism *to which a question was added after the Council of Trent, making a negative judgment on the Catholic Mass: "Thus the Mass is basically nothing but a denial of the one sacrifice and suffering of Jesus Christ and a condemnable idolatry" (HC # 80). The Christian Reformed Church in North America has done a study of Catholic doctrine and has been able to report a change in that evaluation. The study has been recognized by the Catholic bishops as an accurate understanding of Catholic faith and practice.*

Clarification of difference, CRC Report in GA II:

A key difference between the *Heidelberg Catechism* and Roman Catholic teaching:

With regard to veneration, it is important to remember that the Reformed creedal tradition did not embrace the Zwinglian interpretation of the sacrament. *The Belgic Confession*, for example, while recognizing that eating "the living bread" is a matter of appropriating and receiving Christ "spiritually by faith," declares the "manner" of God's working in the sacrament to be "beyond our understanding" and "incomprehensible to us, just as the operation of God's spirit is hidden and incomprehensible." Or, again, while insisting that the "manner in which we eat" is "not by the mouth but by the Spirit, through faith," it declares that "we do not go wrong when we say that what is eaten is Christ's own natural body and what is drunk is his own blood" and, later, that we must therefore "receive the holy sacrament" with "humility and reverence" (art. 35). It seems reasonable to assert that the difference between Roman Catholic and Reformed teaching is not whether the sacramental meal should be treated with reverence but the precise manner in which that reverence is expressed....

As a result of this study, the Interchurch Relations Committee [of the Christian Reformed Church] proposed to the Synod:

If the bishops of the Roman Catholic Church in the United States and Canada endorse the above report as an accurate presentation of official Roman Catholic teaching regarding the sacrament of the Eucharist [which they have], that will have significant implications on whether, and how, the *Heidelberg Catechism* ought to be modified. If Roman Catholic teaching is as it is presented in this report, the committee has serious concerns about the *Heidelberg Catechism*'s conclusion that "the Mass is basically nothing but a denial of the one sacrifice and suffering of Jesus Christ and a condemnable idolatry" (Q. and A. 80). If this report accurately presents Roman Catholic teaching, there are also serious questions about the *Heidelberg Catechism*'s representation, in Q. and A. 80, of what "the Mass teaches." Thus, if this report accurately presents Roman Catholic teaching, significant changes in the *Heidelberg Catechism* may be warranted.

———

Editor's Notes: Reformed and Catholic scholars in the international bilateral dialogue have been able to articulate a new level of agreement on the Eucharist.

Convergence, Ref–C I in GA I:

70. If this [biblical, historical, and theological] background is taken seriously, new possibilities of mitigating the traditional confessional quarrels emerge from the understanding of the New Testament accounts of the institution: for example,

—In the words of institution the emphasis is on the fact of the personal presence of the living Lord in the event of the memorial and fellowship meal, not on the question as to how this real presence (the word "is") comes about and is to be explained. The eating and drinking and the memorial character of the Passover meal, with which the New Testament links Jesus' last meal, proclaim the beginning of the new covenant.

—When Christ gives the apostles the commission "Do this in remembrance of me!" the word "remembrance" means more than merely a mental act of "recalling."

—The term "body" means the whole person of Jesus, the saving presence of which is experienced in the meal....

84. The Reformed and Roman Catholics are convinced of the centrality of this common christological confession. The specific mode of Christ's real presence in the Eucharist is thus to be interpreted as the presence of the Son who is both consubstantial with us in our human and bodily existence while being eternally consubstantial with the Father and the Holy Spirit in the Godhead (Jn 17:21–23)....This doctrine, that the logos is at the same time incarnate and present in the whole world, is not a Calvinist specialty, but is common to the Christology of pre-Chalcedonian as well as post-Chalcedonian orthodoxy, East and West. What clearly matters is the fully Trinitarian context which is guarded by this doctrine and the Christological presuppositions on which there are no fundamental disagreements between Roman Catholic and Reformed traditions.

[The text goes on to explore our common faith in the mission dimension of the Eucharist, and urges theological work to resolve differences, so better to serve this gospel imperative.]

89. In the course of history certain formulae have been taken up in dogmatic and liturgical usage, primarily as protective devices to safeguard the faith against misinterpretation....Such formulations need to be re-examined in order to see whether they are still adequate as safeguards against misunderstanding, or have themselves become sources of misunderstanding, especially in the ecumenical situation.

There is therefore a pastoral responsibility on the churches to see that such formulae contribute to the genuine communication of the Gospel to the contemporary world....

91. The terminology which arose in an earlier polemical context is not adequate for taking account of the

extent of common theological understanding which exists in our respective churches. Thus we gratefully acknowledge that both traditions, Reformed and Roman Catholic, hold to the belief in the Real Presence of Christ in the Eucharist; and both hold at least that the Eucharist is, among other things:

(1) a memorial of the death and resurrection of the Lord;

(2) a source of loving communion with him in the power of the Spirit (hence the epiclesis in the Liturgy), and

(3) a source of the eschatological hope for his coming again.

92. It is clear that this international dialogue outlines the imperative for Eucharistic agreement, in service to the mission of the church, but does not itself provide more than a biblical groundwork and some suggested lines of inquiry.

Editor's Notes: The Methodist churches, being heirs of the Anglican Church, have a heritage of faith in the real presence of Christ in the Lord's Supper and an understanding of the sacrificial nature of the Eucharist. This has enabled a high level of agreement in the dialogue, while articulating continuing differences. The Methodist practice of "open communion" is significantly different from the Catholic and Orthodox practice—which sees communion in faith as a basis for sacramental communion—because of a different understanding of the relationship of the Eucharist to the mission of the church and full ecclesial communion.

Methodist

Convergence, difference, WMC–RC I in GA I:

83. POINTS OF AGREEMENT

I. The real presence

1. Both Methodists and Roman Catholics affirm as the primary fact the presence of Christ in the Eucharist, the Mass, or the Lord's Supper.

2. This is a reality that does not depend on the experience of the communicant.

3. It is only by faith that we become aware of the presence of Christ in the Eucharist.

4. Within the worship of the Church, this is a distinctive mode or manifestation of the presence of Christ.

5. Christ in the fullness of His being, human and divine, crucified and risen, is present in this sacrament.

6. The presence of Christ is mediated through the sacred elements of bread and wine over which the words of institution have been pronounced.

7. Bread and wine do not mean the same outside the context of the Eucharistic celebration as they do within that context. Within the eucharistic celebration they become the sign par excellence of Christ's redeeming presence to His people. To the eyes of faith, they now signify the Body and Blood of Jesus, given and shed for the world; as we take, eat and drink, and share the bread and wine, we are transformed into Him. The eucharistic bread and wine are therefore efficacious signs of the Body and Blood of Christ.

II. The sacrifice

1. The Eucharist is the celebration of Christ's full, perfect and sufficient sacrifice, offered once and for all, for the whole world.

2. It is a memorial which is more than a recollection of a past event. It is a re-enactment of Christ's triumphant sacrifice and makes available for us its benefits.

3. For this reason Roman Catholics call the Eucharist a sacrifice, though this terminology is not used by Methodists.

4. In this celebration we share in Christ's offering of Himself in obedience to the Father's will.

III. Communion

1. The perfect participation in the celebration of the Eucharist is the communion of the faithful.

2. By partaking of the Body and Blood we become one with Christ, our Savior, and one with one another in a common dedication to the redemption of the world.

84. POINTS OF DIFFERENCE

I. The presence

1. Presence in the Eucharist for the Methodists is not fundamentally different from the presence of Christ in other means of grace, i. e. preaching.

2. For some Methodists the preaching of the Word provides a more effective means of grace than the Eucharist.

3. To the faith of the Roman Catholic, the bread and wine within the context of the Eucharistic celebration are transformed into another reality, i. e. the Body and Blood of the glorified Jesus. The external of the bread and wine remain unchanged. For the Roman Catholic this transformation takes place through the words of institution pronounced by a validly ordained priest.

4. The worship of the Blessed Sacrament is linked with the Roman Catholic doctrine of the transformation of the elements, and does not obtain in Methodism.

II. Intercommunion

1. In Methodism any Christian who can conscientiously accept the invitation is welcomed to the Lord's table. Except in cases of urgent necessity, eucharistic communion is extended by Roman Catholics only to those who share the same faith. We welcome the ongoing study of this problem in actual dialogue, and look forward to the day when we can partake of the Eucharist together. We rejoice in the increasing agreements in doctrine between the two communions which are working to bring this about.

Editor's Notes: Disciples, like Methodists and Reformed, practice "open communion." In fact, their own origins and ecumenical hopes emerged out of a dedication to the Eucharist as a means of grace bringing Christians together with no barriers.

Disciples

Convergence, CC–C II in GA II:

29. Both Disciples of Christ and Roman Catholics celebrate the Eucharist regularly and frequently—at least every Sunday. Although they have differences in the understanding of the Eucharist, they are one in the conviction that the communion willed by God takes on a specific reality at the Lords Supper. In fact, the celebration of the Eucharist renews, makes real and deepens visible fellowship with God....

30. The Eucharist is an act through which a divine reality otherwise more or less hidden emerges and is made present. What is revealed is the plan of salvation, the good news that Jesus Christ reconciles humanity to the Father. The Eucharist both symbolizes and makes present, together with the gift of Christ himself, the salvation offered through him. In it faith is freshly evoked and is further nourished in the participant; for the community the essential elements of Christian faith and life are expressed.

[While Catholics and Disciples continue to have different approaches to eucharistic hospitality, they are able to say the following together:]

32. God in Christ invites to the Eucharist, and through the Holy Spirit binds together into one body, all who break the one loaf and share the one cup. At the Lord's table the unity of the Church is accomplished, for believers are joined to Christ and to one another. Thus, precisely because the celebration of the Eucharist is the climax of the Church's life, disunity among Christians is felt most keenly at the Eucharist; and their inability to celebrate the Lord's Supper together makes them less able to manifest the full catholicity of the Church.

Editor's Notes: Baptists, Pentecostals, and some evangelical churches are not sacramental churches. However, there are many evangelical Christians (such as Anglican and Methodist) who are members of sacramental churches. Therefore, generalizations about the theology of these groups are difficult.

Evangelicals

Convergence, ERCDOM in GA II:

4., 3) Church members need constantly to be strengthened by the grace of God. Roman Catholics and Evangelicals understand grace somewhat differently, however, Roman Catholics thinking of it more as divine life and Evangelicals as divine favor....Both sides also understand the Eucharist (or Lord's Supper) as a sacrament (or ordinance) of grace. Roman Catholics affirm the real presence of the body and blood of Jesus Christ and emphasize the mystery of Christ and his salvation becoming present and effective by the working of the Holy Spirit under the sacramental sign, whereas Evangelicals (in different ways according to their different Church traditions) view the sacrament as the means by which Christ blesses us by drawing us into fellowship with himself, as we remember his death until he comes again (1 Cor 11:26).

Despite the lack of full accord which we have just described, both Evangelicals and Roman Catholics agree that the Eucharist is spiritual food and spiritual drink (1 Cor 10:3–4, 16), because the unifying Spirit is at work in this sacrament. As a memorial of the New Covenant, the Eucharist is a privileged sign in which Christ's saving grace is especially signified and/or made available to Christians. In the Eucharist the Holy Spirit makes the words Jesus spoke at the Last Supper effective in the Church and assures Christians that through their faith they are intimately united to Christ and to each other in the breaking of the bread and the sharing of the cup.

Southern Baptists

Difference, SBC–CUSA II in BU:

> 2., [D] We attach different significance to the elements of the Lord's Supper, that is to say, to the bread and wine of communion. Both groups agree that the celebration of the Lord's Supper, or eucharist, includes the memorializing of Jesus' passion and death, the proclamation of his resurrection and ascension, and the anticipation of his return for the gathering of the faithful into glory. But Catholics would add that, through the power of the Spirit, bread and wine actually become the body and blood of Christ, thus enabling a unique mode of Christ's real presence in the community.

Why It Matters

If unity is ever to be reached between churches, then believers from the various traditions need to learn to treat each church's beliefs and practices with respect. Respect does not mean blind acceptance. Rather, respect for other church's practices and beliefs means listening and watching carefully, seeking to understand how God is present and active in the church's life and ritual. When there are questions related to practices or beliefs, inquiry, not ridicule, is much preferred. Catholics need to learn to explain their beliefs and practices and to ask questions of members of other churches.

When explaining the Catholic practice of infant baptism to members of churches that practice only adult baptism, consider the advice from the BEM (no. B16): "express more visibly the fact that children are placed under the protection of God's grace…and take more seriously [the] responsibility for the nurture of baptized children to mature commitment to Christ." That is, Catholics and other churches who baptize infants entrust the infant to God's care at baptism, just as the parent has entrusted the child's welfare to the church. They do so with the full intent and purpose of raising the child to Christian discipleship and love for the Lord.

The practice of "conditional baptism"—rebaptizing a person from another Christian tradition "just in case" the person's previous baptism was not legitimate—is now rarely practiced by most Christian churches. Because of the agreements on the sacrament of baptism between many of the churches, law, policies, and practices have changed. Now, conditional baptism is held only when no record of a previous baptism can be found or in cases where the Catholic Church considers the baptism invalid. For example, the Catholic Church has determined that people who were previously baptized as Mormons should be baptized when they formally enter the Catholic Church.

Eastern Catholic churches celebrate the sacraments of initiation—baptism, confirmation, and Eucharist—at the time of the person's baptism. In this they follow the practice of the Eastern Orthodox Church. This is important because while there is not a sharing of sacraments between the Eastern Orthodox and the Roman Catholic Churches, there is a sharing between the Eastern Catholic and Roman Catholic churches and many Eastern Catholics celebrate the sacraments in a Latin church because Eastern Catholic churches are few and far between in some areas of the country. Pastors and religious educators should know that an Eastern Catholic or an Eastern Orthodox who participates in the Latin Church absolutely should not be rebaptized, reconfirmed, or even placed in a catechumenate program or in a confirmation or first communion class. They definitely should not be dismissed from the Eucharist, or enrolled in the book of the elect. They are already members of Christ's body and may be admitted into full participation in the Catholic Church at anytime during the year. Eastern Catholic children may receive the Eucharist whenever their parents feel it is appropriate and do not need to wait until their peers receive the sacrament. Of course, as you may already know, people who enter the Catholic Church from one of the Eastern churches do not become "Roman Catholics," even if they are baptized in a Roman Catholic Church. Rather, members from the Eastern churches would become members of the corresponding Eastern Catholic church.

That being said, admission into the Catholic Church should not be rushed or haphazard. It's important that people who change churches fully understand the beliefs of the Catholic Church and the ways in which they differ from the beliefs of other Christian churches. This applies not only to sacramental preparation, but also to the differences in our understanding of the creed and Catholic Church teaching. We will return to the catechumenate in the next chapter when we look at other churches' treatment of divorce and remarriage.

The Catholic Church has published guidelines for when members of other Christian churches may receive the Eucharist in a Catholic service. And while the dialogues have moved the theology of the Eucharist of the Catholic, Lutheran, Anglican, Presbyterian, Methodist, and Disciples churches closer to unity, Catholics do not receive the Eucharist in these other churches. This lack of sharing should not be understood as a lack of respect for the Eucharist in other churches, however. Catholics who participate in the Eucharist in other Christian churches should hold the eucharistic elements in the highest esteem and treat them with the greatest respect. And while the Catholic Church accepts the validity of the Eucharist in the Eastern churches, many of the Eastern and Oriental Orthodox churches discourage Catholics from receiving the sacrament from their churches.

7

CELEBRATING THE MYSTERIES: SACRAMENTS AT THE SERVICE OF COMMUNION

Felix and Anastasia are preparing for marriage. They come from Methodist and Catholic churches, but are committed to each other and to the faith and tradition of their individual churches. They want a wedding that is truly Christian and that incorporates as much as possible the heritages of both of their families.

From their discussions about marriage and family life they feel they have a similar understanding about the sacredness of marriage and the lifelong commitment they intend to make. In working with their Catholic priest and Methodist minister, they are surprised to learn that their churches have such different doctrines about the same Christian ceremony. They are delighted that they will be married in Anastasia's Methodist Church and that Felix's Catholic pastor will have a role in the service; however, they are intrigued that their ministers cannot preside together at the wedding or in the Eucharist.

In spite of our common convictions and respect for one another's understanding of marriage and ordained ministry, there are still differences that keep Christians divided. What are some of these differences in ministry and marriage? What developments are taking place to help to bridge these divisions?

The Sacrament of Holy Orders (CCC #1536–1589; see also #874 ff.)

Editor's Notes: Churches involved in ecumenical discussion have developed a wide consensus on the diversity of ministries in the New Testament, the history of the development of the threefold ministry of deacon, presbyter, and bishop, and the rite of ordination. While much work has been done, much more work remains to be done before full agreement is reached on the relationship of the ordained and lay ministry to the governance of the church, the transmission of the ministry from the apostles, and the ordering of ministry.

Reflection Questions:

- How does the ordained ministry relate to the priesthood of all believers?
- How do the Catholic Church and its dialogue partners understand the succession of the ministry from the apostles?
- What are some of the proposals for Catholics and other churches for reconciling their ordained ministries?

Editor's Notes: Churches of the Reformation generally do not use the word sacrament *for holy orders, as Catholics and Orthodox do. The Lutheran/Catholic and ARCIC I statements clarify why this is the case and in what way this is not considered a Church-dividing distinction. These clarifications are characteristic of many of the other dialogues.*

Lutheran

Convergence, L–RC VI:
32. The Catholic tradition speaks of this act of the church, in which the Holy Spirit works through word and signs, as a sacrament. In the Catholic Church this sacramental understanding of ordination is binding. The Lutheran tradition uses a more restricted concept of sacrament and therefore does not speak of the sacrament of ordination. Yet in principle a sacramental understanding of the ministry is not rejected. Wherever it is taught

that through the act of ordination the Holy Spirit gives grace strengthening the ordained person for the life-time ministry of word and sacrament, it must be asked whether differences which previously divided the churches on this question have not been overcome. For both Catholics and Lutherans it is incompatible with this understanding of ordination to see ordination merely as a mode or manner of ecclesiastical appointment or installation in office.

33. This fundamental mutual understanding also leads Catholics and Lutherans to common statements about the minister of ordination. Ordination is primarily the act of the exalted Lord who moves, strengthens and blesses the ordained person through the Holy Spirit. Since the ministry expresses the priority of the divine initiative, and since in the service of unity it stands in and between the local churches, its transmission takes place through those who are already ordained. Thus the fact that ministers can perform the service of unity only in community with other ordained ministers is expressed in this way. It is also important, however, that the congregation be involved in the calling and appointment of ministers because the ministry is for the congregation and must carry out its mission in concert with the whole congregation.

Anglican

Agreement, Final Report, Elucidation on Ministry in GA I:

The phrase "in this sacramental act" in para. 15 [of the section on Ministry of the Final Report] has caused anxiety on two different counts: that this phrase seems to give the sacrament of ordination the same status as the two "sacraments of the Gospel"; and that it does not adequately express the full sacramentality of ordination.

Both traditions agree that a sacramental rite is a visible sign through which the grace of God is given by the Holy Spirit in the Church. The rite of ordination is one of these sacramental rites. Those who are ordained by prayer and the laying on of hands receive their ministry from Christ through those designated in the Church to hand it on; together with the office they are given the grace needed for its fulfilment (cf. para. 14). Since New Testament times the Church has required such recognition and authorization for those who are to exercise the principal functions of episcope in the name of Christ. This is what both traditions mean by the sacramental rite of ordination.

Both traditions affirm the pre-eminence of baptism and the eucharist as sacraments "necessary to salvation." This does not diminish their understanding of the sacramental nature of ordination, as to which there is no significant disagreement between them.

World Council of Churches Faith and Order

Editor's Notes: Convergences in the biblical understanding of ordained ministry and its historical development have been dramatic, but they have not yet reached levels of agreement achieved on baptism and the Eucharist. The renewal, reconciliation, and recognition of ordained ministries challenge all of the churches, including the Catholic Church.

Convergence, BEM in GA I:

M7. Differences in terminology are part of the matter under debate. In order to avoid confusion in the discussions on the ordained ministry in the Church, it is necessary to delineate clearly how various terms are used in the following paragraphs.

a) The word *charism* denotes the gifts bestowed by the Holy Spirit on any member of the body of Christ for the building up of the community and the fulfillment of its calling.

b) The word *ministry* in its broadest sense denotes service to which the whole people of God is called, whether as individuals, as a local community, or as the universal Church. Ministry or ministries can also denote the particular institutional forms which this service may take.

c) The term *ordained ministry* refers to persons who have received a charism and whom the church appoints for service by ordination through the invocation of the Spirit and the laying on of hands.

d) Many churches use the word *priest* to denote certain ordained ministers. Because this usage is not universal, this document will discuss the substantive questions in paragraph 17....

M13. The chief responsibility of the ordained ministry is to assemble and build up the body of Christ by proclaiming and teaching the Word of God, by celebrating the sacraments, and by guiding the life of the community in its worship, its mission and its caring ministry.

M14. It is especially in the eucharistic celebration that the ordained ministry is the visible focus of the deep and all-embracing communion between Christ and the members of his body....

A variety of titles are used by churches for those who hold ordained ministry in the church. Following the scripture, some churches do not see a distinction between presbyter and bishop. Other churches prefer to use the title of pastor, presbyter, or minister for the ordained.]

M17. Jesus Christ is the unique priest of the new covenant. Christ's life was given as a sacrifice for all....Ordained ministers are related, as are all Christians, both to the priesthood of Christ, and to the priesthood of the Church. But they may appropriately be called priests because they fulfill a particular priestly service by strengthening and building up the royal and prophetic priesthood of the faithful through word and sacraments, through their prayers of intercession, and through their pastoral guidance of the community....

M22. Although there is no single New Testament pattern, although the Spirit has many times led the Church to adapt its ministries to contextual needs, and although other forms of the ordained ministry have been blessed with the gifts of the Holy Spirit, nevertheless the three-fold ministry of bishop, presbyter and deacon may serve today as an expression of the unity we seek and also as a means for achieving it. Historically, it is true to say, the threefold ministry became the generally accepted pattern in the Church of the early centuries and is still retained today by many churches. In the fulfillment of their mission and service the churches need people who in different ways express and perform the tasks of the ordained ministry in its diaconal, presbyteral and episcopal aspects and functions….

M25. The traditional threefold pattern thus raises questions for all the churches. Churches maintaining the threefold pattern will need to ask how its potential can be fully developed for the most effective witness of the Church in this world. In this task churches not having the threefold pattern should also participate. They will further need to ask themselves whether the threefold pattern as developed does not have a powerful claim to be accepted by them….

M36. Under the particular historical circumstances of the growing Church in the early centuries, the succession of bishops became one of the ways, together with the transmission of the Gospel and the life of the community, in which the apostolic tradition of the Church was expressed. This succession was understood as serving, symbolizing and guarding the continuity of the apostolic faith and communion.

M37. In churches which practice the succession through the episcopate, it is increasingly recognized that a continuity in apostolic faith, worship and mission has been preserved in churches which have not retained the form of historic episcopate. This recognition finds additional support in the fact that the reality and function of the episcopal ministry have been preserved in many of these churches, with or without the title "bishop." Ordination, for example, is always done in them by persons in whom the Church recognizes the authority to transmit the ministerial commission....

M41. The act of ordination by the laying on of hands of those appointed to do so is at one and the same time invocation of the Holy Spirit *(epiklesis)*; sacramental sign; acknowledgment of gifts and commitment....

[The most vexing challenges among the churches of the West to restoring full eucharistic communion is to find a way for ordained ministries to be recognized and reconciled, and to find ways of talking about differences over the ordination of women.]

M52. Among the issues that need to be worked on as churches move towards mutual recognition of ministries, that of apostolic succession is of particular importance. Churches in ecumenical conversations can recognize their respective ordained ministries if they are mutually assured of their intention to transmit the ministry of Word and sacrament in continuity with apostolic times. The act of transmission should be performed in accordance with the apostolic tradition, which includes the invocation of the Spirit and the laying on of hands.

M53. In order to achieve mutual recognition, different steps are required of different churches. For example:

a) Churches which have preserved the episcopal succession are asked to recognize both the apostolic content of the ordained ministry which exists in churches which have not maintained such succession and also the existence in these churches of a ministry of *episkope*, in various forms.

b) Churches without the episcopal succession, and living in faithful continuity with the apostolic faith and mission, have a ministry of Word and sacrament, as is evident from the belief, practice, and life of those churches. These churches are asked to realize that the continuity with the Church of the apostles finds profound expression in the successive laying on of hands by bishops and that, though they may not lack the continuity of the apostolic tradition, this sign will strengthen and deepen that continuity. They may need to recover the sign of the episcopal succession.

M54. Some churches ordain both men and women, others ordain only men. Differences on this issue raise obstacles to the mutual recognition of ministries. But those obstacles must not be regarded as substantive hindrance for further efforts towards mutual recognition. Openness to each other holds the possibility that the Spirit may well speak to one church through the insights of another. Ecumenical consideration, therefore, should encourage, not restrain, the facing of this question.

M55. The mutual recognition of churches and their ministries implies decision by the appropriate authorities and a liturgical act from which point unity would be publicly manifest. Several forms of such public act have been proposed: mutual laying on of hands, eucharistic concelebration, solemn worship without a particular rite of recognition, the reading of a text of union during the course of a celebration. No one liturgical form would be absolutely required, but in any case it would be necessary to proclaim the accomplishment of mutual recognition publicly. The common celebration of the eucharist would certainly be the place for such an act.

Editor's Notes: Catholic and Orthodox churches share a common understanding of the threefold ministry of presbyter, bishop, and deacon.

Orthodox

Consensus, Ox–C III in GA II:

28. Episcopal ordination confers on the one who receives it by the gift of the Spirit, the fullness of the priesthood. During the ordination the concelebration of the bishops expresses the unity of the Church and its identity with the apostolic community. They lay hands and invoke the Holy Spirit on the one who will be ordained as the only

ones qualified to confer on him the episcopal ministry. They do it, however, within the setting of the prayer of the community.

29. Through his ordination, the bishop receives all the powers necessary for fulfilling his function….

32. Throughout the entire history of our Churches, women have played a fundamental role, as witnessed not only by the most Holy Mother of God, but also by the holy women mentioned in the New Testament, by the numerous women saints whom we venerate, as well as by so many other women who up to the present day have served the Church in many ways. Their particular charisms are very important for the building up of the Body of Christ. But our Churches remain faithful to the historical and theological tradition according to which they ordain only men to the priestly ministry….

41. It is in presiding over the eucharistic assembly that the role of the bishop finds its accomplishment. The presbyters form the college grouped around him during that celebration. They exercise the responsibilities the bishop entrusts to them by celebrating the sacraments, teaching the Word of God and governing the community, in profound and continuous communion with him. The deacon, for his part, is attached to the service of the bishop and the priest and is a link between them and the assembly of the faithful….

45. The importance of this [apostolic] succession comes also from the fact that the apostolic tradition concerns the community and not only an isolated individual, ordained bishop. Apostolic succession is transmitted through local Churches ("in each city," according to the expression of Eusebius of Caesarea; "by reason of their common heritage of doctrine," according to Tertullian in the *De Praescriptione*, 32, 6). It is a matter of a succession of persons in the community, because the Una Sancta is a communion of local Churches and not of isolated individuals. It is within this mystery of *koinonia* that the epis-

copate appears as the central point of the apostolic succession.

— ∞∞ —

Editor's Notes: In the 1982 Final Report, Anglican and Catholic scholars claimed full agreement in ordained ministry, short of resolving the issue of the ordination of women. The agreement was affirmed, after clarification, by the bishops of the Lambeth Conference and by the Holy See.

Anglican

Agreement, Final Report in GA I:

9. An essential element in the ordained ministry is its responsibility for "oversight" *(episcope)*. This responsibility involves fidelity to the apostolic faith, its embodiment in the life of the Church today, and its transmission to the Church of tomorrow. Presbyters are joined with the bishop in his oversight of the church and in the ministry of the word and the sacraments; they are given authority to preside at the Eucharist and to pronounce absolution. Deacons, although not so empowered, are associated with bishops and presbyters in the ministry of word and sacrament, and assist in oversight….

13. Because the eucharist is the memorial of the sacrifice of Christ, the action of the presiding minister in reciting again the words of Christ at the Last Supper and distributing to the assembly the holy gifts is seen to stand in a sacramental relation to what Christ himself did in offering his own sacrifice. So our two traditions commonly used priestly terms in speaking about the ordained ministry….[T]heir ministry is not an extension of the common Christian priesthood but belongs to another realm of the gifts of the Spirit….

16. Both presbyters and deacons are ordained by the bishop. In the ordination of a presbyter the presbyters present join the bishop in the laying on of hands, thus signifying the shared nature of the commission entrusted to them. In the ordination of a new bishop, other bishops

lay hands on him, as they request the gift of the Spirit for his ministry and receive him into their ministerial fellowship. Because they are entrusted with the oversight of other churches, this participation in his ordination signifies that this new bishop and his church are within the communion of churches. Moreover, because they are representative of their churches in fidelity to the teaching and mission of the apostles and are members of the episcopal college, their participation also ensures the historical continuity of this church with the apostolic church and of its bishop with the original apostolic ministry. The communion of the churches in mission, faith and holiness, through time and space, is thus symbolised and maintained in the bishop. Here are comprised the essential features of what is meant in our two traditions, by ordination in the apostolic succession....

17. We are fully aware of the issues raised by the judgment of the Roman Catholic Church on Anglican Orders. The development of the thinking in our two Communions regarding the nature of the Church and of the Ordained Ministry, as represented in our Statement, has, we consider, put these issues in a new context. Agreement on the nature of ministry is prior to the consideration of the mutual recognition of ministries. What we have to say represents the consensus of the Commission on essential matters where it considers that doctrine admits no divergence....

Agreement, Final Report, Elucidation on Ministry in GA I:
6. Mutual recognition presupposes acceptance of the apostolicity of each other's ministry. The Commission believes that its agreements have demonstrated a consensus in faith on eucharist and ministry which has brought closer the possibility of such acceptance. It hopes that its own conviction will be shared by members of both our communions; but mutual recognition can only be achieved by the decision of our authorities. It has

been our mandate to offer to them the basis upon which they may make this decision.

———⊶⊷———

Editor's Notes: The Lutheran/Catholic dialogue, in contributing to developing a common ground on holy orders, illustrates approaches of Catholic dialogues with other Protestant churches whose ordinations we do not yet recognize and who do not claim to have retained the apostolic succession of bishops from the pre-Reformation Church.

Lutheran

Consensus, L–RC VI in GA II:

40. In the late Middle Ages the distinction between bishop and presbyter was seen almost exclusively from the point of view of jurisdiction. In addition it was of far reaching practical importance that spiritual and secular powers were generally intermingled in the episcopal office in the Middle Ages. For all these reasons, the relationship between episcopate and presbyterate long remained unclarified. Jerome's opinion that bishops and priests were originally one and the same also played a role and was later referred to by the Lutheran Confessional Writings.

The Second Vatican Council for the first time introduced greater clarity on this point in the Roman Catholic Church. The Council tried to do justice to the development of the ancient church by calling the diocese over which the bishop presides a "local congregation." Accordingly, the fullness of the ministry belongs to the bishop alone; the sacramental character of the episcopal consecration is expressly affirmed by the Council. According to the teaching of the Council the presbyters in exercising their ministry depend on the bishop; they are co-workers, helpers and instruments of the bishop and form in community with their bishop a single presbyterate. Yet even after the Second Vatican Council, questions regarding the more precise determination of the relationship of episcopate and presbyterate still remain open.

41. The Lutheran Confessions wanted to retain the episcopal polity of the church....The fact that it was impossible at this time to arrive at an agreement in doctrine and to persuade the bishops to ordain Reformation ministers led perforce to forsaking continuity with previous order....

42. In view of the emergency situation, the Lutheran Confessions avoided prescribing any specific form of *episcopé* in the sense of regional church leadership. Episcopacy, to be sure, was normal at least for the *Confessio Augustana*. The loss of this office in its historic character has nevertheless had certain consequences for the Lutheran understanding of the church's ministerial structure. The Lutheran office of pastor, comparable to that of presbyter, has really taken over the spiritual functions of the bishop's office and was even at times theologically interpreted as identical with it. This was seen as a return to an earlier ministerial structure in church history in which the bishop's office was a local one....In some Lutheran areas, where this was possible, the historical continuity of the episcopal office has been maintained....

48. If both churches acknowledge that for faith this historical development of the one apostolic ministry into a more local and a more regional ministry has taken place with the help of the Holy Spirit and to this degree constitutes something essential for the church, then a high degree of agreement has been reached....

60. As regards the succession of the ministers, the joint starting point for both Catholics and Lutherans is that there is an integral relation between the witness of the gospel and witnesses to the gospel. The witness to the gospel has been entrusted to the church as a whole. Therefore, the whole church as the *ecclesia apostolica* stands in the apostolic succession. Succession in the sense of the succession of ministers must be seen within

the succession of the whole church in the apostolic faith....

[The urgency of reestablishing full communion led the Catholic and Lutheran members of the dialogue to propose unity by stages.]

84. [T]he next step could consist of a mutual recognition that the ministry in the other church exercises essential functions of the ministry that Jesus Christ instituted in his church, and which one believes, is fully realized in one's own church. This as yet incomplete mutual recognition would include the affirmation that the Holy Spirit also operates in the other church through its ministries and makes use of these as means of salvation in the proclamation of the gospel, the administration of the sacraments, and the leadership of congregations. Such a statement is possible on the basis of what has been said up to now. It would be an important step in helping us through further reciprocal reception to arrive eventually at full mutual recognition of ministries by the acceptance of full church and eucharistic fellowship....

Editor's Notes: Many Lutheran churches around the world have entered into episcopal apostolic succession as Anglicans understand it. Since 2000, all episcopal installations in the Evangelical Lutheran Church in America take place with the participation of bishops in the apostolic succession. Catholics and Lutherans in dialogue have suggested a similar process.

Convergence, L–RC VIII in GA II:

Editor's Notes: The text spells out the common basis in faith, a joint collegial exercise of episcopacy between Lutheran and Catholic bishops, and a "mutuality in Magisterium," so that a process of integration of ministry, including episcopal ministry, would take place before full communion was established. The steps regarding ordination are included here.

132. The joint exercise of the ministry of *episcopé*, which includes ordaining, leads to the gradual establishment of a common ordained ministry.

133. The formation of the ordained church ministry would be the result of individual ordinations which would take place whenever there is a candidate to ordain. All neighbouring bishops, Lutherans and Catholics, on the basis of the jointly exercised *episcopé* would ordain the new minister together. At the end of this process— within a reasonable space of time—the common ordained ministry would be realized.

134. Each of these ordinations must be understood and undertaken as an event which is at the same time (a) confessional, (b) epicletic, (c) communal and (d) juridical:

a. At the moment of taking up his ministry, the new minister confesses the apostolic faith before the entire worshiping community which, together with the Catholic and Lutheran bishops (or other ministers exercising *episcopé*) present on that occasion, witnesses to the correctness of his faith.

b. Within this liturgical action the gift of the spirit, necessary for the exercise of the ministry, is imparted through the imposition of hands by the Catholic and Lutheran bishops.

c. Not everything, however, can depend on the common imposition of hands. The whole congregation is also involved.…Finally, ordination also concerns the fellowship among the churches since it is one of the tasks of those ordained to further this fellowship.

d. Ordination sets one immediately into the service of the church and confers the authority inherent in such service.…

135. It must be clearly understood that at stake in joint ordinations by Catholic and Lutheran bishops is a gift of grace of the Holy Spirit received in common by Catholics and Lutherans. In a confession of gratitude the two partners recognize together that the common and collegial ordained ministry is a gift of the Spirit to the apostolic church. At this juncture it would therefore be wrong to pose the question of what the one partner has given to the other.

136. A common ordained ministry would thus grow out of the jointly exercised *episcopé*. This transition would be a process which is so irrevocably rooted in a truly joint exercise of *episcopé* that, should it not take place or be discontinued, one could no longer really speak of a jointly exercised *episcopé*. Ordination constitutes one of the most important functions of *episcopé*.

137. This transition to a common ordained ministry is pre-eminently a gift of God....

138. The dimension of ecclesial reconciliation inherent in this event should be expressed in all local congregations through preparation marked not only by joy and gratitude, but also by penitence; both sides confessing their sins against *koinônia*.

139. In this act of reconciliation and penitence, as is generally characteristic of the path we have proposed, our churches turn resolutely towards the future and leave it to God to judge the past....

140. In filling vacant posts by new ordinations one avoids problems which could encumber other procedures which have been discussed or could allow for misinterpretations:

a. Reordination: Its problems are not only terminological: one would properly speak of "ordination" in the case of an ordination considered null and void. Reordination is primarily a problem, because the church whose ministers were newly ordained, would have to admit the invalidity of all previous ordinations.

b. Supplementary Ordination: In view of the fact that previous ordinations were intended for a particular church and not for the universal church, a "supplementary ordination" has been considered. The problem here is that existing ordinations are not then taken seriously. For the Catholic Church, therefore, a "supplementary ordination" is inconceivable when it recognizes the ordination of a previously separated church, as, for example, the Orthodox Church.

c. Act of "reconciliation of ministries": What is meant here is a comprehensive act of worship during which by mutual imposition of hands forgiveness is asked and the Holy Spirit is invoked in prayer that it would grant to all the gifts they need. The problematic of such a broad act of "reconciliation of ministries" derives from its ambiguity and, consequently, from its unclarity. Is there implicitly an ordination or a supplementary ordination? Is the validity of previous ordinations taken seriously?

d. Mutual commissioning: If previous ordinations in the other church are considered valid, a mutual commissioning of ordained ministers would be conceivable in order to achieve a common church ministry. The problematic here is that this would be a mere administrative act while the establishment of a ministerial fellowship cannot be reduced to a legal action. Moreover, mutual commissioning would be an act among ordained ministers with no attention to the role of the people of God.

141. For the transition period the way proposed makes it imperative to determine precisely the juridical status of the jointly ordained as well as of those bishops and ministers (presbyters) not yet jointly ordained.

[To reach deeper agreement on the ordained ministry of bishop and presbyter/pastor the Lutheran/Catholic dialogue in the United States has made the following recommendations on the basis of thorough biblical and historical argumentation.]

96. We recommend that our churches recognize our common understanding of structures of ministry and church life, namely, the diocese/synod with its bishop and parish/congregation with its pastor or priest. The differences between us in emphasis and terminology need not be church dividing even though they challenge each church to further reflection.

97. We recommend a mutual recognition that our ordained ministries realize, even if imperfectly, the apostolic ministry instituted by God in the church and

thereby share the saving presence of Christ and the Spirit....

99. We recommend a mutual recognition that our communities realize, even if imperfectly, the one church of Jesus Christ, sharing in the apostolic tradition....

103. We recommend a mutual recognition that:

1. our ordained ministries are wounded because the absence of full communion between our ecclesial traditions makes it impossible for them to represent and foster adequately the unity and catholicity of the church; and

2. our communities are wounded by their lack of the full catholicity to which they are called and by their inability to provide a common witness to the gospel.

Editor's Notes: The second Vatican Council speaks of a "defectus" in the sacrament of holy orders in the churches of the Reformation. In some versions of council documents, this word has been translated as "lack." On the basis of their research the dialogue says:

Convergence, LCUSA X in GC II:

109. We recommend that Roman Catholic criteria for assessing authentic ministry include attention to a ministry's faithfulness to the gospel and its service to the communion of the church, and that *defectus ordinis* as applied to Lutheran ministries be translated as "deficiency" rather than "lack."...

123. Lutheran and Roman Catholic bishops are in communion, albeit imperfect, that parallels that imperfect communion that exists between our churches. Therefore, we recommend that common activities between Lutheran and Roman Catholic bishops be promoted in order to signify the level of communion that exists between them, such as joint retreats of Lutheran and Roman Catholic bishops, co-authored pastoral letters on topics of mutual concern, and joint efforts on matters of public good.

124. We also recommend intensification of mutual activity between ordained ministers that builds on joint activities already occurring, such as joint presiding at non-eucharistic prayer services and weddings, common sponsorship of events or services in the life of the church. We recommend, in light of our common baptism into the people of God, that members share in joint catechetical, publishing, witnessing, and social ministry ventures, and attendance at diocesan and synodical assemblies.

The Sacrament of Matrimony (CCC #1601–1658)

Editor's Notes: Both the Catechism *(#1633–1637) and the Directory for the Application of Principles and Norms on Ecumenism treat the practice and theology of interchurch marriages. There also has been significant agreement on the nature and sacramentality of marriage. Many Catholic dioceses in the United States have local agreements with Christian partners in their area concerning the sacrament.*

Reflection Questions:

- What are the common theological bases for Christians who marry in Christ?
- What are the differences between Catholics and other Christians on remarriage after divorce? How do all Christians affirm the permanence of marriage in spite of these differences?
- What are the common pastoral concerns all Christians share in their ministry to couples in interchurch families?

Editor's Notes: Marriage is considered a sacrament in Orthodox and Catholic churches, though there are two differences that cause significant pastoral and theological tension. Orthodox permit remarriage after a failed first sacramental marriage and they emphasize the role of the priest pre-

siding at the sacrament. The Catholic Church asserts the role of the marrying couple as the ministers of the sacrament. Neither of these issues has been considered church dividing. The international dialogue has yet to take up the issue, but important contributions have been made in the United States dialogue. (Pastoral resources when working with the Catechism: *Ronald G. Roberson, ed.,* Oriental Orthodox-Roman Catholic Pastoral Relationships and Interchurch Marriages *[Washington, DC: US Catholic Conference, 1995];* A Guide on Catholic-Orthodox Marriages *[Washington, DC: US Catholic Conference, 1998.])*

Eastern Orthodox

Consensus, difference, Ox–CUS V in BU:

I. The Sacramental Character of Marriage: For Christians of both the Orthodox and Roman Catholic Churches marriage is a sacrament. Through the prayers and actions of our wedding rites we profess the presence of Christ in the Spirit and believe that it is the Lord who unites a man and a woman in a life of mutual love. In this sacred union, husband and wife are called by Christ not only to live and work together, but also to share their Christian life so that each with the aid of the other may progress through the Holy Spirit in the life of holiness and so achieve Christian perfection. This relationship between husband and wife is established and sanctified by the Lord. As a sacred vocation, marriage mirrors the union of Christ and the church (Eph. 5:23)….

IV. Theological Clarifications on Christian Marriage: In the teaching of the Orthodox and Roman Catholic Churches a sacramental marriage requires both the mutual consent of the believing Christian partners and God's blessing imparted through the ministry of the church.

At present there are differences in the concrete ways in which this ministry must be exercised in order to fulfill the theological and canonical norms for marriage in our two churches. There are also differences in the theological interpretation of this diversity. Thus the Orthodox Church accepts as sacramental only those marriages sanctified in the liturgical life of the church by being blessed by an Orthodox priest.

The Catholic Church accepts as sacramental the marriages which are celebrated before a Catholic priest or even a deacon, but it also envisions some exceptional cases in which, by reason of a dispensation or the unavailability of a priest or deacon, Catholics may enter into a sacramental marriage in the absence of an ordained minister of the church.

An examination of the diversities of practice and theology concerning the required ecclesial context for Christian marriage that have existed in both traditions demonstrates that the present differences must be considered to pertain more to the level of secondary theological reflection than to that of dogma. Both churches have always agreed that the ecclesial context is constitutive of the Christian sacrament of marriage. Within this fundamental agreement various possibilities of realization are possible as history has shown and no one form of this realization can be considered to be absolutely normative in all circumstances.

Recommendation, Ox–CUS I in BU:

II. Theological Problems: 1. According to the view of the Orthodox Church the marriage of an Orthodox can only be performed by an Orthodox priest as the minister of the sacrament. In the view of the Catholic Church the contracting partners are the ministers of the sacrament, and the required presence of a Catholic major cleric as witness of the Church can be dispensed with for weighty reasons. In view of this, we recommend that the Catholic Church, as a normative practice, allow the Catholic party of a proposed marriage with an Orthodox to be married with the Orthodox priest officiating. This procedure should, however, take place only after consultation by the partners with both pastors.

Recommendation, Ox–CUS VI in BU:

6. Decisions, including the initial and very important one of the children's church membership, rest with both husband and wife and should take into account the good of the children, the strength of the religious convictions of the parents and other relatives, the demands of their consciences, the unity and stability of the family, and other aspects of the specific context. In some cases, when it appears certain that only one of the partners will fulfill his or her responsibility, it seems clear that the children should be raised in that partner's church. In other cases, however, the children's spiritual formation may include a fuller participation in the life and traditions of both churches, respecting, however, the canonical order of each church. Here particularly the decision of the children's church membership is more difficult to make. Yet we believe that this decision can be made in good conscience. This is possible because of the proximity of doctrine and practice of our churches, which enables each to a high degree to see the other precisely as *Church*, as the locus for the communion of men and women with God and with each other through Jesus Christ in the Holy Spirit.

Editor's Notes: Anglicans and Catholics share a canonical and sacramental tradition for dealing with marriage, divorce, and annulment, unlike the differences that exist between East and West or between Catholics and the other churches of the Reformation. Remaining differences both theological and pastoral were discussed in two major dialogues.

Anglican

Convergence, ARCIC–M in BU:

6. ii. That in Christian marriage the man and the woman themselves make the covenant whereby they enter into marriage as instituted and ordained by God; this new unity, the unity of marriage, is sacramental in virtue of their Christian baptism and is the work of God in Christ.

iii. That this marriage once made possesses a unity given by God to respect which is a primary duty; this duty creates secondary obligations for the Church in both its pastoral and its legislative capacity. One is the obligation to discourage marriages in which the unity would be so strained or so lacking in vitality as to be both a source of danger to the parties themselves and to be a disfigured sign of or defective witness to the unity of Christ with his Church. Another is the obligation to concert its pastoral care and legislative provisions to support the unity of the marriage once it is made and to ensure as best it can that these provisions be not even unwittingly divisive....

21. On marriage itself the Commission finds no fundamental difference of doctrine between the two Churches, as regards what marriage of its nature is or the ends which it is ordained to serve. The language of Vatican II in *Gaudium et Spes* (47–52), grounding marriage in the natural order, in the mutual pact or covenant *(pactum, foedus)* of the spouses, is entirely at one with the covenantal interpretation of marriage written into the Anglican liturgies. The sacramental nature of marriage is also affirmed, partly in the moral sense of enduring obligation *(sacramentum)* expressed in the marriage vow, partly in the sense of sign *(signum)*: a sign to the world....It is from all this, with continuance in the sacramental life of the Church, that Christian marriage takes its specific character and achieves its fullness....This substantial convergence in doctrine, despite differences in the language used to express it, is a welcome fact of our time, too precious to permit us to rest on the polarities suggested by the time-conditioned formulations of the Reformation and Counter-Reformation....The differences in these responses are not such as to deny or impair our full agreement on what marriage in its created and sacramental nature is....

27. It follows *[from our different emphases and histories]*, therefore, that in a mixed marriage an acceptance of eccle-

siastical requirements which seems natural to one party might well occasion surprise and even resentment in the other. The Anglican partner would see a wider range of matters which he would think it right that the partners should "work out for themselves" than the Roman Catholic partner, whose disposition is to recognize the authority of his Church in these matters. This difference would inevitably occur whenever questions of Christian conscience arise. We shall point below to the two matters where the difference particularly affects a mixed marriage, namely in the requirement of a promise about the baptism and education of children and the requirement of marriage according to the "canonical form."…

[This dialogue surveys in some detail the Anglican and Catholic theology relating to canon law and the nature of the church as they relate to marriage practice and discipline. It recounts the history disclosing a common theological understanding of sacramentality and a commitment to the indissolubility of marriage. The members of the dialogue recognize the different practices that currently exist in present canonical legislation of the two communities. The following paragraph illustrates the different emphasis.]

45. Roman Catholics take the point that Anglican discipline regarding the indissolubility of marriage was for long among the strictest of all. They are proportionately disconcerted by developments in theory and discipline within the Anglican Communion (of which an extreme case is the recent canon 18 [Tit. 1] of the General Convention of the Episcopal Church in the USA) which appear to them to compromise the Catholic doctrine of indissolubility. Though the Roman Catholic members of the Commission found much of the treatment of marriage in the report *Marriage, Divorce and the Church* profoundly sensitive, scholarly and edifying, the carefully-considered recommendations of the Report concerning the re-marriage of divorced persons led the Commission at its Fourth Meeting to consider the question whether the notion of "irretrievable breakdown" was compatible

with any concept of an indissoluble *vinculum*. This discussion cleared up several misconceptions and pointed to several imprecisions of linguistic usage, yet it left the Catholics and some of the Anglicans in the Commission unconvinced that the proposition "marriage is characteristically indissoluble but some marriages turn out to be dissoluble" allowed any meaning to the notion of life-long commitment.

[This text focuses on how marital breakdown is dealt with in the sacramental and pastoral practices of the churches and how they are linked very intentionally with the quest for unity.]

55. This leads us to say that, in setting this problem of defective marital situations and their pastoral care in the total perspective of the Roman Catholic/Anglican search for unity, one established principle is to be re-called which has underlain all adumbrations of the form that unity might take: it is that any such form of unity must preserve what is integral and acceptable in both our traditions in a variety-in-unity. What is or is not mutually acceptable will emerge in the course of this search. A fact perhaps significant in this context—and in any case one which raises profound questions in itself—is that in the Orthodox Church, whose communion with Rome has been described by Pope Paul VI as "almost perfect," long established marriage discipline includes the practice of re-marriage in church after divorce.

Editor's Notes: One of the most sensitive issues in this dialogue concerned the promise required of couples that they raise their children Catholic. Subsequent Catholic reforms and the 1983 Code of Canon Law have helped to resolve this issue.

The Anglican/Catholic dialogue Life in Christ *treats of morality and human sexuality, but one of the two "test themes" is that of remarriage after divorce. Therefore the convergences and divergences here are important, especially as new issues around marriage emerge that further strain relations between the two churches.*

Convergence, LinC in GA II:

> 55. Neither of our two traditions regards marriage as a human invention. On the contrary, both see it as grounded by God in human nature and as a source of community, social order and stability. Nevertheless, the institution of marriage has found different expression in different cultures and at different times. In our own time, for instance, we are becoming increasingly aware that some forms, far from nurturing the dignity of persons, foster oppression and domination, especially of women. However, despite the distortions that have affected it, both our traditions continue to discern and uphold in marriage a God-given pattern and significance….

> 61. Marriage, in the order of creation, is both sign and reality of God's faithful love, and thus it has a naturally sacramental dimension. Since it also points to the saving love of God, embodied in Christ's love for the Church (cf. Eph 5:25), it is open to a still deeper sacramentality within the life and communion of Christ's own Body.

> *[After an extensive discussion of the pre-Reformation common history and the divergences of the two traditions in pastoral and canonical approaches since separation, the dialogue goes on to say:]*

> 74. Anglicans and Roman Catholics both believe that marriage points to the love of Christ, who bound himself in an irrevocable covenant to his Church, and that therefore marriage is in principle indissoluble. Roman Catholics go on to affirm that the unbreakable bond between Christ and his Church, signified in the union of two baptized persons, in its turn strengthens the marriage bond between husband and wife and renders it absolutely unbreakable, except by death. Other marriages can, in exceptional circumstances, be dissolved. Anglicans, on the other hand, do not make an absolute distinction between marriages of the baptized and other marriages, regarding all marriages as in some sense sacramental. Some Anglicans hold that all marriages are therefore indissoluble. Others, while holding that all

marriages are indeed sacramental and are in principle indissoluble, are not persuaded that the marriage bond, even in the case of marriage of the baptized, can never in fact be dissolved....

76. Our reflections have brought to the fore an issue of considerable importance. What is the right balance between regard for the person and regard for the institution? The answer must be found within the context of our theology of communion and our understanding of the common good. For the reasons which have been explained, in the Roman Catholic Church the institution of marriage has enjoyed the favor of the law. Marriages are presumed to be valid unless the contrary case can be clearly established. Since Vatican II renewed emphasis has been placed upon the rights and welfare of the individual person, but tensions still remain. A similar tension is felt by Anglicans, although pastoral concern has sometimes inclined them to give priority to the welfare of the individual person over the claims of the institution. History has shown how difficult it is to achieve the right balance.

77. Our shared reflections have made us see more clearly that Anglicans and Roman Catholics are at one in their commitment to following the teaching of Christ on marriage; at one in their understanding of the nature and meaning of marriage; and at one in their concern to reach out to those who suffer as a result of the breakdown of marriage. We agree that marriage is sacramental, although we do not fully agree on how, and this affects our sacramental discipline....On the level of law and policy, neither the Roman Catholic nor the Anglican practice regarding divorce is free from real or apparent anomalies and ambiguities. While, therefore, there are differences between us concerning marriage after divorce, to isolate those differences from this context of far-reaching agreement and to make them into an insuperable barrier would be a serious and sorry misrepresentation of the true situation....

Editor's Notes: The dialogue recommends common structures of consultation and communion that can allow for joint pastoral action and approach to pastoral, canonical, and ethical issues. In 2000, such a commission was established: The International Anglican Roman Catholic Commission for Unity and Mission (http://www.prounione.urbe.it/dia-int/iarccum/ e_iarccum-info.html).

⸙

Editor's Notes: The theology and practice of Christian marriage took a very different course in the continental Reformation than in Anglicanism. These texts from the Lutheran/Catholic/Reformed dialogue and the Methodist/Catholic dialogue illustrate the agreements and disagreements with Protestants. The pastoral resource by Bishop Patrick Cooney and Rev. John Bush, Interchurch Families: Resources for Ecumenical Hope *(Washington, DC: U.S. Conference of Catholic Bishops, 2002), developed with the U.S. Reformed churches, can be a helpful companion.*

Lutheran/Reformed

Editor's Notes: Through sacramental renewal after the Second Vatican Council and participation in the ecumenical dialogue, Catholic interchurch marriage practices evolved quickly, as did the pastoral need for direction and mutual understanding on the local level. This text was developed with international Lutheran and Reformed bodies and the Holy See to clarify differences and serve pastoral concerns on local levels.

Convergence, difference, L/R/RC–M in GA I:

Editor's Notes: This dialogue text begins with the context in which marriage is lived, before moving on to the theological content of Christian teaching.

> 8. A description of the exterior reality of marriage leads to a catalogue of complementary characteristics that are common everywhere:
> —Marriage, especially in Western tradition, means a free union based on reciprocity.

—It means cohabitation that involves the life, the work and the interests of the partners.

—It is based on a community of life that embraces and gives security to the persons and becomes enlarged into a community for the begetting and raising of children.

—The description of marriage as a "spiritual community" expresses the fact that in marriage the fundamental and all-embracing questions of life have to be answered jointly by the partners. Since the community regards the binding and all-of-life-embracing nature of such questions, marriage has a religious character which is essential to its nature.

In the case of an individual marriage, these characteristics never constitute an invariable and fixed inventory....

18. This relationship of grace between the mystery of Christ and the conjugal state requires a name. We all of us believe that the biblical term "Covenant" truly characterizes the mystery of marriage. It is this Covenant that the Catholic Church calls a sacrament. The Reformation Churches prefer not to employ this term chiefly because of their definition of what a sacrament is, because of the special character of marriage in relation to the sacraments of baptism and Eucharist, and finally because of the controversies and misunderstandings of the past. We believe, however, that in the light of our different mentalities and historical situations, we can have a view of marriage which is in a profound sense a common one.

19. In fact we are all equally convinced that marriage is closely connected with God's promise. This promise is nothing other than Christ himself turning to look upon the spouses so that their love too should become a real and lasting union....

23. Catholics should envisage grace, not as a kind of purely objective gift which acts unconditionally on the spouses, but as an experience of fidelity and life that Christ stimulates in their hearts through the gift of the Spirit. As for Lutherans and members of the Reformed

Churches, they accept that the promise sealed with the death and resurrection of Christ is active in the hearts and lives of married Christians who live the mystery of Christ, in this way becoming its beneficiaries and witnesses....

24. It is our common conviction that in the conjugal union a man and a woman commit themselves for their whole lives, and that the couple is destined through marriage to remain united "as long as life lasts," as is said in our liturgies....

45. And so we are led to Him whom we have never ceased to discover at the heart and source of Christian marriage: the Christ whose mystery of life and salvation we want to make shine out among us: something we are never completely certain that we are doing, but also never give up hope of doing. It is in any case this desire which should inspire the attitude we have to adopt toward mixed marriage, without minimizing or overstating either our points of agreement or our points of dissent....

[The text outlines a detailed set of suggestions for the pastoral approach of the churches to interchurch couples and families.]

61. It is stressed that the clergy have a duty to exercise a high degree of mutual understanding and trust, which will help better joint pastoral preparation and support for mixed marriage. Furthermore, there is the need to realize that the solution of delicate personal problems involved in mixed marriages, of which no two are alike, is to be found in the maturing and sensitive growing together of the family itself. This sensitiveness must be matched by any source of outside assistance from which, if joint pastoral care is assumed, all hints of competitiveness, suspicion or possessiveness must be banished, since these would inhibit the necessary sensitiveness from the start....

[While Catholics have worked out a clear, detailed approach to interchurch marriages, for the most part, this is not the case

with the Protestant churches. Therefore, the dialogue includes a review of those policies. Since this text was developed, Catholic marriage legislation has continued to evolve, and is now incorporated in the 1983, 1993 Codes of Canon Law, and the 1993 Directory.]

91. In the Lutheran and Reformed Churches we are accustomed to marriages between spouses who belong to different ecclesiastical traditions....

92. In the past there has been, however, a serious and a difficult problem where one of the intending partners was a Catholic: and it can hardly be disputed that the difficulties stemmed from the legal norms imposed on the situation by the Canon Law of the Catholic Church. This idea of legal norms in this connection is foreign to the spirituality of the Lutheran and Reformed Churches. From their point of view these norms seemed to place the first importance upon the fulfillment of the Catholic spouse's obligations on the part of the children: whereas it has been possible for Lutheran and Reformed ministers and Churches to give the first priority to the Christian good and growth in grace of husband and wife together as a married couple and so of the whole family.

96. In the Catholic view, on the contrary, the laws of the Church are a function of theology and an expression of pastoral concern. They express in a practical manner the requirements of the doctrine of faith, and are intended to introduce Christian values into the life of the faithful. It is therefore true that theological convictions about the nature and obligatory character of the faith, as well as about the nature of the Church influence the characteristic spirit of Catholic regulations....

[In spite of these differences, the dialogue encourages common affirmation and pastoral action.]

104. Given the prospect of a theological rapprochement, our Churches should endeavor, especially in the field of the problems of mixed marriages, to abandon the mutual mistrust which still often prevails....

106. But both sides were convinced that the theological agreements attained in the course of the dialogue were of decisive importance for the treatment of these questions, and, indeed, formed a fundamental condition for tackling them....

⟞⟞⟞⟞⟞

Editor's Notes: The Methodist/Catholic dialogue touched upon marriage in several rounds. Rooted as it is in the Anglican tradition, Methodism finds it less difficult to speak of marriage as sacramental, though there are some reservations about Catholic sacramental theology. This dialogue refers to the work of the two above dialogues as a resource for dealing with Methodist/Catholic interchurch families and the church-dividing theological differences.

Methodist

Convergence, WMC–RC III in GA II:

49. In particular we are able to affirm that it is not only the wedding but the whole marriage that is sacramental. The relationship, the continual, lived out, total giving and sharing of the spouses is a genuine sign of God's love for us, Christ's love for us, Christ's love for the Church.

While Catholics speak of marriage as a sacrament and Methodists do not, we would both affirm, in the words of the introduction to the 1979 "Service of Christian Marriage" of the United Methodist Church: "Christian marriage is the sign of a lifelong covenant between a man and a woman. They fulfill each other, and their love gives birth to new life in each and through each...."The Protestant reformers of the sixteenth century were unwilling to call marriage a sacrament because they did not regard matrimony as a necessary means of grace for salvation. Though not necessary for salvation, certainly marriage is a means of grace, thus, sacramental in character. It is a covenant grounded in God's love....

50. Marriage is sacramental in nature because it is the living and life-giving union in which the covenantal love of God is made real....

54. We all subscribe to this teaching on Christ's will for matrimonial permanence and fidelity and this despite our different approaches to the problems of matrimonial nullity and of marital breakdown. We believe that further dialogue on these topics may well reveal closer unity of understanding, since we are all alarmed at the trivialization of marriage and the increase of divorce in the societies from which we come....

Difference, WMC–RC I in GA I:

75. *Divorce.* The Roman Catholic Church does not allow the divorce of baptized partners of a consummated marriage with a view to re-marriage, nor has she allowed the re-marriage of divorced persons. The Methodist Church has taken a different point of view on these matters. Nevertheless, we are well aware that special problems are created by the breakdown of marriages and that these cause great suffering, not least to the children of that marriage....We are greatly concerned with the increasing incidence of divorce and the disintegration of family life and jointly urge both Churches to make common effort to reduce their occurrence....

Why It Matters

Couples from different churches who are preparing for marriage face many added struggles because of the "mixed marriage." In addition to deciding where to hold the wedding and which minister to invite to preside, the couple also has to cope with the different attitudes about marriage that they have learned from their own religious tradition. Decisions about which church to attend after the wedding and where to baptize the children usually won't be solved in marriage-preparation sessions, but the decisions can be made easier if the couple has had a chance to understand each church's theology of matrimony. Time should be taken in the prewedding interview to discuss with the couple where each church stands on the sacrament, the permanence of marriage, and its attitude toward divorce and remarriage.

This also holds true for those seeking to enter the Catholic Church. Divorce and remarriage causes more problems for people seeking to enter the Catholic Church than any other issue. When the seeker is told that they cannot be received into the Catholic Church until their marriage issues are resolved, they are frequently dumbfounded. The Catholic understanding of marriage is not part of their tradition and may be difficult for them to accept. Spending time to review the Catholic understanding of marriage early in the "courtship" may save great hurt later. Be sure to compare the Catholic belief with the belief of the person's original church, and help them to see how and why the beliefs differ.

Be careful never to denigrate the status of the minister from another Christian church. It's not only good manners, it's also good theology. Because Jesus is the "unique priest of the new covenant...ordained ministers are related...both to the priesthood of Christ and the priesthood of the Church...because they fulfill a particular priestly service by strengthening and building up the royal and prophetic priesthood of the faithful through word and sacrament...and through their pastoral guidance" (BEM, M17). While resolution remains to be reached on the validity of orders, there can be no doubts that we treat the orders of each church with respect. This issue comes to the surface most frequently at weddings and funerals. These can be times of great healing for the church's wounded unity.

8

LIFE IN CHRIST: THE DIGNITY OF THE HUMAN PERSON

A ballot initiative to legalize casino gambling is coming before the community in Madisonville in order to improve the school system. Many of the Christian churches in the area seem to have a different point of view on the subject, and some have been quite vocal in advocating for or against the initiative.

The pastors in town realize how polarizing the issue is, so they call a public meeting at which each church can share its positions respectfully with one another without debate. At the meeting, small groups are formed that bring together members from different churches to discuss a wide variety of ethical issues, including gambling. The pastors see this as an opportunity to inform their people's conscience and deepen their interest in the community.

The Christians in these discussion groups all see this as an opportunity to deepen their understanding of the gospel imperative to unity among Christians and to work together to improve their community. Guidelines are provided so that the religious liberty of all concerned is preserved, respectful listening is promoted, and a deepening of Christian fidelity is fostered, even when different perspectives are aired.

Yet, despite all of this attention to detail, the discussions don't go well. The Baptists think that gambling is sinful, the Catholics see it as merely a minor vice. The Lutherans lean toward supporting the government, while the Mennonites feel that a peaceful boycott might be necessary to stop government from intruding on citizen's rights. This Christian dialogue could quickly break out into World War III.

Christian churches hold a variety of beliefs and attitudes about what is appropriate Christian behavior, and each turns to scripture to support their beliefs. Where can they find common ground for a sensitive discussion and serious consideration of what will be best for the community?

Morality (CCC #1749–1770)

Editor's Notes: Anglicans, Orthodox, Protestants, and Catholics agree on most moral issues. However, the issues raised by the Reformers concerning the relationship of grace and good works in the context of Christ's justifying death and resurrection have been a major stumbling block to Christian unity. Just as we have noted in the treatment of faith and of the sacraments, a hierarchy of truths (CCC #90, 2234, 1886) also exists within the ordering of Christian values. An organic relationship exists between the elements of our faith and of our moral teaching.

For all Christians, God's saving grace in Jesus Christ is the central truth of Christian discipleship (CCC #1987–2011). The 1999 signing of the Joint Declaration on the Doctrine of Justification *with the churches of the Lutheran World Federation provides Catholics with a new lens through which to view the Christian life and such issues as sin, law, merit, freedom, and good works. In this section we will continue to follow the outline of the* Catechism, *remembering that Catholic teaching on life in Christ is viewed through this perspective, which gives order and unity to our response to God's free grace in Jesus Christ.*

At the time of the Second Vatican Council, many ecumenists believed that full communion would never occur until all sacramental and faith issues were resolved. If ethical issues were mentioned at all, they were mentioned only in passing—more as an impulse toward common witness than as divisive issues that needed to be resolved.

There are several churches (Anabaptist, Mennonite, Brethren, Quaker) for whom issues of morality were divisive: Their view of church, state, and peace differed markedly from the views of both the Catholic and Orthodox churches, and from the views of the churches of the magisterial Reformation. In the United States, African-American Protestant churches (mostly Methodist, Baptist, and Pentecostal) emerged in reaction against white racism. Reconciliation with these churches entails dealing with these two ethical issues as seriously as we deal with sacramental and creedal issues.

In the years since the council, ecumenical dialogue has revealed a wide area of ethical agreement and the potential for common witness in the social and political realm. While the churches generally agree on the issues, the way each church approaches and responds to those same issues differs greatly. Over the years of alienation different styles developed for approaching the new ethical problems that continue to face the churches. The way in which each church responds to such issues as abortion, euthanasia, approaches to war and peace, homosexuality, and new biotechnology has raised serious and potentially church-dividing questions. Biblical-historical research and dialogue are being used to deal with these issues, just as they are applied to divisive issues of faith and sacraments.

The texts in this section become increasingly important to us as we struggle to deal with modern problems.

Reflection Questions:

- How do God's grace in Jesus Christ and our response in the moral life relate to each other?
- What are the principles and values that lie behind our particular decisions in following Christ?
- What is the relationship of communion in faith and sacraments to communion in moral decision making?

Anglican

Editor's Notes: The learning articulated in the Anglican–Catholic reflection is a good example of what the dialogues on ethics have accomplished.

Consensus, ARCIC II, LinC in GA II:

> 53. [A] deeper understanding of our separated histories
> has enabled us to appreciate better the real character of
> our divergences, and has persuaded us that it has been
> our broken communion, more than anything else, that
> has exacerbated our disagreements. In recent times there
> has been a large measure of cross-fertilization between
> our two traditions. Both our Communions, for example,
> have shared in the renewal of biblical, historical and
> liturgical studies, and both have participated in the ecu-
> menical movement. Our separated paths have once again
> begun to converge. It is in the conviction that we also
> possess a shared vision of Christian discipleship and a
> common approach to the moral life, that we take courage
> now to look directly at our painful disagreement on two
> particular moral issues.

*Editor's Notes: The Catholic dialogue with Orthodox, Protestant, and
Anglican churches in the context of the World Council has provided a
broad overview of what we believe about morality. They flesh out and help
us better understand Catholic teaching as it appears in this section of the*
Catechism *(http://www.prounione.urbe.it/dia-int/jwg/doc/e_jwg_n7db.
html).*

*The guidelines in this selection are a useful resource in dealing with
practical issues in the Christian life. These can also be helpful in establishing dialogues between local groups that differ on ethical issues.*

World Council of Churches–Catholic Church Joint Working Group

Convergence, JWG in GA II:

> I.3. Pressing personal and social moral issues, however,
> are prompting discord among Christians themselves and
> even threatening new divisions within and between
> churches....Dialogue should replace diatribe....
>
> I.4. Therefore, if some ethical issues arouse passionate
> emotions and create awkward ecumenical relations, the

churches should not shun dialogue, for these moral issues also can become church-reconciling means of common witness....In a prayerful, non-threatening atmosphere, dialogue can locate more precisely where the agreements, disagreements and contradictions occur. Dialogue can affirm those shared convictions....

I.5. Attentive concern for the complexities of the moral life should not cause Christians to lose sight of what is most fundamental for them all: the starting and ending point is the grace of God in Jesus Christ and the Spirit as mediated in the Church and in creation....Only God's initiating and sustaining grace enables Christians to transcend moral differences, overcome divisions and live their unity in faith....

II. 2. In real but imperfect communion with one another, each church expects itself and other churches to provide a moral environment through formation and deliberation.

III. Common Sources and Different Pathways of Moral Deliberation: For those pathways of moral reflection and deliberation which churches use in coming to ethical decisions, the churches share the Scriptures and have at their disposal such resources as liturgy and moral traditions, catechisms and sermons, sustained pastoral practices, the wisdom distilled from past and present experiences, and the arts of reflection and spiritual discernment. Yet church traditions configure these common resources in different ways.

III. 1. The biblical vision by itself does not provide Christians with all the clear moral principles and practical norms they need. Nor do the Scriptures resolve every ethical case....

Nevertheless, there is general consensus that by prayerfully studying the Scriptures and the developing traditions of biblical interpretations, by reflecting on human experiences, and by sharing insights within a community, Christians can reach reasonable judgments and decisions in many cases of ethical conduct.

III.2. Within the history of the Church, Christians have developed ways of reflecting systematically on the moral life by the ordering of biblical concepts and images and by rational argument....Or more recently, the language of "hierarchy of values" distinguishes between those core values at the heart of Christian discipleship and those other values which are less central yet integral to Christian morality. By emphasizing the "first-order principles" or the "core values," Christians can discover how much they already share, without reducing moral truth or searching for a least common denominator.

III.3. Christian traditions, however, have different estimates of human nature and of the capacity of human reason. Some believe that sin has so corrupted human nature that reason cannot arrive at moral truths. Others maintain that sin has only wounded human nature, and that with divine grace and human discipline, reason can still reach many universally applicable truths about moral living....

V. Ecumenical Challenges to Moral Formation and Deliberation: Churches which share real but imperfect *koinonia* face new challenges as communities of moral formation and deliberation: the pluralism of moral positions, the crisis of moral authority, changing moral judgments on traditional issues, and positions on new ones.

V.1. Christians agree that there is a moral universe which is grounded in the wisdom and will of God, but they may have different interpretations of God's wisdom, of the nature of that universe, and of the degree to which human beings are called to fashion it as co-creators with God.

We cannot deny three facts:

—First, Christians do share a long history of extensive unity in moral teaching and practice, flowing in part from a shared reflection on common sources, such as Ten Commandments and the Beatitudes.

—Second, divided Christian communities eventually did acquire some differences in ways of determining moral principles and acting upon them.

—Third, these differences have led today to such a pluralism of moral frameworks and positions within and between the ecclesial traditions that some positions appear to be in sharp tension, even in contradiction....

V.3. The process of the formulation and reception of ethical decisions also poses a major challenge of participation: who forms and formulates the churches' moral decisions, using which powers of influence and action, and which instruments of consultation? How do church members and the society at large assess, appropriate and respond to official church pronouncements? What are the channels of such a response, and what kinds of response are encouraged or discouraged?

V.4. Are not the conditions and structures of dialogue themselves prime ethical issues for churches? They are potentially either divisive or reconciling....Structures, offices, and roles express moral values or disvalues. Ways of exercising power, governance, and access have moral dimensions....

V.6. Several new ethical issues especially challenge ecumenical collaboration when the churches have no clear and detailed precedents, much less experience and consensus. Only to begin a long list of examples: economic policies in a world of "haves" and "have-nots"; immigration and refugee regulations within and between nations; industrialization and the environment; women's rights in society and in the churches; in vitro fertilization, genetic engineering and other biomedical developments. Christians and others experience the urgency of these unavoidable, complex ethical issues. They expect the churches to offer moral guidance on them....

Guidelines for the Ecumenical Dialogue on Moral Issues

The acceptance and practice of these suggested guidelines for dialogue can promote the goal of the ecumenical movement: the visible unity of Christians in one faith and one Eucharistic fellowship, expressed in worship, common life and service, in order that the world may believe....

A lack of ecumenical dialogue on personal and social moral issues, and a weak will to overcome whatever divisiveness they may prompt, place yet another stumbling block in the proclamation of the one gospel of Jesus Christ, who is "the Way the Truth and the Life" (Jn 14:6).

Guidelines

1. In fostering the *koinonia* or communion between the churches, we should as much as possible consult and exchange information with one another....

2. In dialogue we should try first to understand the moral positions and practices of others as they understand them....

3. In comparing the good qualities and moral ideals or the weaknesses and practices of various Christian communities, one should compare ideals with ideals and practice with practice....

4. By placing ethical issues within this inheritance of moral unity, we can more carefully understand the origin and nature of any present disagreement or division....

6. We should seek from the empirical sciences the best available knowledge on specific issues, and if possible agree on the data and their ethical implications before offering moral guidance.

7. We should acknowledge that various church traditions in fact sometimes agree, sometimes differ in the ways they:

—use Scriptures and other common resources, as well as the data of empirical sciences;

—relate moral vision, ethical norms and prudential judgments;

—identify a specific moral issue and formulate the problems;

—communicate within a church those values and disciplines which help to develop its own moral environment in the shaping of Christian character;

—understand and exercise ministerial leadership and oversight in moral guidance.

8. We should be ever alert to affirm whatever is shared in common, and to admit where there are serious divergent, even contrary stances....

10. When the dialogue continues to reveal sincere but apparently irreconcilable moral positions, we affirm in faith that the fact of our belonging together in Christ is more fundamental than the fact of our moral differences. The deep desire to find an honest and faithful resolution of our disagreements is itself evidence that God continues to grace the *koinonia* among disciples of Christ.

Editor's Notes: In the context of our common understanding of grace (JDDJ), Lutherans and Catholics have resolved their differences over good works. This agreement in faith does not destroy the contribution of the different emphases within the two traditions, given here as an "internally differentiated consensus."

Lutheran

Agreement, JDDJ in GA II:

37. We confess together that good works—a Christian life lived in faith, hope and love—follow justification and are its fruits. When the justified live in Christ and act in the grace they receive, they bring forth, in biblical terms, good fruit. Since Christians struggle against sin their entire lives, this consequence of justification is also for them an obligation they must fulfill. Thus both Jesus and the apostolic Scriptures admonish Christians to bring forth the works of love.

38. According to Catholic understanding, good works, made possible by grace and the working of the Holy Spirit, contribute to growth in grace, so that the righteousness that comes from God is preserved and communion with Christ is deepened. When Catholics affirm the "meritorious" character of good works, they wish to say that, according to the biblical witness, a reward in heaven is promised to these works....

39. The concept of a preservation of grace and a growth in grace and faith is also held by Lutherans. They do emphasize that righteousness as acceptance by God and sharing in the righteousness of Christ is always complete....When they view the good works of Christians as the fruits and signs of justification and not as one's own "merits," they nevertheless also understand eternal life in accord with the New Testament as unmerited "reward" in the sense of the fulfillment of God's promise to the believer.

Editor's Notes: The Anglican/Catholic dialogue on the moral life is the most extensive international report on this subject. Even while there is a broad agreement, new issues—such as homosexual unions or the ordination of women as priests—have emerged that are divisive and require attention. The principles enunciated in this statement are proposed as a common ground in the context of which these new challenges may be discussed. The preface here outlines the hopes of the dialogue.

Anglican

Convergence, ARCIC II, LinC in GA II:

3. In what follows we shall attempt to display the basis and shape of Christian moral teaching and to show that both our Communions apprehend it in the same light. We begin by reaffirming our common faith that the life to which God, through Jesus Christ, calls women and men is nothing less than participation in the divine life, and we spell out some of the characteristics and implications of our shared vision of life in Christ....Finally, we re-affirm our belief that differences and disagreements are exacerbated by a continuing breach of communion, and that integrity of moral response itself requires a movement towards full communion....

Shared Vision...

8. Ignorance and sin have led to the misuse and corruption of human freedom and to delusive ideas of

human fulfillment. But God has been faithful to his eternal purposes of love and, through the redemption of the world by Jesus Christ, offers to human beings participation in a new creation, recalling them to their true freedom and fulfillment....

11. Approached in this light the fundamental questions with which a Christian morality engages are such as these:

—What are persons called to be, as individuals and as members one of another in the human family?

—What constitutes human dignity, and what are the social as well as the individual dimensions of human dignity and responsibility?

—How does divine forgiveness and grace engage with human finitude, fragility and sin in the realization of human happiness?

—How are the conditions and structures of human life related to the goal of human fulfillment?

—What are the implications of the creatureliness which human beings share with the rest of the natural world?

At this fundamental level of inquiry and concern, we believe, our two Communions share a common vision and understanding....It will put in proper perspective any disagreement that may continue to exist....

[The text goes on to detail Anglican and Catholic common moral sources and principles and divergent emphases and applications within these, and concludes with a call for a common journey together in Christ.]

36. In the sixteenth century...[t]he Roman Catholic Church and the Churches of the Reformation went their different ways and fruits of shared communion were lost. It is in this context of broken communion and diverging histories that the existing differences between Anglicans and Roman Catholics on matters of morality must be located if they are to be rightly understood.

37. These differences, we believe, do not derive from disagreement on the sources of moral authority or on

fundamental moral values. Rather, they have arisen from the different emphases which our two Communions have given to different elements of the moral life. In particular, differences have occurred in the ways in which each, in isolation from the other, has developed its structures of authority and has come to exercise that authority in the formation of moral judgment. These factors, we believe, have contributed significantly to the differences that have arisen in a limited number of important moral issues....

Conscience (CCC #1776–1794)

Editor's Notes: As the Catechism *emphasizes (1777–1794), conscience is at the core of Christian morality. The emphasis placed on conscience in our different traditions has made for differing conclusions among the churches. The Joint Working Group of the World Council and the Holy See gives a comparison of the churches' roles in conscience formation. Several dialogues with particular churches have attempted to clarify these differences.*

Reflection Questions:

- How do Christians understand human conscience?
- What are the roles of freedom and authority in forming moral judgment?
- How do the different churches balance the role of the church in moral teaching?
- What are the different roles of the individual and the church in the formation of conscience?

World Council of Churches–Catholic Church Joint Working Group

Convergence, JWG in GA II:

IV. 1. The formation of conscience and the development of connected positions on specific ethical issues follow various pathways among different traditions, such as the Orthodox or Roman Catholic, Reformed or Lutheran, Baptist or Friends (Quaker). Every church believes that its members have the task of rightly applying their faith more fully to daily life. All traditions have their own ways of beginning, moving through and concluding their moral deliberations, and of acting upon them. There are different ways of discussing, consulting and arriving at decisions and of transmitting and receiving them. Influencing this process are the different ways in which they understand the action of the Holy Spirit and the exercise of the specific role of ministerial leadership in moral discernment and guidance.

In the Roman Catholic Church, bishops, according to the gift received from the Holy Spirit, and under His guidance, in their ministry of oversight (*episkope*), are the authoritative guardians and interpreters of the whole moral law, that is, both the law of the Gospel and the natural law. Bishops have the pastoral responsibility and duty of offering moral guidance, even sometimes definitive judgment that a specific action is right or wrong. Moral theologians provide ethical discernment within the community. Confessors, pastoral counselors and spiritual directors seek to take account of the unique needs of the individual person.

In the Orthodox Church decisions on ethical issues rest with the hierarchy, whether a Synod of bishops or an individual bishop, who are inspired by the Scriptures and the long tradition of the Church's pastoral care and moral guidance. The main concern is the spiritual welfare of the person in his or her relationship to God and to fellow human beings. The prudential application of church law and general norms (*oikonomia*) sometimes temper strictness, sometimes increase severity. It is a principal means for both spiritual growth and moral guidance. Orthodox tradition cherishes also the role of experienced spiritual fathers and mothers, and in the process of moral reflection, it stresses prayer among both laity and ordained.

Other churches do not ascribe to ministerial leadership this competency in interpretation or such authority of judgment. They arrive at certain ethical judgments by different polities of consulting and decision-making which involve clergy and laity. The Reformed traditions, for example, hold that the living Word of the sovereign God is always reforming the church in faith and life. Doctrinal and ethical judgments should be based on the Holy Scripture and informed by the whole tradition of the Church catholic and ecumenical. But no church body has the final authority in defining of Word of God. Redeemed and fallible human beings within the church faithfully rely on the process, inspired by the Holy Spirit, whereby they select their ordained and lay leaders and reach authoritative but reformable expressions of faith and positions on personal and social ethics.

Anglican

Difference, ARCIC II, LinC in GA II:

48. Reflection on the divergent histories of our two Communions has shown that their shared concern to respond obediently to God's Word and to foster the common good has nevertheless resulted in differing emphases in the ways in which they have nurtured Christian liberty and exercised Christian authority. Both Communions recognize that liberty and authority are essentially interdependent, and that the exercise of authority is for the protection and nurture of liberty. It cannot be denied, however, that there is a continuing temptation—a temptation which the continued separation of our two Communions serves only to accentuate—to allow the exercise of authority to lapse into authoritarianism and the exercise of liberty to lapse into individualism.

49. All moral authority is grounded in the goodness and will of God. Our two Communions are agreed on this principle and on its implications. Both our Communions, moreover, have developed their own structures and institutions for the teaching ministry of the Church, by which the will of God is discerned and its implications for the common good declared. Our Communions have diverged, however, in their views of the ways in which authority is most fruitfully exercised and the common good best promoted. Anglicans affirm that authority needs to be dispersed rather than centralized, that the common good is better served by allowing to individual Christians the greatest possible liberty of informed moral judgment, and that therefore official moral teaching should as far as possible be commendatory rather than prescriptive and binding. Roman Catholics, on the other hand, have, for the sake of the common good, emphasized the need for a central authority to preserve unity and to give clear and binding teaching.

Disciples

Convergence, CC–C III:
Conscience, Freedom and Being in Christ

4.2. The mission of the Church is to proclaim the Word of God. As it does so, the Church respects the freedom of every human being created "in the image and likeness of God" (*cf.* Gen 1:26–27). Both Roman Catholics and Disciples agree that the Church affirms each person's freedom; but the Church also has a responsibility to help its members make informed decisions, not to misuse the freedom that is God's gift, but use it for following God's will....

4.4. What is the role of conscience in matters of belief? Disciples of Christ and Roman Catholics agree that what we call human conscience is rightly described by the classical image of a voice of God, present in the heart of every human being. This is shown by St. Paul's discussion of the position of Gentiles in relation to the Mosaic law when he writes, "They show that what the law requires is written on their hearts, to which their own conscience bears witness" (Rom 2:15)....This first level of conscience is the work of God and, although sin can cloud conscience, it cannot destroy it.

4.5. The Church has a truth to teach which its members cannot discover only by themselves: it has been revealed in the person and work of Jesus Christ and kept in the memory which is guarded by the community of believers....It is their responsibility to form a conscience which is open to what God is saying. Nothing can oblige them to act against their perception of the will of God. Family, school, friends, and the culture all play a part in influencing human decisions. Because the Church has received from God the mission to teach the Gospel, it has a duty to help its members to make the faith of the Church their own in order to inform their conscience. This is therefore the second level of Christian conscience—to make a reasoned response to the revelation of God in Jesus Christ....

4.7. If men and women want to be in harmony with God, they have to hear and obey the voice of their conscience, informed and enlightened by the Word of God, assisted by the gifts of the Holy Spirit and prudent advice, and guided by the teaching of the Church....

4.8. The Commission's discussion has been important in dispelling old stereotypes, such as the idea that the Roman Catholic Church has no place for freedom of conscience, or the idea that Disciples place no limits on the freedom of conscience. Both communions teach the place of the freedom of conscience and both see limits to its exercise within the community. This leads to two important agreements. Disciples and Roman Catholics both recognize that commitment to the Gospel should be freely made. They also recognize that living the

Christian life is a continuous process of receiving and living by the teaching handed on in the Church and making personal decisions which are themselves shaped by life in communion with other believers.

⁕

Methodist

Convergence, WMC–C III in GA II:
> 43. Whether we see conscience as a separate faculty or as the mobilizing of all our faculties to discern the good and shun evil, we agree that the human capacity we call conscience is the gift of God and is of vital significance for the moral life.
>
> Conscience does not act as an independent source of moral information. Since people have the responsibility of fostering, protecting and following their conscience, it needs to be formed and informed and must therefore be open to guidance from authority. Therefore in moral decision-making, as in coming to terms with doctrinal formulations, the Christian is one who stands under authority. The normative authority is Scripture interpreted in the light of Tradition (the living voice of the Church), Reason and Experience.
>
> 44. People have both the responsibility to see that their conscience is open to authoritative guidance and the right freely and faithfully to follow that conscience. Thus we agree that no one is to be forced to act in a manner contrary to conscience, or to be restrained from acting according to conscience, "as long as the just requirements of public order are observed" (Vatican II: Declaration on Religious Freedom, n. 2) and the rights of others are not infringed. We are agreed that "freedom of conscience" does not mean "make up your mind on moral matters with no reference to any other authority than your own sense of right and wrong." There may come a point when the Church is compelled to say, "If

you persist in exercising your freedom of conscience in this way you put yourself outside the Church."

⁕

Virtues (CCC #1803–1832)

Editor's Notes: A central idea to the Reformation was the role of the virtue of faith in the process of salvation. With the resolution of the question of justification between Lutherans and Catholics, the issue of salvation by "faith alone" has also been resolved. The emphasis of both traditions has not been lost, however, as the texts below will demonstrate. Through the dialogues what each church teaches about "faith" has been clarified. Today, both recognize that their understandings of faith, while focusing on different dimensions, are grounded in the scripture.

Lutheran

Agreement, JDDJ in GA II:

25. We confess together that sinners are justified by faith in the saving action of God in Christ.…They place their trust in God's gracious promise by justifying faith, which includes hope in God and love for him. Such a faith is active in love and thus the Christian cannot and should not remain without works. But whatever in the justified precedes or follows the free gift of faith is neither the basis of justification nor merits it.

26. According to Lutheran understanding, God justifies sinners in faith alone *(sola fide)*.…God himself effects faith as he brings forth such trust by his creative word. Because God's act is a new creation, it affects all dimensions of the person and leads to a life in hope and love. In the doctrine of "justification by faith alone," a distinction but not a separation is made between justification itself and the renewal of one's way of life that necessarily follows from justification and without which faith does not exist.…

27. The Catholic understanding also sees faith as fundamental in justification. For without faith, no justification can take place. Persons are justified through baptism as hearers of the word and believers in it. The justification of sinners is forgiveness of sins and being made righteous by justifying grace, which makes us children of God. In justification the righteous receive from Christ faith, hope, and love and are thereby taken into communion with him. This new personal relation to God is grounded totally on God's graciousness and remains constantly dependent on the salvific and creative working of this gracious God, who remains true to himself, so that one can rely upon him. Thus justifying grace never becomes a human possession to which one could appeal over against God. While Catholic teaching emphasizes the renewal of life by justifying grace, this renewal in faith, hope, and love is always dependent on God's unfathomable grace and contributes nothing to justification about which one could boast before God (Rom 3:27).

Reformed

Consensus, Ref–C II in GA II:

78. To speak in this way of our justification and reconciliation with God is to say that faith is above all a reception (Rom 5:1–2): it is received and in turn it gives thanks for grace.…We receive from Christ our justification, that is our pardon, our liberation, our life with God. By faith, we are liberated from our presumption that we can somehow save ourselves; by faith, we are comforted in spite of our terror of losing ourselves. We are set at liberty to open ourselves to the sanctification which God wills for us.

79. The person justified by the free gift of faith, i.e. by a faith embraced with a freedom restored to its fullness, can henceforth live according to righteousness.…And so, justification by faith brings with it the gift of sanctification, which can grow continuously as it creates life, justice

and liberty. Jesus Christ, the one mediator between God and humankind, is also the unique way which leads toward pleasing God. Faith receives freely and bears testimony actively, as it works itself out through love (Gal 5:6).

———∞∞———

Sin (CCC #1849–1869)

Editor's Notes: In the Western churches that have emerged from the Reformation, belief in original sin was a key common element. Their understanding of the human person is shaped by their common belief. Differences about faith emerged because of different biblical emphases. That is, in some of his letters Paul emphasizes the sinful aspect of the human person, in others, God's gifts in creation. With Lutherans, Catholics have come to a common understanding of the relationship of sin, freedom, and righteousness, while retaining the differences of emphasis outlined in the texts below. Reformed/Catholic discussions have taken a similar direction in reconciling Reformation differences over the sinful and graced nature of the human person.

Reflection Questions:

- What is the relationship of sin and concupiscence in Catholic understanding?
- How does one distinguish and relate original sin and the sins committed by the conscious believer?
- What is the relationship among grace, cooperation, and human freedom?

Lutheran

Agreement, JDDJ in GA II:

19. We confess together that all persons depend completely on the saving grace of God for their salvation. The freedom they possess in relation to persons and the things of this world is no freedom in relation to salvation, for as sinners they stand under God's judgment and

are incapable of turning by themselves to God to seek deliverance, of meriting their justification before God, or of attaining salvation by their own abilities. Justification takes place solely by God's grace. Because Catholics and Lutherans confess this together, it is true to say:

20. When Catholics say that persons "cooperate" in preparing for and accepting justification by consenting to God's justifying action, they see such personal consent as itself an effect of grace, not as an action arising from innate human abilities.

21. According to Lutheran teaching, human beings are incapable of cooperating in their salvation, because as sinners they actively oppose God and his saving action. Lutherans do not deny that a person can reject the working of grace. When they emphasize that a person can only receive (mere passive) justification, they mean thereby to exclude any possibility of contributing to one's own justification, but do not deny that believers are fully involved personally in their faith, which is effected by God's Word.

22. We confess together that God forgives sin by grace and at the same time frees human beings from sin's enslaving power and imparts the gift of new life in Christ. When persons come by faith to share in Christ, God no longer imputes to them their sin and through the Holy Spirit effects in them an active love. These two aspects of God's gracious action are not to be separated, for persons are by faith united with Christ, who in his person is our righteousness (1 Cor 1:30): both the forgiveness of sin and the saving presence of God himself. Because Catholics and Lutherans confess this together, it is true to say that:

23. When Lutherans emphasize that the righteousness of Christ is our righteousness, their intention is above all to insist that the sinner is granted righteousness before God in Christ through the declaration of forgiveness and that only in union with Christ is one's life

renewed. When they stress that God's grace is forgiving love ("the favor of God"), they do not thereby deny the renewal of the Christian's life. They intend rather to express that justification remains free from human cooperation and is not dependent on the life-renewing effects of grace in human beings.

24. When Catholics emphasize the renewal of the interior person through the reception of grace imparted as a gift to the believer, they wish to insist that God's forgiving grace always brings with it a gift of new life, which in the Holy Spirit becomes effective in active love. They do not thereby deny that God's gift of grace in justification remains independent of human cooperation.

Reformed

Consensus, Ref–C II in GA II:

> 69. b) The death and resurrection of Jesus also reveal to us who we are: not merely creatures who are object of God's benevolence, but also human beings capable of sin, historically imprisoned in the bonds of a sin which is our curse. From the beginning we hid ourselves from God, and this is why God is hidden from us.…This awareness of alienation and exile in the midst of faith we call sin. We recognize that there is a betrayal of God's trust in us and that God's heart is saddened by our separation. From this condition we cannot free ourselves by our own strength.…Because of sin, the law intended for life judges, condemns and leads to death. Substitute sacrifices are endlessly repeated. Prophecies lag, bide their time, fall silent. Wisdom remains an ideal. In Jesus, the unique mediator, in his death and resurrection, we are radically freed from this situation: the way of true life is opened to us anew.

Editor's Notes: Evangelical and Catholic differences about original sin still remain strong, even in the light of progress made with other Protestant and Anglican churches.

Evangelical

Divergence, ERCDOM in GA II:

3., 1) Evangelicals insist that original sin has distorted every part of human nature, so that it is permeated by self-centeredness. Consequently, the Apostle Paul describes all people as "enslaved," "blind," "dead" and "under God's wrath," and therefore totally unable to save themselves.

Roman Catholics also speak of original sin as an injury and disorder which has weakened—though not destroyed—human free will. Human beings have "lifted themselves up against God and sought to attain their goal apart from him." As a result this has upset the relationship linking man to God and "has broken the right order that should reign within himself as well as between himself and other men and all creatures." Hence human beings find themselves drawn to what is wrong and of themselves unable to overcome the assaults of evil successfully, "so that everyone feels as though bound by chains."

Clearly there is some divergence between Roman Catholics and Evangelicals in the way we understand human sin and need, as well as in the language we use to express them. Roman Catholics think Evangelicals over-stress the corruption of human beings by affirming their "total depravity" (i.e. that every part of our humanness has been perverted by the Fall), while Evangelicals think Roman Catholics underestimate it and are therefore unwisely optimistic about the capacity, ability and desire of human beings to respond to the grace of God. Yet we agree that all are sinners, and that all stand in need of a radical salvation which includes deliverance from the power of evil, together with reconciliation to God and adoption into his family.

Social Justice (CCC #1928–1942)

Editor's Notes: Catholics generally are in agreement with the classical Reformation churches on issues of human rights, peace, race, and economic solidarity. The few brief examples provided here illustrate this agreement.

Reformed

Convergence, Ref–C I in GA I:

23. We were all agreed that the ethical decisions which necessarily follow from the Gospel of the Kingdom of God and the believing acceptance of this Gospel extend also to the realm of politics. In both confessions there were those who inclined to place greater emphasis on the need for a certain caution and those who stressed the need to derive concrete political decisions from the New Testament message and the possibility of doing so.

Methodist

Convergence, WMC–RCI in GA I:

46. Methodists find in the statements of Vatican II on human dignity and autonomy many echoes of their own tradition (Cf. GS, Ch. 1). Combining objectivity with a steady relation of human activity to God, these statements offer opportunities for development and application which Catholics and Methodists should exploit together, recognizing that amid the threat of dehumanization here is an approach to man's secular achievements which promises better fruit….There is no more eloquent witness the Church can give to the dignity of man than intelligent support of and scope to his highest activities, and she has a remarkable history in this.

Evangelicals

Editor's Notes: Because of their emphasis on personal salvation and evangelism, evangelical Christians are generally reluctant to engage in social witness. However, Catholics and Evangelicals have worked together on issues of personal morality and pro-life witness.

Convergence, ERCDOM in GA II:

> 7., 2), c) Common Witness in Community Service....In the name of Christ, Roman Catholics and Evangelicals can serve human need together, providing emergency relief for the victims of flood, famine and earthquake, and shelter for refugees; promoting urban and rural development; feeding the hungry and healing the sick; caring for the elderly and the dying; providing a marriage guidance, enrichment and reconciliation service, a pregnancy advisory service and support for single parent families; arranging educational opportunities for the illiterate and job creation schemes for the unemployed; and rescuing young people from drug addiction and young women from prostitution. There seems to be no justification for organizing separate Roman Catholic and Evangelical projects of a purely humanitarian nature, and every reason for undertaking them together. Although faith may still in part divide us, love for neighbor should unite us.

> d) Common Witness in Social Thought and Action. There is a pressing need for fresh Christian thinking about the urgent social issues which confront the contemporary world. The Roman Catholic Church has done noteworthy work in this area, not least through the social encyclicals of recent Popes. Evangelicals are only now beginning to catch up after some decades of neglect. It should be to our mutual advantage to engage in Christian social debate together. A clear and united Christian witness is needed in face of such challenges as the nuclear arms race, North-South economic inequality, the environmental crisis, and the revolution in sexual mores....

There are many such areas in which Roman Catholics and Evangelicals can both think together and take action together. Our witness will be stronger if it is a common witness.

⸙

Editor's Notes: Among the unique tasks of reconciliation among churches in the United States is healing the schisms caused by white racism and slavery. The historic African-American churches, orthodox in this Protestant faith and "independent" not of their own choosing, see their own witness as a unique, confessional testimony to the apostolicity of the church in the midst of a sinful, racially divided, ecclesial community. For these churches reconciliation is not "merely" an ethical issue, it partakes of the very core of the Gospel. The question of the history of white racism and the churches' complicity in slavery must be addressed, along with issues of sacraments and church order.

Black Churches

Convergence, Black Ch in GC II:

IV. APOSTOLICITY

We affirm the Apostolic tradition that recognizes the transmission of authentic faith down the centuries by all those who have faithfully lived it, whether or not they have been officially designated as apostles....We recognize, therefore, the apostolicity of what we have received from our slave ancestors who, though "unlearned and ignorant" men and women, reinterpreted the distorted Christianity they received from the slave masters and passed down to succeeding generations of Black believers the story of Jesus....But we acknowledge the importance of the Apostolic tradition being engaged and not merely passed on. Apostolicity must be lived out in the context of contemporary events. It is not the recitation of past formulations, but the living of the present commandments of the Risen Lord.

In the final analysis the test of apostolicity is the experiencing of the life, death and resurrection of Jesus

Christ in our daily struggle against demonic powers that seek to rob us of our inheritance as children of God redeemed by the blood of Jesus Christ. Our deeds, more than our creeds, determine whether we have fully received and acted upon the faith of the apostles….

It is in the Black Church's historic identification with marginality that Jesus is appropriated as the Black Messiah, the paradigm of our existential reality as an oppressed people and the affirmation of our survival and liberation.

Finally, for Black Christians, the search for an expression of the Apostolic faith must be multiracial and multicultural rather than captive to any one race, sex, class or political ideology. The Church and the ecumenical movement must no longer submit to domination by social, economic or intellectual elites….

CONCLUSION AND RECOMMENDATIONS

1. The Afro-American Christian tradition, embodied particularly in Black Baptist, Methodist and Pentecostal Churches, but continuing also in other Black-led Protestant and Roman Catholic congregations, has been and continues to be an indigenous expression of the faith of the apostles in North America….

3. We invite the other churches participating in the Faith and Order movement to give greater study and recognition to how God has maintained the continuity of the Apostolic Faith primarily through the oral character and noncreedal styles of the African American tradition expressed in worship, witness and social struggle.

4. We urge the other…churches…to take note of the unity of faith and practice that the Black Church has historically emphasized and to engage the Faith and Order movement in greater involvement in the struggle against racism and all forms of oppression as an essential element of the Apostolic confession.

5. We call upon Black churches in North and South America, the Caribbean and in Africa to confess boldly the faith we received from the Apostles, despite every

effort made to distort and falsify it and, joining with us who were a part of this historic consultation in Richmond, to intensify their involvement in the Faith and Order movement by sharing the "gift of Blackness" with those of other traditions....

Law (CCC #1950–1974)

Editor's Notes: Christians use "law" in a variety of ways: God's law revealed in scripture, but also discernable in nature; human positive law in the church (canon law/constitutional discipline) or in society. For Christians, law is always understood within the context of God's grace in Jesus Christ and the common good of the community. Reformation differences, at least with Lutherans and Anglicans, have been resolved with the Joint Declaration and in the dialogues.

Reflection Questions:

- What is the role of law in the following of Christ?
- What are the different roles of church law and the divine law revealed by God in Jesus Christ?
- In what way is God's law "good news" in the Christian life?

Lutheran

Agreement, JDDJ in GA II:

31. We confess together that persons are justified by faith in the gospel "apart from works prescribed by the law" (Rom 3:28). Christ has fulfilled the law and by his death and resurrection has overcome it as a way to salvation. We also confess that God's commandments retain their validity for the justified and that Christ has by his teaching and example expressed God's will which is a standard for the conduct of the justified also.

32. Lutherans state that the distinction and right ordering of law and gospel is essential for the under-

standing of justification. In its theological use, the law is demand and accusation. Throughout their lives, all persons, Christians also, in that they are sinners, stand under this accusation which uncovers their sin so that, in faith in the gospel, they will turn unreservedly to the mercy of God in Christ, which alone justifies them.

33. Because the law as a way to salvation has been fulfilled and overcome through the gospel, Catholics can say that Christ is not a lawgiver in the manner of Moses. When Catholics emphasize that the righteous are bound to observe God's commandments, they do not thereby deny that through Jesus Christ God has mercifully promised to his children the grace of eternal life.

Anglican

Convergence, ARCIC II, LinC in GA II:

52. [D]ifferences there are and differences they remain. Both Anglicans and Roman Catholics are accustomed to using the concept of law to give character and form to the claims of morality. However, this concept is open to more than one interpretation and use, so causing real and apparent differences between our two traditions. For example, a notable feature of established Roman Catholic moral teaching is its emphasis on the absoluteness of some demands of the moral law and the existence of certain prohibitions to which there are no exceptions. In these instances, what is prohibited is intrinsically disordered and therefore objectively wrong. Anglicans, on the other hand, while acknowledging the same ultimate values, are not persuaded that the laws as we apprehend them are necessarily absolute. In certain circumstances, they would argue, it might be right to incorporate contextual and pastoral considerations in the formulation of a moral law, on the grounds that fundamental moral values are better served if the law sometimes takes into account certain contingencies of nature and history and

certain disorders of the human condition. In so doing, they do not make the clear-cut distinction, which Roman Catholics make, between canon law, with its incorporation of contingent and prudential considerations, and the moral law, which in its principles is absolute and universal. In both our Communions, however, there are now signs of a shift away from a reliance on the concept of law as the central category for providing moral teaching. Its place is being taken by the concept of "persons-in-community." An ethic of response is preferred to an ethic of obedience. In the desire to respond as fully as possible to the new law of Christ, the primacy of persons is emphasized above the impersonalism of a system of law, thus avoiding the distortions of both individualism and utilitarianism. The full significance of this shift of emphasis is not yet clear, and its detailed implications have still to be worked out. It should be emphasized, however, that whatever differences there may be in the way in which they express the moral law, both our traditions respect the consciences of persons in good faith.

Editor's Notes: None of the international Catholic/Orthodox dialogues have yet taken up ethical issues. However, in areas like divorce and remarriage and the evaluation of one another's sacraments, the role of law—divine and canon—becomes important. This United States text on the economy demonstrates this importance.

Orthodox

Convergence, Ox–CUS IV in BU:
> 4. Our investigation has shown:
> —The wealth of meanings which economy has had over the centuries;
> —Some weaknesses in recent presentations of economy;
> —The significance of economy for our ongoing ecumenical discussion.

5. At the most basic level, the Greek word *oikonomia* means management, arrangement, or determination in the strictly literal sense. A few overtones add to this basic meaning. *Oikonomia* may imply accommodation, prudent adaptation of means to an end, diplomacy and strategy and even dissimulation and the "pious lie." But *oikonomia* can also have highly positive connotations. It suggests the idea of stewardship, of management on behalf of another, on behalf of a superior....

7. God is seen as arranging all for the purpose of man's salvation and eternal well-being; and man fashioned in the image and likeness of God is viewed as being called to imitate this divine activity.

8. The word *oikonomia* later acquired additional uses in ecclesiastical contexts, in particular:

—The administration of penance, the arranging or managing of a penitent's reconciliation to the church;

—The reception of those turning to the church from heresy or schism;

—The restoration of repentant clergy and the reception of heretical or schismatic clergy as ordained.

9. In all these areas, however, the understanding of economy as responsible stewardship, imitating the divine economy, is maintained, excluding arbitrariness or capriciousness.

Recent presentations of economy often have included the following elements:

—Economy understood as a departure from or suspension of strict application *(akribeia)* of the church's canons and disciplinary norms, in many respects analogous to the West's dispensation.

—Economy applied not only to canon law and church discipline, but to the sacraments as well. In this context, it has been argued, for example, that all non-Orthodox sacraments, from the point of view of strictness, are null and void but that the Orthodox Church can, by economy, treat non-Orthodox sacraments as valid. These views imply that the application of economy to the sacraments may vary according to circumstances, including such pastoral considerations as the attitude of the non-Orthodox group toward Orthodoxy, the well-being of the Orthodox flock, and the ultimate salvation of the person or groups that contemplate entering Orthodoxy.

10. These recent interpretations do not, in the judgment of the Consultation, do justice to the genuine whole tradition underlying the concept and practice of economy. The church of Christ is not a legalistic system whereby every prescription has identical importance, especially when ancient canons do not directly address contemporary issues. Nor can the application of economy make something invalid to be valid, or what is valid to be invalid. Because the risen Christ has entrusted to the church a stewardship of prudence and freedom to listen to the promptings of the Holy Spirit about today's problems of church unity, a proper understanding of economy involves the exercise of spiritual discernment.

Why It Matters

Christian churches hold a variety of positions on moral and ethical issues. Each church bases its position more or less on its reading of scripture and its own historical development. While these differences can "arouse passionate emotions and create awkward ecumenical relations," they can also be appropriate opportunities for dialogue and reconciliation (JWG in GA II).

Careful planning must be used when organizing interchurch discussions on moral issues. Establish a prayerful, nonthreatening atmosphere in which to hold the conversation. Study the scriptures and discuss their meaning, have members of each church leading the discussion. Set simple ground rules for the discussion. No name-calling or judgments would be high on the list, along with "frame questions seeking understanding, not put-down or embarrassment." Seek to affirm shared convictions. Where there is disagreement, focus on explaining how the churches reached their various decisions.

These discussions may not lead to solutions, but they can lead to understanding and a willingness to work together on the shared issues. The "Guidelines for the Ecumenical Dialogue on Moral Issues" (taken from JWG in GA II, and found in this volume on pages 182–87) can be used to foster productive conversations between churches on moral issues.

The way in which a person forms his or her conscience or makes a moral decision may differ significantly between churches. The same is true when it comes to their understanding of sin or living the Christian virtues. A discussion on these issues can be very productive when preparing interchurch couples for marriage or seekers for reception into full communion in the Catholic Church.

The Catholic emphasis on living the Christian virtues may be seen by some as promoting a "justification by works" faith. While we know that's not true, care must be used when explaining Catholic practices to avoid such misunderstandings. An added area for discussion in these settings is the mercy of God and how we should seek forgiveness.

9

LIFE IN CHRIST: SALVATION AND THE CHURCH

In Rogerstown a serious set of racial tensions has emerged in the public schools that has alarmed the city elders and the religious leadership. The Christian pastors call a meeting to see how the churches might be sources of healing and reconciliation in this deeply divided community. Catholic, Orthodox, and Protestant; African-American, Asian, and white ethnic congregations have lay and clergy meetings together to analyze the problem and begin developing approaches that will help Christians take leadership roles in healing the community.

A group of Pentecostal and fundamentalist churches refuses to join the group, saying that Catholics claim to be saved by good works and not by Christ and therefore are not Christian. Some of the Catholics and Orthodox are cautious because they fear that this sort of collaborative work will make newly immigrated Hispanic and Eastern European members become subject to proselytism. Some Protestants who attend the meeting are reluctant to have the group speak out actively, because they see the role of the church as saving souls and not social action. Some Catholics refuse to attend because some of the Orthodox and Protestant churches do not agree with their church's position on contraception.

How do Christians come to understand different ways of being saved and different approaches to ethical action—differences that divide them? How is the doctrine of grace and salvation related to human works in this world? What are appropriate forms of evangelization and social witness of the churches together in the community?

Grace and Justification (CCC #1987–2016)

Editor's Notes: As we have noted, all Christians agree that our salvation comes solely through the death and resurrection of Jesus Christ. This salvific act is the source and heart of our understanding of the Christian life and its moral implications. While the churches agree on Jesus' saving act, what they understand or mean by the words justification *and* grace *led to the Reformation and to the subsequent developments among the separated churches.*

With the 1999 signing of the Joint Declaration on the Doctrine of Justification, the Catholic and Lutheran churches find themselves in a new context. We now understand our teaching on grace in a whole new light. We have a more positive view of the Reformation and the churches that emerged from it. We can appreciate more deeply the faith taught in the Catechism. *Agreements with other churches also illuminate our common faith in God's free grace in Jesus Christ.*

Reflection Questions:

- What does it mean to say that our salvation is totally dependent on Christ and that we cannot merit our own justification?
- How do we understand grace as a gift of the Holy Spirit?
- How do we reconcile the free response of the Christian to God's initiative in Jesus Christ?

JUSTIFICATION

Reformed

Consensus, Ref–C II in GA II:

> 79. The person justified by the free gift of faith, i.e., by a faith embraced with a freedom restored to its fullness, can henceforth live according to righteousness. The person who has received grace is called to bear fruits worthy of that grace. Justification makes him or her an "heir of God, co-heir with Christ" (Rom 8:17). The one who has freely received is committed to gratitude and service. This is not a new form of bondage but a new way forward….
>
> 80. Together we confess the church, for there is no justification in isolation. All justification takes place in the community of believers or is ordered toward the gathering of such a community. Fundamental for us all is the presence of Christ in the church, considered simultaneously as both a reality of grace and a concrete community in time and space. Christ himself acts in the church in the proclamation of the word, in the celebration of the sacraments, in prayer, and in intercession for the world. This presence and this action are enabled and empowered by the Spirit, by whom Christ calls to unite human beings to himself, to express his reality through them, to associate them in the mystery of his self-offering for them.

Lutheran

Agreement, JDDJ in GA II:

> *[On the basis of extensive biblical, historical, and theological research, the churches are able to say officially:]*
>
> 15. In faith we [Lutheran and Catholic churches] together hold the conviction that justification is the work of the triune God. The Father sent his Son into the world to save sinners. The foundation and presupposition of justification is the incarnation, death, and resurrection of

Christ. Justification thus means that Christ himself is our righteousness, in which we share through the Holy Spirit in accord with the will of the Father. Together we confess: By grace alone, in faith in Christ's saving work and not because of any merit on our part, we are accepted by God and receive the Holy Spirit, who renews our hearts while equipping and calling us to good works….

[For the Catholic Church and the Lutheran churches signing this Declaration, the whole ecclesial context has changed and thus provided implications for our relationships, our teaching, and our interpretation of the faith.]

41. Thus the doctrinal condemnations of the 16th century, in so far as they relate to the doctrine of justification, appear in a new light: The teaching of the Lutheran churches presented in this Declaration does not fall under the condemnations from the Council of Trent. The condemnations in the Lutheran Confessions do not apply to the teaching of the Roman Catholic Church presented in this Declaration.

42. Nothing is thereby taken away from the seriousness of the condemnations related to the doctrine of justification. Some were not simply pointless. They remain for us "salutary warnings" to which we must attend in our teaching and practice.

Editor's Notes: Since the nineteenth century such Anglo-Catholics as John Henry Newman (before he became Catholic) have claimed that there was a harmony between Anglican and Catholic theology on the issues of salvation and justification. Evangelical Anglicans have contested this claim, so the dialogue has taken up the issue. These paragraphs are exemplary of the far reaching consensus claimed in the full text.

Anglican

Consensus, ARCIC II, S&C in GA II:

14. Roman Catholic interpreters of Trent and Anglican theologians alike have insisted that justification and

sanctification are neither wholly distinct from nor unrelated to one another. The discussion, however, has been confused by differing understandings of the word *justification* and its associated words....Thus the Catholic understanding of the process of justification...tended to include elements of salvation which the Reformers would describe as belonging to sanctification rather than justification. As a consequence, Protestants took Catholics to be emphasizing sanctification in such a way that absolute gratuitousness of salvation was threatened. On the other side, Catholics feared that Protestants were so stressing the justifying action of God that sanctification and human responsibility were gravely depreciated.

Justification and sanctification are two aspects of the same divine act (1 Cor 6:11). This does not mean that justification is a reward for faith or works: rather, when God promises the removal of our condemnation and gives us a new standing before him, this justification is indissolubly linked with his sanctifying recreation of us in grace. This transformation is being worked out in the course of our pilgrimage, despite the imperfections and ambiguities of our lives. God's grace effects what he declares: his creative word imparts what it imputes. By pronouncing us righteous, God also makes us righteous. He imparts a righteousness which is his and becomes ours.

Editor's Notes: While most evangelical Christians are not yet able to claim agreement with Catholics on justification, remarkable convergence has been articulated in the dialogue. Some evangelicals have said that Catholics are not "Christian" because they think we believe we are saved by our own good works rather than by Jesus Christ. For many evangelicals, however, the dialogue has demonstrated that Catholics believe that we are saved by Christ and not by our own actions.

Evangelicals

Convergence, ERCDOM in GA II:

3., 5) The Meaning of Salvation

In the Old Testament salvation meant rescue, healing and restoration for those already related to God within the covenant. In the New Testament it is directed to those who have not yet entered into the new covenant in Jesus Christ.

Salvation has to be understood in terms of both salvation history (the mighty acts of God through Jesus Christ) and salvation experience (a personal appropriation of what God has done through Christ). Roman Catholics and Evangelicals together strongly emphasize the objectivity of God's work through Christ, but Evangelicals tend to lay more emphasis than Roman Catholics on the necessity of a personal response to, and experience of, God's saving grace. To describe this, again the full New Testament vocabulary is needed (for example, the forgiveness of sins, reconciliation with God, adoption into his family, redemption, the new birth—all of which are gifts brought to us by the Holy Spirit), although Evangelicals still give paramount importance to justification by grace through faith.

We agree that what is offered us through the death and resurrection of Christ is essentially "deliverance," viewed both negatively and positively. Negatively, it is a rescue from the power of Satan, sin and death, from guilt, alienation (estrangement from God), moral corruption, self-centeredness, existential despair and fear of the future, including death. Positively, it is a deliverance into the freedom of Christ. This freedom brings human fulfillment. It is essentially becoming "sons in the Son" and therefore brothers to each other. The unity of the disciples of Jesus is a sign both that the Father sent the Son and that the Kingdom has arrived. Further, the new community expresses itself in eucharistic worship, in serving the needy (especially the poor and disenfranchised), in open fellowship with people of every age, race and culture, and in conscious continuity with the historic Christ through fidelity to the teaching of his apostles....

Roman Catholics draw attention to the three dimensions of evangelization which *Evangelii nuntiandi* links. They are the anthropological, in which humanity is seen always within a concrete situation; the theological, in which the unified plan of God is seen within both creation and redemption; and the evangelical, in which the exercise of charity (refusing to ignore human misery) is seen in the light of the story of the Good Samaritan.

We all agree that the essential meaning of Christ's salvation is the restoration of the broken relationship between sinful humanity and a saving God; it cannot therefore be seen as a temporal or material project, making evangelism unnecessary....

ASSURANCE

Editor's Notes: Among the Reformation concerns about justification and salvation was what appeared to the Reformers to be Catholics' lack of trust in God's grace. Many Reformers felt that Catholics relied on their own good works rather than on the grace of Christ, and therefore Catholics seemed to them to be insecure about God's saving love in their life. With agreement on justification, the issue of reliance on God's promises is also resolved without losing the gifts of both traditions.

Lutheran

Agreement, JDDJ in GA II:

34. We confess together that the faithful can rely on the mercy and promises of God. In spite of their own weakness and the manifold threats to their faith, on the strength of Christ's death and resurrection they can build on the effective promise of God's grace in Word and Sacrament and so be sure of this grace.

35. This was emphasized in a particular way by the Reformers: in the midst of temptation, believers should not look to themselves but look solely to Christ and trust only him....

36. Catholics can share the concern of the Reformers to ground faith in the objective reality of Christ's promise, to look away from one's own experience, and to trust in Christ's forgiving word alone (cf. Mt 16:19; 18:18)....Every person, however, may be concerned about his salvation when he looks upon his own weaknesses and shortcomings. Recognizing his own failures, however, the believer may yet be certain that God intends his salvation.

Editor's Notes: Evangelical Christians have not participated in the Joint Declaration process. Nevertheless, remarkable agreement on the issue of grace has improved mutual understanding. Evangelicals held the stereotype that Catholics believed they were saved by their own works. Catholics often returned the stereotype by believing that Evangelical Protestants held "once saved, always saved," without any need to change one's behavior or actions after accepting Christ as a personal savior.

Evangelical

Convergence, ERCDOM in GA II:

4., 4) Assurance of Salvation

It has always been traditional among Evangelicals to stress not only salvation as a present gift, but also the assurance of salvation enjoyed by those who have received it....Yet in daily life we live in the tension between what is already given and what is still awaited as a promise, for "your life is hid with Christ in God. When Christ who is our life appears, then you will also appear with him in glory" (Col 3:3, 4).

Roman Catholics and Evangelicals are agreed that the only ground for assurance is the objective work of Christ; this ground does not lie in any way in the believer. We speak somewhat differently about the work of Christ, however, and relate it differently in terms of practical piety. Evangelicals refer to the "finished" work of Christ on the cross and rest their confidence wholly upon it. Roman Catholics also speak of Christ's work as having been done "once for all"; they therefore see it as beyond repetition....

Roman Catholics and Evangelicals both claim an authentic religious experience, which includes an awareness of the presence of God and a taste for spiritual realities. Yet Evangelicals think Roman Catholics sometimes lack a visible joy in Christ, which their assurance has given them, whereas Roman Catholics think Evangelicals are sometimes insufficiently attentive to the New Testament warnings against presumption. Roman Catholics also claim to be more realistic than Evangelicals about the vagaries of religious experience. The actual experience of Evangelicals seldom leads them to doubt their salvation, but Roman Catholics know that the soul may have its dark nights. In summary Evangelicals appear to Roman Catholics more pessimistic about human nature before conversion, but more optimistic about it afterwards, while Evangelicals allege the opposite about Roman Catholics. Roman Catholics and Evangelicals together agree that Christian assurance is more an assurance of faith (Heb 10:22) than of experience, and that perseverance to the end is a gratuitous gift of God.

Church (CCC #2030–2046)

Editor's Notes: The church is engaged in moral formation and leadership on many levels. The question of how the churches together form their members for life in Christ provides a basis for common witness. The role of church authority in formation of conscience differs among the churches.

In the church's mission there are tensions over the balance between dialogue and proclamation, and over proselytism and evangelization. A variety of dialogues have contributed to resolving these issues.

Reflection Questions:

- What is the church's role in moral formation? In giving authoritative guidance to conscience?
- What are the prospects for common mission in the world? What are the challenges to this common witness?
- How do the very divisions among the churches testify to their weakness and the limitations of Christ's mission in the world?

World Council of Churches–Catholic Church Joint Working Group

Convergence, JWG in GA II:

II.5. The task of moral formation and deliberation is one which the churches share. All churches seek to enhance the moral responsibility of their members for living a righteous life and to influence positively the moral standards and well-being of the societies in which they live.

This identifies an ecumenical objective: the quality of the moral environment that churches create together in and through worship, education and nurture, and social witness.…On the other hand, churches can also distort character and mal-form conscience. They have at times undergirded national chauvinism and ethnocentrism, and actively discriminated against persons on the basis of race or nationality, class or gender….

[In addition to the task of the church in moral formation, the church's teaching authority also plays an important role, albeit in different ways. This text is meant as a guide to discussion more than a statement of agreement.]

IV. Different Authoritative Means of Moral Discernment: Different understandings and exercise of church polities and structures of authority mean that moral formation and concrete ethical positions are themselves developed in different ways, even when similar attitudes and outcomes often emerge....

IV.2. Thus, ecumenical dialogue on moral issues should include the nature, mission and structures of the Church, the role of ministerial authority and its use of resources in offering moral guidance, and the response to the exercise of such authority within the Church. These subjects will in turn help to locate ecumenical gifts and opportunities for common witness, as well as tensions and conflicts.

First, the tensions and conflicts. Is there anxiety and unease because many fear the erosion of the foundational sources of Scripture and Tradition, and of church authority which they believe to be most reliable in guiding Christian conscience and conduct? Or are the ways in which particular church traditions understand, accept and use the sources and authorities themselves the source of tension and divisiveness? Does deliberation of ethical issues generate anxiety and anger because some persons negatively experience these sources and their use? For example, the interpretation of Scripture and Tradition in such ways that they present the oppressive face of social and theological patriarchy? One often best understands persistent unchanging stands on a specific issue not by focusing narrowly on it, but by considering what people sense is at stake for life together in society if certain sources, structures, and authorities are ignored or even ridiculed. For example, in some settings questions about the beginning and ending of life—abortion and euthanasia—carry such moral freight.

Furthermore, some churches stress more than others the structures of authority and formal detailed statements on belief and morality. This can create an imbalance and lack of realism in the dialogue if one easily compares the official teachings of some churches with the more diffuse estimates of the general belief and practice of others. Thus, awareness of the moral volatility which surround the sources and authorities used—which they are, by whom and how they are interpreted, and with what kinds of concerns they are associated—is critical for understanding why some moral issues are difficult and potentially divisive among Christians....

VI. Christian Moral Witness in a Pluralistic Society: Christians are called to witness in the public forum to their common moral convictions with humility and with respect for others and their convictions. They should seek dialogue and collaboration with those of other faith-communities, indeed with all persons of good will who are committed to the well-being of humanity.

1. In the political process of legislation and judicial decision, churches may rightly raise their prophetic voice in support or in protest. In common witness they can take a firm stand when they believe that public decisions or laws affirm or contradict God's purposes for the dignity of persons or the integrity of creation....

In fact, such moral issues of human rights and equality have been community-building experiences of *koinonia* in faith and witness, which some perceive as profound experiences of "Church."

VI.2. Sometimes churches and Christian advocacy groups may agree on the basic values which they should promote, yet they disagree about the means that should be used, especially in the political arena. In such situations, they should seek collaboration as much as their agreement allows, and at the same time articulate the reasons for their disagreement. Disagreement over some particular points or means to an end should not rule out all collaboration. In these cases, however, it is all the more important to be open and explicit about the areas of disagreement, so as to avoid confusion in common witness.

VI.3. In the public arena, the churches are one family of moral community among others, whether religious or secular. Moral discernment is not the exclusive preserve of Christians. Christian moral understandings and approaches to ethical issues should be open to evaluate carefully the moral insights and judgments of others....

⸺

Anglican

Convergence, ARCIC II, LinC in GA II:

33. Guided by the Holy Spirit, believer and believing community seek to discern the mind of Christ amidst the changing circumstances of their own histories. Fidelity to the Gospel, obedience to the mind of Christ, openness to the Holy Spirit—these remain the source and strength of continuity. Where communities have separated, traditions diverge; and it is only to be expected that a difference of emphasis in moral judgment will also occur. Where there has been an actual break in communion, this difference cannot but be the more pronounced, giving rise to the impression, often mistaken, that there is some fundamental disagreement of understanding and approach.

34. Moral discernment is a demanding task both for the community and for the individual Christian. The more complex the particular issue, the greater the room for disagreement. Christians of different Communions are more likely to agree on the character of the Christian life and the fundamental Christian virtues and values. They are more likely to disagree on the consequent rules of practice, particular moral judgments and pastoral counsel.

101. Working together, however, has convinced us that the disagreements on moral matters, which at present exist between us, need not constitute an insuperable barrier to progress towards fuller communion. Painful and perplexing as they are, they do not reveal a fundamental divergence in our understanding of the moral implications of the Gospel.

⸺

Methodist

Convergence, WMC–C III in GA II:

> 47. In both our Churches we have various procedures for offering guidance on moral issues....In neither Church does the following out of these procedures always match the ideal, for each Church recognizes "how great a distance lies between the message she offers and the human failings of those to whom the Gospel is entrusted" (GS, 43).
>
> In both our Churches we are under ecclesiastical authority, but we recognize a difference in that some pronouncements of the Catholic Church are seen as requiring a higher degree of conscientious assent from Catholics than the majority of pronouncements of the responsible bodies of Methodism require of Methodists.
>
> Where there are differences between us on what decisions should be made and what actions taken on particular moral and ethical issues, we need to look not just at these differences but at what gives rise to them, in each case enquiring whether they reflect only social and historical conditions or fundamental divisions over issues of conscience and authority.

EVANGELIZATION, PROSELYTISM, AND COMMON WITNESS

Editor's Notes: Many common dialogue statements of Catholics, Baptists, and other evangelicals, as well as texts from the Joint Working Group of the World Council, touch on themes of mission, evangelism, proselytism, and common witness. This selection from the Pentecostal/Catholic dialogue is exemplary of the recommendations and conclusions.

Pentecostals

Convergence, Pent–C IV in GA II:

> 70. Still members of the Dialogue think that Pentecostals and Catholics already agree on critical points of faith.

Recognition of this fact makes it possible for each of our communities to act in ways that do not impede the growth of the other....

75. Conflict erupts when another community of Christians enters into the life of an already religiously-impacted community and begins to evangelize without due consideration of the price that has been paid for witness to the Gospel by believers who have preceded them....They have not spoken with one another. Certain assumptions have been made by each about the other. Judgments have taken place without proper consultation between them.

76. Even if the motives of newcomers are irreproachable with respect to the welfare of the people in this region, including a genuine concern to see that the citizens of the region have really heard the Gospel, their method of entry into the region often contributes to misunderstanding and conflict, and perhaps even to a violent response. Courtesy would seem to call for some communication with the leaders of the older church by the new evangelizers....

77. The conflicts which have occurred between us demonstrate clearly the problem which disunity creates even for well-intentioned Christians. Disunity isolates us from one another. It leads to suspicion between us. It contributes to a lack of mutual understanding, even to an unwillingness for us to try to understand each other....

78. If each perceives the other through the lens of this disunity the result is all too often that one sees the other as an adversary to its own mission and may, therefore, feel the need to place impediments in the way of the other. There may be public denunciations, even persecution, of one another. Both sides have suffered, Pentecostals in particular since they have usually been the minority. But the main tragedy, and on this both the Catholic and Pentecostal teams agree, is that the conflict resulting from the disunity of Christians always "scandalizes the world, and damages that most holy cause, the

preaching of the Gospel to every creature" (UR, 1)....Most of our conflicts would diminish if we agreed that this is what evangelization is all about.

79. Instead of conflict, can we not converse with one another, pray with one another, try to cooperate with one another instead of clashing with one another? In effect, we need to look for ways in which Christians can seek the unity to which Christ calls his disciples (cf. John 17:21) starting with basic respect for one another, learning to love one another....

[The issue that most concerns Catholics and Pentecostals about mission and witness is the different styles we bring to evangelism.]

93. Attempts to define proselytism reveal a broad range of activities and actions that are not easily interpreted. These tend to be identified and evaluated differently by the parties involved. In spite of these difficulties, we have concluded that both for Catholics and for Pentecostals, proselytism is an unethical activity that comes in many forms. Some of these would be:

—all ways of promoting our own community of faith that are intellectually dishonest, such as contrasting an ideal presentation of our own community with the weaknesses of another Christian community;

—all intellectual laziness and culpable ignorance that neglect readily accessible knowledge of the other's tradition;

—every willful misrepresentation of the beliefs and practices of other Christian communities;

—every form of force, coercion, compulsion, mockery or intimidation of a personal, psychological, physical, moral, social, economic, religious or political nature;

—every form of cajolery or manipulation, including the exaggeration of biblical promises, because these distortions do not respect the dignity of persons and their freedom to make their own choices;

—every abuse of mass media in a way that is disrespectful of another faith and manipulative of the audience;

—all unwarranted judgments or acts which raise suspicions about the sincerity of others;

—all competitive evangelization focused against other Christian bodies (cf. Rom 15:20).

94. All Christians have the right to bear witness to the Gospel before all people, including other Christians.…Both the Pentecostal and Catholic members of this Dialogue view as proselytism such selfish actions as an illegitimate use of persuasive power. Proselytism must be sharply distinguished from the legitimate act of persuasively presenting the Gospel. Proselytism must be avoided.

95. At the same time we acknowledge that if a Christian, after hearing a legitimate presentation of the Gospel, freely chooses to join a different Christian community it should not automatically be concluded that such a transfer is the result of proselytism.…

[Pentecostals' key concern in common mission and witness is the issue of religious liberty, especially in countries where Catholics are the majority and may have carried a historic relationship to the state.]

102. Because of these convictions, members of the Dialogue reject:

—all violations of religious freedom and all forms of religious intolerance as well as every attempt to impose belief and practices on others or to manipulate or coerce others in the name of religion;

—inequality in civil treatment of religious bodies, although, we affirm, as Vatican II affirmed, that in exercising their rights individuals and social groups "are bound by the moral law to have regard to the rights of others, to their own duties toward others and for the common good of all" (DH, 7)….

113. Individual Christians have the right and responsibility to proclaim the Gospel boldly (Acts 4:13, 29; Eph 6:19) and persuasively (cf. Acts 17:3; Rom 1:14). All people have the right to hear the Gospel preached in their own "language" in a culturally sensitive fashion.

The Good News of Jesus Christ addresses the whole person, including his or her behavioral, cognitive, and experiential dimensions. We also affirm responsible use of modern technology as a legitimate means to communicate the Gospel.

—⁂—

Life/Peace (CCC #2258–2275)

Editor's Notes: While there is a great deal of agreement among the churches on the principles of morality, the biblical basis for ethics, and the root of all moral action in the grace and justifying love of Christ, there are particular conclusions that often leave the churches divided in their public witness. Human sexuality, abortion, war and peace, and euthanasia are among these. These texts outline some areas of discussion whereby these issues might become less divisive.

Reflection Questions:

- What are some of the issues in the community that are the most divisive among Christians?
- Where does the church stand in witness to society?
- How can churches respect one another and understand one another when ethical issues divide them?

LIFE ISSUES

Anglican

Convergence, ARCIC II, LinC in GA II:

85. Roman Catholic teaching rejects all direct abortion. Among Anglicans the view is to be found that in certain cases direct abortion is morally justifiable. Anglicans and Roman Catholics, however, are at one in their recognition of the sanctity, and right to life, of all human persons, and they share an abhorrence of the growing practice in many countries of abortion on

grounds of mere convenience. This agreement on fundamentals is reflected both in pronouncements of bishops and in official documents issued by both Communions....

86. We cannot enter here more fully into this debate, and we do not wish to underestimate the consequences of our disagreement. We wish, however, to affirm once again that Anglicans and Roman Catholics share the same fundamental teaching concerning the mystery of human life and the sanctity of the human person. They also share the same sense of awe and humility in making practical judgments in this area of profound moral complexity....For Roman Catholics, the rejection of abortion is an example of an absolute prohibition. For Anglicans, however, such an absolute and categorical prohibition would not be typical of their moral reasoning. That is why it is important to set such differences in context. Only then shall we be able to assess their wider implications.

Methodist

Difference, WMC–C I in GA I:

77. *Abortion*. We agree that the Holy Scripture affirms the sacredness and dignity of human life and that we have, therefore, a duty and obligation to defend, protect and preserve it. Our two Churches are at present confronted with complex moral issues relative to abortion and with wide differences between them in their teaching and interpretations. We have a responsibility to explore, clarify and emphasize the moral and ethical issues involved in abortion and confront our people with them as the ultimate basic for decision.

Reformed

Convergence, Ref–CUSA in BU:

> Touched by the tragic personal and social dimensions of decisions regarding abortion, the members of the Roman Catholic/Presbyterian Reformed Consultation wish to express our common concerns....We believe that our defining traditions have much to contribute through dialogue towards the clarification of principles and the exercise of charity in this matter....
>
> Abortion decisions exist in a milieu of closely related social evils which limit peoples' choices. Social, educational, and economical inequities suffered by women are part of the problem. Any discussion of abortion in our times should proceed with a recognition of the pervasive bias of cultural and ecclesial traditions which devalue women....
>
> If our churches are to be credible in addressing abortion, they must take the lead in accepting women as full and contributing members of the human and ecclesial communities....
>
> Some of the basic principles on which the Consultation was able to reach agreement include the following:
>
> 1. the transcendent basis for respect for human life is the image and likeness of God in which human beings are created;
>
> 2. the ultimate responsibility for moral decision making rests with the individual conscience guided by reason and grace;
>
> 3. authentic moral decisions can never be exclusively subjective or individualistic but must take account of the insights and concerns of the broader religious, social, and familial community;
>
> 4. judicial and legislative standards are not always coterminous with moral demands, and therefore the legalization of abortion does not of itself absolve the Christian conscience from moral responsibility; and

5. religious groups have the right to use licit means to influence civil policy regarding abortion.

Some of the areas in which substantial differences were discovered and which call for further dialogue between our two traditions including the following

1. the moment and meaning of personhood;
2. the rights of the unborn in situations where rights are in conflict;
3. the role of civil law in matters pertaining to abortion; and
4. the interrelation of individual versus communal factors in decision making.

In the light of our common Christian heritage...[w]e will always respect the personal dignity of those involved in making decisions about abortion. Regardless of the ultimate decision reached, we will offer pastoral support insofar as our personal conscience and moral convictions allow. We will not resort to stereotypes and abusive language. We will work to transform societal arrangements which press people into untenable moral dilemmas. We will attempt to create compassionate community which overcomes alienation, loneliness, and rejection and which makes real a genuine community of moral discourse and decision. We will take responsibility as part of the mission of the church to create an ethos which values all life and which works toward a society where abortion need not occur.

PEACE

Editor's Notes: The question of the Christian's role in violent conflict and the church's role in support of the state are issues that have been discussed within the church from the beginning, with pacifist and just war positions able to survive for centuries within the same church. However, the historic peace churches (Mennonite, Quaker, Brethren) have taken the pacifist position—to a lesser or greater degree—as a confessional standard. Catholic dialogues with these churches, usually in a conciliar context, have produced some modest convergences.

The Catholic social teaching on war, as on other elements of our moral life, has evolved in such a way that a reexamination of the biblical and historical tradition and its implications in the modern context have created a ground for deeper ethical convergences, as we see in these World Council and the two Faith and Order texts.

World Council of Churches–Catholic Church Joint Working Group

Convergence, JWG–GAII 73:

> III.5. The Christian stance towards war is another example of different pathways which lead to different conclusions. Every tradition accepts the biblical vision of peace between neighbors; and, more specifically, the New Testament witness to nonviolent attitudes and acts. A major division has arisen, however, from different judgments concerning the Church's collaboration with civic powers as a means of influencing human history. Those churches which have opted for collaboration accept some versions of the "just war" theory; they tolerate, even encourage, the active participation of patriotic Christians in some wars between nations and in armed revolutions within a country. But groups within these same churches agree with those other churches which choose to witness within the political order as non-compromising opponents to all use of military force, because it is contrary to the non-violent, peace-making way of Christ. These Christians abstain from bearing arms, even if that be civil disobedience.
>
> Here one can identify the precise point of difference in major theological options which have fundamental consequences for the policy of a church towards war and the conduct of its members.

⸺∞⸺

Peace Churches

Convergence, Peace II in GC II:

4. The divisions in the Body of Christ in the world are a counter witness to the peace sought and proclaimed by the church as the follower of the Prince of Peace who prayed that his disciples might be one. The movement toward unity among the churches is itself a sign and model of their peacemaking vocation....

Editor's Notes: The scriptural basis for the churches' convictions on peace was thoroughly studied to provide a common platform for articulating agreements and disagreements.

Difference, Peace I in GC II:

We acknowledge that those Christian groups historically opposing church involvement with the state and especially with its violent defense have claimed to be doing nothing less than preserving the faith delivered to the apostles....These divisions are a matter of vital importance, like the church order, sacramental, and creedal differences that have already been widely recognized as separating Christians....

The statements [of the churches produced during the 1980s] generally agree that peace is a central theme in Scripture, that it is rooted in some way in the eschatological reign of God, and that Jesus did not resort to violence. They differ in their estimate of the relevance of biblical views of peace, war and violence for church in the contemporary context....It may be that the statements' shared concern for peacemaking is beginning to inform the churches' appropriation of Scripture in ways that relativize the traditional interpretations that have undergirded confessional divisions along just war and pacifist lines. The fact that all these statements have recently been produced by these groups does seem to indicate that concern for peace witness, which had earlier been left largely to the historic peace churches, has now become important for virtually all Christian groups....

The recent church peace statements appear to share several characteristics that may indicate movement toward a new model: a focus on creating conditions for peace and preventing war, a central concern for nonviolence and finding alternatives to war, a presumption that all (not only national leaders) are responsible for making peace and preventing war, and a concern to learn from rather than to ignore or condemn pacifists....

[This text ends by raising specific questions to the U.S. churches.]

Convergence, difference, Peace II in GC II:

6. We lament that Christians have used their faith to further hate and violence. Nevertheless, events of the last decade have also shown that the peacemaking efforts in the world and the responses of the churches have made a difference in human history. While areas of disagreement continue, peacemaking as an essential element of the apostolic faith is acknowledged by all. We continue to recognize divergences in the approach to this apostolic mandate in our pilgrimage toward full communion.

[Rather than agreements, this dialogue produced "learnings" to be shared with the churches.]

7. We are agreed, on the basis of the Apostolic Tradition, that Christians, following our Lord and Savior Jesus Christ, are called to be peacemakers. We consider this a common confession of the faith once delivered to the apostles, basic to our Christian unity....Peacemaking is most deeply rooted in Christ and the unity of the church, and such unity is a gift of the Holy Spirit linked to repentance and forgiveness. Through the power of the Holy Spirit, we are enabled to practice peacemaking as a way of participation in the life and death of Christ. A primary vocation of every believer is love, out of which peacemaking flows....

8. In the face of the fragmentation of the church we are agreed on the importance of spiritual formation for unity in peacemaking....

9. Among many represented at this meeting, criticism of the just war theory has deepened.…For some, the just war tradition is an unused resource that can enhance peacemaking if seriously taken into account by Christians.…

12. We are agreed that some form of critical participation in civil government and in the surrounding society is appropriate. We are interested neither in complete withdrawal from society nor in uncritical absorption into the dominant culture.

13. We are agreed that, at some point, Christians may be called to obey God rather than human authorities.…Peacemaking is dependent on hope in God's deliverance of the righteous, God's judgment on the unjust and fulfillment of peace in God's reign.

Points of Contention

14. A) While we are in agreement that all Christians should be striving for peace, there continues to be significant disagreement over the best ways to pursue peace. Some individuals and traditions hold that to follow Jesus is to relinquish all contemplation and taking of violent action toward another human being, created in the image of God, for whom Christ died. Others wonder if the love of neighbor may at times call for effective intervention—even armed intervention—to save innocent parties from hostile aggression. Would this action be an honorable means of action or cause Christians to become what we hate?

15. B) While the various churches may come to embrace clear positions on peace and nonviolence as normative for Christians, churches also struggle with what to do with members who chose another path. What is the significance of this diversity within each church for the unity and healing of divisions among the churches? Should particular strategies and stances toward peacemaking become obligatory, or should churches simply give clear witness to the truth they have received? Then again, how meaningful can a testimony be if it goes

unheeded by the church's members? While churches do not want to become dictatorial, they clearly desire to provide accountability for maintaining their convictions, while at the same time providing pastoral care for those who dissent for reasons of conscience.

16. C) Marks of the church are of central concern, but as of yet, we have no full agreement as to what are the necessary marks. Some wonder if they should include gathering in the name of Jesus and Christ-like disciple-ship—even leading to suffering. This being the case, a clear connection between the death and resurrection with Christ experienced in the eucharist and baptism may be understood to extend to ethical stances in the world. For the Christian, one must be willing that self should suffer for truth, and not that truth should suffer for self.

17. D) Understandings of church and state continue to be matters of concern....We recognize the tensions between the polarities of charisma and institution within the church, and affirm at each step solidarity with Jesus and his teachings.

Marriage and Human Sexuality (CCC #2331–2391)

Editor's Notes: Many issues concerning human sexuality, marriage, and celibacy have been discussed among the churches. Here, several texts are selected to show approaches on the issues of contraception and homosexuality. These will need to be read in the context of the dialogue results noted above on the sacramentality of marriage.

Reflection Questions:

- In the Christian tradition, what is the goal and context for human sexuality?

- What are the reasons given by the churches for their different views on contraception? What is the Catholic position that is brought to these discussions?

Anglican

Convergence, ARCIC II, LinC in GA II:

57. Both our traditions offer comparable accounts of chastity, which involves the ordering of the sexual drive either towards marriage or in a life of celibacy. Chastity does not signify the repression of sexual instincts and energies, but their integration into a pattern of relationships in which a person may find true happiness, fulfillment and salvation. Anglicans and Roman Catholics agree that the new life in Christ calls for a radical break with the sin of sexual self-centeredness, which leads inevitably to individual and social disintegration. The New Testament is unequivocal in its witness that the right ordering and use of sexual energy is an essential aspect of life in Christ (cf. Mk 10:9; Jn 8:11; 1 Cor 7; 1 Pt 3:1-7; Heb 13:4), and this is reiterated throughout the common Christian tradition, including the time since our two Communions diverged.

CONTRACEPTION

Anglican

Convergence, difference, ARCIC II, LinC in GA II:

79. Both Roman Catholics and Anglicans agree, too, that God calls married couples to "responsible parenthood"....Broader questions concerning the pressure of population, poverty, the social and ecological environment, as well as more directly personal questions concerning the couple's material, physical and psychological resources, may arise. Situations exist in which a couple would be morally justified in avoiding bringing children into being. Indeed, there are some circumstances in which it would be morally irresponsible to do so. On this

our two Communions are also agreed. We are not agreed, however, on the methods by which this responsibility may be exercised.

80. The disagreement may be summed up as follows. Anglicans understand the good of procreation to be a norm governing the married relationship as a whole. Roman Catholic teaching, on the other hand, requires that each and every act of intercourse should be "open to procreation" (cf. *Humanae Vitae*, 11). This difference of understanding received official expression in 1930. Before this, both churches would have counseled abstinence for couples who had a justifiable reason to avoid conception. The Lambeth Conference of Anglican bishops, however, resolved in 1930 that "where there is a clearly felt moral obligation to limit or avoid parenthood, and where there is a morally sound reason for avoiding complete abstinence...other methods may be used." The encyclical of Pope Pius XI (*Casti Connubii*, 1930), which was intended among other things as a response to the Lambeth resolution, renewed the traditional Roman Catholic position....

Methodist

Difference, WMC–C I:

76. *Contraception.* We agree that human sexual intercourse has two equal and inter-related functions, namely fostering love, affection, unity and fidelity between husband and wife as well as that of reproduction. Under the stress and strain of modern social and economic conditions, parents have a right and duty before God to decide the number of children they may bear, support, rear and educate. How this decision is to be implemented is a moral matter, a matter of conscience which should be the subject of prayerful consideration by the parents who are to seek help and guidance from the Church. We recognize, however, that at present there exist differences

between the official positions of our respective Churches on the application of contraceptive methods by responsible parents. As we take cognizance of existing movements within our two Churches and of the sociological, ecological and demographic conditions of mankind, we would encourage further dialogue on this matter.

⸺ ∝∞∝ ⸺

HOMOSEXUALITY

Anglican

Convergence, ARCIC II, LinC in GA II:

85. This is not the time or place to discuss such further issues in detail. However, confining ourselves to the two issues of abortion and homosexual relations, we would argue that, in these instances too, the disagreements between us are not on the level of fundamental moral values, but on their implementation in practical judgments....

87. In the matter of homosexual relationships a similar situation obtains. Both our Communions affirm the importance and significance of human friendship and affection among men and women, whether married or single. Both affirm that all persons, including those of homosexual orientation, are made in the divine image and share the full dignity of human creatureliness. Both affirm that a faithful and lifelong marriage between a man and a woman provides the normative context for a fully sexual relationship. Both appeal to Scripture and the natural order as the sources of their teaching on this issue. Both reject, therefore, the claim, sometimes made that homosexual relationships and married relationships are morally equivalent, and equally capable of expressing the right ordering and use of the sexual drive. Such ordering and use, we believe, are an essential aspect of life in Christ. Here again our different approaches to the formulation of law are relevant. Roman Catholic teaching holds that homosexual activity is "intrinsically disordered," and concludes that it is always objec-

tively wrong. This affects the kind of pastoral advice that is given to homosexual persons. Anglicans could agree that such activity is disordered; but there may well be differences among them in the consequent moral and pastoral advice they would think it right to offer to those seeking their counsel and direction.

88. Our two Communions have in the past developed their moral teaching and practical and pastoral disciplines in isolation from each other. The differences that have arisen between them are serious, but careful study and consideration has shown us that they are not fundamental. The urgency of the times and the perplexity of the human condition demand that they now do all they can to come together to provide a common witness and guidance for the well-being of humankind and the good of the whole creation.

Why It Matters

Catholics don't usually think about justification by faith. The emphasis placed upon living a moral life can, at times, make one's personal response to God's grace seem more important than God's giving of that grace. The dialogue with Evangelicals on the meaning of salvation makes clear the Catholic emphasis on the salvific nature of God's grace. "We agree that what is offered us through the death and resurrection of Jesus is essentially 'deliverance,' ...a rescue from the power of Satan, sin and death...(and) a deliverance into the freedom of Christ. This freedom brings human fulfillment....We all agree that the essential meaning of Christ's salvation is the restoration of the broken relationship between sinful humanity and a saving God" (ERCDOM, no. 3, 5).

As the Lutheran dialogue goes on to say, "Catholics can share the concern of the Reformers to ground faith in the objective reality of Christ's promise, to look away from one's own experience, and to trust in Christ's forgiving word alone" (JDDJ, no. 36).

Christian churches agree that the "task of moral formation and deliberation is one which the churches share," seeking to "enhance the moral responsibility of their members for living a righteous life and to influence positively the moral standards and well-being of the societies in which they live" (JWG in GA II, II.5).

The dialogues make clear that Christians are encouraged to work together for common moral goals, but recognize that deciding how best to accomplish the goals may be difficult to achieve because of the different ways we understand scripture and God's salvific action. In these cases, Christians have to take the time to name the differences that divide them and work to find common ground for action.

When working with people seeking to enter the Catholic Church, look for ways to help them understand the Catholic belief in God's merciful and saving grace. Help them to see that Catholic action for others is done in imitation of Christ and not out of a desire to save one's self.

The dialogues offer strong language in support of efforts to evangelize those who have not heard the gospel and strong language against those who attempt to "steal" believers from other communities. Those who actively engage in evangelical efforts should be aware of the guidelines presented in Pent–C IV in GA II, no. 93 (see pages 225–29), which begins, "proselytism is an unethical activity that comes in many forms." Those who evangelize should abstain from name-calling, lying, force or coercion, manipulation, acts that raise questions about the other's sincerity, and intellectual dishonesty. People must be free to enter another Christian community of their own free will, attracted to it by the way the community lives and proclaims the gospel.

In matters of moral action, people of good faith may disagree on the appropriate actions to take. When we catechize on moral issues it is important that we not paint those who disagree with us as being evil or sinful. Such attitudes will lead to greater division. Instead, the dialogues encourage each side to present what it believes and encourage the other side to engage in fruitful conversation seeking a change in understanding or a conversion of heart. It is essential, however, that those who seek to enter the Catholic Church or those who will be marrying a Catholic be aware of what Catholics believe on such important matters as life issues and issues of human sexuality. By helping new Catholics understand what the Catholic belief is and why, you will be preparing them more effectively to live as Catholic followers of Christ.

10
CHRISTIAN PRAYER AND SPIRITUALITY (CCC #2558–2856)

Tom Fleming is a new employee at Jerry's print shop. He fits in very well and is quite popular. A group forms around him to share prayer over the lunch hour. Tom is a natural leader, but he does not dominate the group. Everyone is able to take turns leading the prayer, but some are uncomfortable because the prayers seem "too Catholic."

One member of the group suggests that they go to his church for a Saturday prayer breakfast. This is very successful for those who can make the occasion. Another member suggests that there be a celebration of Mass for the group, although not everyone is Catholic. Will everyone be able to participate? An Orthodox member feels very isolated by both of these invitations and stops attending the group.

What are the ground rules for a common spirituality that recognizes the differences among Christians? How are prayer services, liturgies, and even sacramental events planned to take account of the sensibilities of all concerned? How do people develop a respect for, sensitivity toward, and understanding of appropriate levels of participation in others' worship and in worship that is prepared ecumenically?

Editor's Notes: Spiritual ecumenism is at the heart of the Catholic Church's zeal for unity among Christians. Christians unite our prayer with that of Christ "that they all may be one" (Jn 17:21).

The prayer and spiritual life of Catholics is strengthened by the common spiritual journey toward unity, sharing the gifts of other churches and ecclesial communities, and common prayer. The exuberance and social commitment of African-American worship, the silence of the Quaker meeting, the glories of Orthodox liturgies, the rich biblical basis of Protestant devotion, and the spiritual vitality of Pentecostal praise all enrich Catholic faith and commitment to God. As we come closer to Christ in prayer, we come closer to one another by the power of the Holy Spirit.

Since the Vatican Council, common prayer has been encouraged, and guidelines for common worship, both nonliturgical and sacramental, have been clearly enunciated (Directory for the Application of Principles and Norms on Ecumenism, *ch. 4, see http://www.vatican.va/roman_curia/pontifical_councils/chrstuni/documents/rc_pc_chrstuni_doc_). Included here are selections from the dialogues on ecumenical spirituality and on common prayer.*

Central to Catholic prayer life is the participation with other Christians in the Week of Prayer for Christian Unity (http://www.prounione.urbe.it/att-act/e_week-prayer.html).

This section of the Catechism *is devoted to Christian prayer. The differences in faith among the Christian churches are minimal when we speak of prayer to God—Father, Son, and Holy Spirit—but the diversity is rich. However, the imperative to common prayer with and for one another and for our still divided churches is a central mandate of the gospel.*

Ecumenical Spirituality

Editor's Notes: These excerpts from dialogues that have touched on ecumenical spirituality are examples of the common foundation on which our churches together build their common prayer life. Penitence and conversion characterize ecumenical spirituality, since we are all called to repent for the sin of division and to pray for overcoming the scandal of separation.

Reflection Questions:

- How would you define the words *repentance* and *conversion*? Why would these words be important in an ecumenical setting?
- What healing needs to take place in my community with neighboring churches if ecumenism is to take root? What can I do to bring about this healing?
- How do people in other churches pray? How is that prayer similar to or different from the ways in which Catholics pray? Are these similarities or differences significant or trivial?

Lutheran

Consensus, LCUSA X:

105. Addressing these wounds in our churches will require repentance and conversion. Each church must examine its theology and practice of ministry and ask whether they truly serve the mission and unity of the church. Division offers occasions for sin, to which our churches have sometimes succumbed. The Second Vatican Council teaches, "There can be no ecumenism worthy of the name without a change of heart." Pope John Paul II concluded on this basis, "The Council calls for personal conversion as well as for communal conversion."

106. We recommend that our churches pray together for the grace of repentance and conversion needed for healing the wounds of our division.

Disciples

Convergence, CC–C I in GA I:

12. The Spirit of God draws the Church towards full unity. God's Spirit also works in the world for a new humanity through the liberation of human beings from the oppression and alienation that comes from sin. Both realms of the work of the Spirit are integral parts of one plan of salvation.

13. The unity God has given and continues to give the Church has its origins in God's own life. The Spirit of God is the author of the Church's unity. Through the Spirit, all who are one in the Church are drawn into the loving communion of the Father and Son and in that communion are united to one another. Thus, they are being made one in mind and understanding, since through faith they adhere to the one eternal Word in whom the wisdom of God is fully expressed. In this unity, the divine plan of salvation accomplished in Christ is expressed in the world and is being ever more fully revealed.

16. Spiritual ecumenism does not permit us to avoid the pain of our separated existence, being content to remain as we are. Indeed, the Spirit gives us the courage to confront our divided state.

17. Spiritual ecumenism does not allow us to leave aside the need to deal with the visible manifestation of the unity of the Church. Indeed, we understand that just as the Word of God became flesh in Jesus, so in a similar way, the power of the Spirit of God is manifested in the Church as a visible communion.

18. Nor does spiritual ecumenism relieve us of the Gospel concern for the poor, the alienated and the oppressed. Indeed, Christians often become truly aware of the bonds that unite them and hear the call to conversion of heart as they meet the challenge to promote a society of justice, freedom and charity serving the dignity of every human being.

19. Spiritual ecumenism arises from the realization that the one Spirit of God has already brought us into Christ and continues to move us towards full visible unity. Spiritual ecumenism gives us hope that the Spirit will lead us from the imperfect unity we know painfully in our divided condition to a wholeness we shall experience in joy.

20. Spiritual ecumenism implies a clear consciousness of the sinfulness of division among Christians. Through

spiritual ecumenism we are set free as communities and as individuals from seeking to justify our divisions and we are moved to seek a shared life in a reconciled community. Spiritual ecumenism impels us to a quality of evangelical life marked by the will to be faithful to Christ and open to one another. It also implies repentance and renunciation of egoism, as well as newness of mind, humility and gentleness in the service of others, that is conversion of heart. This *metanoia* thus provides what might be called an "evangelical space"—an arena for the operation of the Gospel—in which we find God's grace newly available to bind us together in praising, blessing, beseeching the God who makes us one. In this evangelical space, we discover new possibilities for genuine exchange and sharing and for seeing in a new light these affirmations that find historical expression in our still separated communities.

21. Thus, spiritual ecumenism allows us to be open to the grace of God. The Holy Spirit is freeing us to experience together his unifying power in the many ways open to us in the ongoing life of the Church, that is, accepting and proclaiming together the Word of God in the Scriptures, confessing together the same Lord, praying together, attending one another's celebration of the Lord's Supper and having a common mission as the priestly people of God in the whole human community. Although we do not yet fully share these experiences owing to our desire to be authentic and faithful to the Church as we have known it heretofore in our communions, we nevertheless realize that God makes the power of his unifying love felt even now. He speaks to us about the contradictions of our divisions when together we open ourselves to Him in prayer and worship, in our joint efforts at articulating a common theological language in ecumenical dialogue, and in the common struggle for justice and peace in the world.

Consensus, CC–C III:

> 5.9. Speaking and telling are not the only ways to evangelize. The witness of holy lives, strengthened by the Eucharist, is also integral to the mission of the Church. God's good news can be expressed in sacrificial lives and acts of mercy, before any word is spoken. Authentic witness to the Gospel takes place through lives of faithfulness to God sustained by prayer, self-denial and acts of love.

Methodist

Consensus, WMC–RC IV in GA II:

> 47. Devotion is the form that faith takes in prayer. It inspires new life and manifests the Spirit's enablement of weak human wills to do good. It leads on to discipline, when the desire to follow the Lord organizes personal life, regulates the use of resources, and places personal enthusiasm and passion at the service of the Gospel.
>
> 48. Personal life and devotion find their proper setting in the light of the Word faithfully preached and of the sacraments administered in accordance with the Gospel. Thus faith, devotion, and discipline are located within the worship and liturgy of the community
>
> 3. Worship
>
> 49. In the presence of the self-revealing God, people feel awe and joy and are moved to express this in praise, prayer, confession and commitment. They wish to recall the message of grace they have heard; to celebrate the acts of God with words, gestures and song; to express in prayer their fears, needs and hopes; and to re-enact the story of salvation in liturgy and drama
>
> 50. The Scriptures amply attest the centrality of private and public worship for God's people. When God's revelation of himself came to its fulfillment in Jesus Christ, the people of the New Covenant held on to their heritage of worship in a new way. The psalms became a

hymnal for the Christian Church; the passover meal acquired fuller meaning as a sacrament of salvation in Jesus Christ. Moreover new hymns were formed (cf. Phil 2:6–11; Col 1:15–20), and baptism in the name of the tri-une God became the sign of new creation in Christ and incorporation into his body

51. As the Gospel spreads, entering new cultures, different languages and expressions are used and the Church's worship is enriched and diversified. The Church welcomes both developments in liturgical traditions and new and spontaneous expressions of faith and worship as signs of the fruitfulness of God's message and the ever-present action of the Holy Spirit. At the same time the Church seeks to ensure that they are genuine manifestations of the Spirit, and faithfully reflect and proclaim the Gospel.

Anglican

Consensus, ARCIC II, S&C in GA II:

22. The believer's pilgrimage of faith is lived out with the mutual support of all the people of God. In Christ all the faithful, both living and departed, are bound together in a communion of prayer. The Church is entrusted by the Lord with authority to pronounce forgiveness in his name to those who have fallen into sin and repent. The Church may also help them to a deeper realization of the mercy of God by asking for practical amends for what has been done amiss. Such penitential disciplines, and other devotional practices, are not in any way intended to put God under obligation. Rather, they provide a form in which one may more fully embrace the free mercy of God.

23. The works of the righteous performed in Christian freedom and in the love of God which the Holy Spirit gives us are the object of God's commendation and receive his reward (Mt 6:4; 2 Tim 4:8; Heb

10:35, 11:6). In accordance with God's promise, those who have responded to the grace of God and consequently borne fruit for the Kingdom will be granted a place in that Kingdom when it comes at Christ's appearing. They will be one with the society of the redeemed in rejoicing in the vision of God. This reward is a gift depending wholly on divine grace. It is in this perspective that the language of "merit" must be understood, so that we can say with Augustine: "When God crowns our merits it is his own gifts that he crowns" (Ep 194, 5.19). Christians rest their confidence for salvation on the power, mercy and loving-kindness of God and pray that the good work which God has begun he will in grace complete. They do not trust in their own merits but in Christ's. God is true to his promise to "render to everyone according to his works" (Rm 2:6); yet when we have done all that is commanded we must still say: "We are unprofitable servants, we have only done our duty" (Lk 17:10).

51. One of the most important ways in which there has already been a sharing of gifts is in spirituality and worship. Roman Catholics and Anglicans now frequently pray together. Alongside common participation in public worship and in private prayer, members of both churches draw from a common treasury of spiritual writing and direction. There has been a notable convergence in our patterns of liturgy, especially in that of the eucharist. The same lectionary is used by both churches in many countries. We now agree on the use of the vernacular language in public worship. We agree also that communion in both kinds is the appropriate mode of administration of the eucharist. In some circumstances, buildings are shared. (ARCIC II CaC in GA II)

Evangelicals

Convergence, ERCDOM in GA II:

7., 2), f) Common Witness in Worship

The word "worship" is used in a wide range of senses from the spontaneous prayers of the "two or three" met in Christ's name in a home to formal liturgical services in church.

We do not think that either Evangelicals or Roman Catholics should hesitate to join in common prayer when they meet in each other's homes. Indeed, if they have gathered for a Bible study group, it would be most appropriate for them to pray together for illumination before the study and after it for grace to obey. Larger informal meetings should give no difficulty either. Indeed, in many parts of the world Evangelicals and Roman Catholics are already meeting for common praise and prayer, both in charismatic celebrations and in gatherings which would not describe themselves thus. Through such experiences they have been drawn into a deeper experience of God and so into a closer fellowship with one another. Occasional participation in each other's services in church is also natural, especially for the sake of family solidarity and friendship.

It is when the possibility of common participation in the Holy Communion or Eucharist is raised, that major problems of conscience arise. Both sides of our dialogue would strongly discourage indiscriminate approaches to common sacramental worship.

The Mass lies at the heart of Roman Catholic doctrine and practice, and it has been emphasized even more in Catholic spirituality since the Second Vatican Council. Anyone is free to attend Mass. Other Christians may not receive Communion at it, however, except when they request it in certain limited cases of "spiritual necessity" specified by current Roman Catholic legislation. Roman Catholics may on occasion attend a Protestant Communion Service as an act of worship. But there is no ruling of the Roman Catholic Church which would permit its members to receive Communion in a Protestant Church service, even on ecumenical occasions. Nor would Roman Catholics feel in conscience free to do so.

Many Evangelical churches practice an "open" Communion policy, in that they announce a welcome to everybody who "is trusting in Jesus Christ for salvation and is in love and charity with all people," whatever their church affiliation. They do not exclude Roman Catholic believers. Most Evangelicals would feel conscientiously unable to present themselves at a Roman Catholic Mass, however, even assuming they were invited. This is because the doctrine of the Mass was one of the chief points at issue during the 16th century Reformation, and Evangelicals are not satisfied with the Roman Catholic explanation of the relation between the sacrifice of Christ on the Cross and the sacrifice of the Mass….Since both Roman Catholics and Evangelicals believe that the Lord's Supper was instituted by Jesus as a means of grace and agree that he commanded his disciples to "do this in remembrance" of him, it is a grief to us that we are so deeply divided in an area in which we should be united, and that we are therefore unable to obey Christ's command together.

Reformed

Consensus, Ref–C I in GA I:

> 54. The Church was founded by Christ to share in the life which comes from the Father and it is sent to lead the world to Jesus Christ, to its full maturity for the glory and praise of the Father. It is therefore called to be the visible witness and sign of the liberating will of God, of the redemption granted in Jesus Christ, and of the kingdom of peace that is to come. The Church carries out this task by what it does and what it says, but also simply by being what it is, since it belongs to the nature of the

Church to proclaim the word of judgment and grace, and to serve Christ in the poor, the oppressed and the desperate (Mt 25:31–40). More particularly, however, it comes together for the purpose of adoration and prayer, to receive ever new instruction and consolation and to celebrate the presence of Christ in the sacrament; around this center, and with the multiplicity of the gifts granted by the Spirit (cf. 1 Cor 12:4–11, 28–30; Rom 12:6–8; Eph 4:11) it lives as a koinonia of those who need and help each other. We consequently believe in a special presence of Christ in the Church by which it is placed in a quite special position in relation to the world and we believe that the Church stands under the special aid of the Holy Spirit, above all in its ministry of preaching and sacraments (cf. Jn 14:16, 25f, 15:26, 16:7–14)....

60. The Church is a worshiping community whose prayers are inseparable from its prophetic and diaconal service. In worship and witness the Church celebrates the central fact of Christ's unity with his people. Being united to Christ in his death and resurrection, the Church is empowered with the Spirit to walk in newness of life and so to be a converted and converting presence in Christ's world. By living as a new people persuaded of God's acceptance in Christ, the Church is a persuasive sign of God's love for all his creation and of his liberating purpose for all men.

⚬

Black Churches

Convergence, Black Ch in GC II:

[H]oliness in the Black Church is not coterminous, as in some expressions of white liberalism, with frenetic social activism. Personal encounter with God as a prerequisite of sanctification and commitment to social transformation are both necessary, but the obligation to "give glory to God," to "glorify the holiness of God" is an essential corollary of the obligation to be engaged in "building the

Kingdom" that continues to be frustrated by racism and oppression. The Black Church is sustained by prayer and praise. It exists in and for the glory of God and not the glorification of human institutions. We know that to struggle in the midst of the world is to experience the glory of God that is thwarted by racism and oppression, but, we also know that we need to praise God in the sanctuary in order to struggle! One of our spirituals has the refrain: "Have you got good religion?" The response is, "Certainly, certainly, certainly Lord!" Good religion is, therefore, understood to make worldly things that were formerly dubious better, and bad religion ruins the best of all possible worlds where there is no acknowledgement of God's presence. Without holiness no one shall see the Lord.

Ultimately, the holiness of the Church is a work of the Holy Spirit. We affirm that the One, Holy Church cannot exist apart from ministries of justice and liberation. We also affirm that true liberation is inseparable from deep spirituality. The intimate involvement of Christians with the Holy Spirit is expressed first in worship that celebrates the manifest presence, goodness and glory of God and moves from the sanctuary to the streets where it empowers the world to goodness, transfigures its wretchedness and need, and creates the quality of life that is symbolized by the nimbus that encircles the throne of God.

World Council Assembly

Convergence, Canberra 1991:

4.1 The Holy Spirit as promoter of *koinonia* (2 Cor. 13:13) gives to those who are still divided the thirst and hunger for full communion. We remain restless until we grow together according to the wish and prayer of Christ that those who believe in him may be one (John 17:21). In the process of praying, working and struggling for unity, the Holy Spirit comforts us in pain, disturbs us when are satisfied to remain in our division, leads us to repentance, and grants us joy when our communion flourishes.

———

Common Prayer

Editor's Notes: Early on in Catholic participation in the ecumenical movement it was important to clarify together, and for the Catholic Church itself (as has been done most clearly in the 1993 Directory), *the principles on which this common prayer takes place. This was done in the Joint Working Group document with which this section begins, and which is still an important guide in planning common prayer.*

After 1989 and the opening of the Orthodox world to the West, a review of common principles was necessary; thus we have also included here sections from the 2002 report of the World Council Orthodox Commission. In both of these reports the question of eucharistic worship is also treated in this context of common prayer.

These two texts support and give background to the Catechism's *elaboration of Christian prayer. It brings the Catholic understanding into the more ample context of the Christian tradition. Many of the Orthodox concerns elaborated in the second report are also issues for Catholics as they approach common worship with fellow Christians.*

Reflection Questions:

- Why is common prayer at the center of God's call to unity among Christians?
- What are some of the sensitivities and priorities in common prayer and common worship?
- How does collaboration with fellow Christians enhance Catholics' life of prayer?
- What is the role of the Holy Spirit in the process of reconciliation among the churches?

World Council of Churches–Catholic Church Joint Working Group

Convergence, JWG JW:

There is an increasing number of occasions on which Christians of different communions meet together and the need is felt by many that some guidelines should be worked out as to how worship on such ecumenical occasions may be arranged.

[On the basis of Catholic directives and World Council experience some common principles are proposed:]

1. When Christians meet together they experience a certain unity in a deep fellowship despite their separations which are still very real. The experience of this fellowship and an actual growth in it is particularly evident when they pray together and praise God, when they repent and ask for God's gift of forgiveness, when they listen to the Word of God together. What often cannot be grasped and formulated in thoughts and words proves to be a reality in the common movement to God….

2. Common prayer however should not give the impression that a fellowship exists where this is not so. Nothing, therefore, should be done which is against the conviction and the discipline of a church….

6. Any agreement on common worship must be based on theological and ecclesiological considerations…. Though common prayer is generally to be encouraged, pastoral considerations are necessary where local churches are not yet prepared for ecumenical fellowship. Worship is for the glorification of God's name. Our attention cannot be directed to Him if there is no real inner freedom felt for worshiping together….

[The following guidelines apply to WCC–Catholic situations of common prayer, but may be a resource in other situations:]

1) The participants must be able to experience both the existing oneness in Christ and the difficulties still to be overcome. Solutions which hide the differences must be avoided.

As far as possible the various traditions represented at a gathering should have the opportunity to participate actively in worship, even if practical considerations seem to make it difficult.

2) There are various forms of worship which must be distinguished:

a) Services in which representatives of several traditions participate. It is important that such services are prepared together and are carried out in a representative way....

b) Services composed in a form which can be adopted by the members of any church tradition, e.g., prayers of adoration, Bible readings, prayers of intercession, etc.

c) Services which are conducted for all those participants in the meeting by one or several members of one church according to the rules of this church....

d) Eucharistic services which are held by one church within the context of a meeting. It should not become the rule that the problem of the Eucharist be bypassed at ecumenical meetings and if Eucharistic services are held solutions should not be sought which make visible only one aspect of the problem....

(1) The meeting itself cannot be responsible for the celebration of a Eucharistic service. Only a church can issue an invitation for such a service....

(3) A preparatory service for all participants in the gathering has proved to be a significant common act on many occasions. It can contribute to a deeper awareness of the scandal of division....

Editor's Notes: Concerns raised by the Orthodox after the fall of Communism (1989) and the resurgence of antiecumenical forces in Eastern Europe have enabled a more thorough ecumenical review of some principles related to common prayer and worship. These guidelines, and the 2002 report of the dialogue between Orthodox and other Christian churches, come as no surprise. In each generation it is important to revisit our understanding with one another as situations change. This has been particularly urgent after the decades of persecution and isolation experienced by the churches of Eastern Europe.

We deepen our prayer life as we deepen our understanding of the prayer of fellow Christians and our understanding of what is or is not possible for us to do together before God. For Catholics, as for Orthodox Christians, prayer to God in common is a profound ecclesial act. Therefore, sensitivity to the Christ in whom we are praying and to our understanding of church enhances the quality of our relationship with God. The distinctions and sensitivities outlined here may assist Catholics who facilitate common prayer with fellow Christians.

World Council of Churches–Orthodox Joint Commission

Convergence, OJC:

Introduction

1. Prayer lies at the center of our identity as Christians, both in our separate communions and in the conciliar ecumenical movement....Many of our divisions become apparent precisely in our common prayer.

2. To help clarify some of the concerns and ambiguities raised by common prayer at WCC gatherings, it has been found useful to distinguish between "confessional common prayer" and "interconfessional common prayer."...

6. Christians from divided ecclesial traditions offer prayer together because of our shared belief in the Holy Trinity and in Jesus Christ as God and Saviour, and because of our common commitment to the quest for Christian unity....As we pray together we give gifts to and receive gifts from each other. Most fundamentally, we offer ourselves to God in all our brokenness, and receive God's offer to heal, teach and lead us.

7. The experience of praying together is not always a comfortable one, nor should it be, for we approach God together before we have been fully reconciled with each other.

8. Indeed, for some, prayer with Christians outside one's own tradition is not only uncomfortable, but con-

sidered to be impossible. For example, Orthodox Christians must take into account canons which may be interpreted as forbidding such prayer, although there is no consensus on how to apply these canons today. Historically, many Protestants have also faced obstacles to common prayer….

[Sharing common prayer in public and attending worship with those who were not Catholic was discouraged by the Catholic Church before the Second Vatican Council.]

10. The goals of these considerations are twofold. One is to clarify that interconfessional common prayer at WCC gatherings is not the worship of an ecclesial body. The other is to make practical recommendations for common prayer….

Challenges of common prayer in ecumenical settings

11. Common prayer at ecumenical events, particularly when combining elements from different traditions, is a source of joy and encouragement to many. It also poses challenges. The challenges have to do in part with issues of unfamiliarity, of adaptation to different worship styles, and even with a different "spiritual ethos." But the challenges of such common prayer go beyond issues of unfamiliarity; they are ecclesiological and theological as well.

Ecclesiological

12. Just as the World Council of Churches does not constitute "the Church" or an ecclesial body itself, the common prayer of Christians from the different member churches is not the prayer of a church or "the Church."…[C]onfusion can result from the way in which a service is organized, presided over, and celebrated, as well as in its content—such as when the gathering is referred to as "church."

Theological

13. There is an inherent and deep connection between theology and prayer. The ancient dictum *lex orandi est lex credendi* says that we pray that which we believe….

Confessional and interconfessional common prayer

15. When we gather to pray together at WCC events, there are occasions when the prayer has been identified with one confession or church within a confessional tradition; hence the term "confessional common prayer." More often, common prayer in ecumenical settings is prepared from a combination of traditions….

Considerations for preparation of common prayer….

Confessional common prayer

19. Confessional common prayer arises from the living worship experience of a particular tradition within the fellowship of the WCC. It will normally be planned by an individual or group from within that tradition, who will discern carefully how best to present the distinctive character of their worship within an ecumenical context. Confessional common prayer is a way of offering the spirituality of one group to others, and therefore should be representative of that group, although the prayer of one group may not be easily distinguished from some others (e.g. Methodist and Reformed)….

Interconfessional common prayer

20. All participants enjoy equal status in interconfessional common prayer. [W]e share a belief in God—Father, Son and Holy Spirit—and a common commitment to Christian unity. Whether clergy or lay, male or female, whatever our confessional background—as fellow pilgrims in the ecumenical journey, we participate as equals in interconfessional common prayer….

Considerations on responsible approaches to some sensitive issues

25. All planners of common prayer should attempt to be sensitive to those issues which might cause difficulty for some participants, and to strive to avoid offense wherever possible. The following considerations can help raise awareness to potential difficulties….

27. Use of symbols and symbolic action: Symbols and symbolic actions chosen for prayer in ecumenical set-

tings ought to be readily understood by a culturally and confessionally diverse ecumenical gathering. When using elements which are particular to one tradition, these should be presented in a way that honors the integrity of that tradition and is meaningful in ecumenical usage. Some symbols may not translate well between particular cultures and ecumenical settings, and some may be too contrived to be useful for common prayer....

30. Leadership of women:...For interconfessional common prayer, a decentralized leadership and equality of participation allow for any participant—male or female, clergy or lay—to take any role. In an ecumenical context, we come together with a range of positions on the question of ordination of women, both between and sometimes within our churches, and we are not yet ready to reconcile these differences....

31. Unfamiliarity: Care should be taken that our common prayer invites participants into particular contexts and symbols rather than asking them to watch it done as a cultural display. For major events (and especially for first time attenders), this will probably entail an orientation to the experience, explaining what will happen and what it means....The elements of common prayer should not themselves become the focus of common prayer, but rather should serve to facilitate the genuine prayers of the community.

32. Social and political themes: Our common prayer rightly entails elements of moral formation and prophetic proclamation. We are called to pray for justice and peace, yet we can distinguish between thematic prayer and prayer used to divide us further on social and political issues over which we have deep disagreement. Our common prayer is addressed to God, and is an invitation to listen to what God is trying to teach us.

Use of language

33. Language matters....In view of the profound connection between theology and prayer, issues of gender in language need careful consideration. The term "inclu-

sive language" is sometimes used broadly and imprecisely. In fact, there are several separate issues involved.

34. We can make a clear distinction between language referring to God and language referring to human beings, and affirm that language for humans should always be inclusive of women and men. Language referring to the entire human community should also be sensitive to matters of race, class, and other potential categories of exclusion.

35. Scripture and Tradition offer a variety of metaphors and images for God. These metaphors and images can be used in common prayer to describe God and God's activity in history....

Eucharistic practice...

36. Eucharistic worship at ecumenical events has been a difficult issue for the fellowship of churches in the World Council of Churches. We cannot all receive from the same table and there exists a range of views and disciplines among member churches on the offering and receiving of the eucharist. Whatever one's views on the eucharist and how it may or may not be shared, the pain of all not being able to receive at the same table is felt by all.

37. From an Orthodox perspective, the eucharist can only be celebrated by the Church and shared by those in sacramental communion. For some Protestants, the eucharist is not only a sign of visible unity to be worked for, but also one of our greatest spiritual resources for the journey toward unity. For the latter, it is therefore appropriate to share it now. Some churches have an "open table" for all who love the Lord. Others offer hospitality at ecumenical occasions or in other clearly defined circumstances. It is important to understand and be sensitive to the different views held by the member churches and also to welcome the convergence in understanding the eucharist that is registered in *Baptism, Eucharist and Ministry* and in some bilateral dialogues.

38. The common prayer life of the ecumenical movement must have truthfulness and integrity. We cannot

pray in a way which pretends we are something different from what we are, or that we are at a further stage in the quest for Christian unity than we actually are….

Conclusion

40. Worship lies at the center of our Christian identity. Yet in worship we also discover our brokenness. In an ecumenical context, common prayer can be a source of both joy and sorrow. When the pain of our disunity is compounded by an insensitivity to a particular ethos, a further deepening of division may result. As brothers and sisters committed to the quest for Christian unity, we seek not to offend but to encourage each other. We are called to approach common prayer with a spirit of generosity and love for one another….

43. Yet we continue on our ecumenical quest. Our divisions will not be resolved solely with theological dialogue and common service to the world. We must also pray together if we are to stay together, for common prayer is at the very heart of our Christian life, both in our own communities and as we work together for Christian unity.…We look forward to the day when our divisions will be overcome, and we can all stand united before the throne of God, singing praises together with one voice.

Why It Matters

Nothing prevents Christians of all communities from joining together for shared, personal prayer. Nothing. Opportunities also abound for Catholics and other Christians to join in shared liturgical and sacramental prayer that is conducted using guidelines developed by the Holy See. All that's missing is a willingness to participate in such prayer experiences.

Indeed, shared prayer between Christians is a perfect opportunity to seek forgiveness for the sin of division and the scandal of separation suffered by the church. Guidelines for such services can be found on pages 257–64 in this chapter.

The seasons of Advent and Lent are celebrated in similar fashion by Catholics, Lutherans, Anglicans, and Methodists. Shared prayer between communities would be especially appropriate during these seasons. You may want to prepare parishioners for this shared prayer by holding several catechetical sessions prior to the event to study those things that divide the church and those things that we hold in common.

Be sure to incorporate information about how the other communities pray and their belief about prayer. Also include in these sessions time to pray for personal conversion and forgiveness. Prayer services involving Christians from several communities during these liturgical seasons can be the start of a long-lasting relationship between churches. Planning a discussion session following the prayer to hear parishioners' perspectives on the service will be well worthwhile.

For joint prayer services to work well, they should be planned by members from each community. The prayers should take into account the sensibilities of each tradition, and yet remain faithful to the style and experience of each church. Those who gather to plan the services should have a deep understanding of their own tradition's liturgical practice and be familiar with its policies about shared ecumenical prayer. These members should also be familiar with the prayer practices of the other communities. Obviously, it will take time to prepare Catholic laymen and laywomen to participate fully in such prayer.

Such services would do well to avoid eucharistic celebrations. Until Catholics and members of other churches can freely celebrate the sacrament of unity together, it is best to avoid these services in ecumenical settings. While avoiding the Eucharist can be painful, there are many other rich prayer traditions in the treasury of the various churches that can be used.

Catholics have much to learn from the prayer traditions of other churches and we have much that we can share. The only thing preventing this sharing is a willingness of church members to work to establish the relationships between churches needed for such prayer to occur.

For those preparing baptized seekers to enter the Catholic Church, prayer can be a pivotal point of entry. Start by having them talk about their current prayer life and how they pray. Then teach them how to pray as a Catholic prays and introduce them to the richness of the Catholic prayer tradition. When doing this, be sure to respect and affirm the prayer traditions of the churches they are leaving. Help them to recognize that they bring with them a richness of prayer that will be enhanced by their full participation in Catholic practices. They should know that they may continue the prayer practices of their former community once they enter the Catholic Church.

Couples preparing for marriage are encouraged to pray together. For couples from different churches, such experiences of shared prayer can help to strengthen the marriage bond. Help them to accept the validity of the prayer of each tradition, and give them permission to share in such prayer together.